GLUTEN-FREE
KITCHEN

GLUTEN-FREE
KITCHEN

How to enjoy pasta, breads, cakes, cookies and more on a gluten-free diet

A practical guide for healthy eating, with 165 recipes

Catherine Atkinson

LORENZ BOOKS

Contents

Introduction 6

Breads & doughs 40

Pasta & noodles 76

Savoury pastry 98

Batters 126

Scones & savoury crackers 160

Cookies & slices 172

Sweet pastry & desserts 194

Small cakes & traybakes 230

Large cakes & gateaux 246

Index 270

Introduction

More than a tenth of the UK population and up to one-third in the USA say that they currently avoid eating food containing gluten. Many people are gluten-intolerant while others find wheat-based and high-gluten products difficult to digest and simply feel better and healthier eating a diet without, or containing less of, these foods. An estimated one in a hundred people have coeliac disease, an incurable, lifelong, autoimmune reaction to gluten, and a similar number have a wheat allergy.

Embarking on any restricted diet can be daunting, but especially when you need to exclude all foods containing gluten. Buying ready-prepared gluten-free foods can be very expensive and monotonous, and the range of gluten-free products, including all kinds of flours and more unusual ingredients such as xanthan gum, somewhat bewildering.

The aim of this book is to demystify gluten-free cooking and show you that it's surprisingly easy to create foods that you may have thought would be off the menu for good. The introductory section contains clear advice on all aspects of gluten-free eating, from how to get diagnosed, to how to avoid gluten in processed foods and protect against cross-contamination both at home and when eating out.

You'll find information on all the different types of gluten-free flours and how to combine them to make your own blends for different types of food, and which flour works best for which type of cooking and baking. Gluten-free flours handle differently to wheat flours, and there are techniques and tips to help you get great results. It is not uncommon to find dairy intolerances alongside gluten, so a guide to common dairy-free ingredients is also given, as well as alternatives to refined sugar.

The recipe section features lots of traditional recipes that have been reworked to make them gluten free, as well as some classic, inherently gluten-free dishes that everyone should have in their repertoire, and also plenty of delicious new ideas to explore. Wholesome breads, pasta, pastries, puddings and all manner of other sweet and savoury bakes are included, many of which are also dairy-free, vegetarian and/or vegan, or easily adaptable. Enjoy your gluten-free kitchen.

What is gluten?

Gluten gives foods elasticity and strength and 'holds' food products together. The most obvious ways it is used is in breads, pasta, pastry, pizza bases, cereals, cakes and cookies, but it is also used for crumb coatings and for binding foods and thickening, so can be found in many processed foods such as sausages, soups, sauces and ready meals.

Types of gluten

Gluten is a collective name for a group of proteins that occur naturally in wheat, rye and barley. In wheat (and all wheat relatives including spelt, kamut, emmer, einkorn and farro), the gluten protein is primarily made of **gliadin** (believed to be one of the main culprits of gluten allergies and intolerances), which gives bread the ability to rise during baking; and **glutenin**, which makes the dough springy and supple. Other types are **secalin**, which occurs in rye, and **hordelin**, which is found in barley; both these grains also contain gliadin, although in much smaller quantities than wheat.

It is these gluten proteins that cause a reaction in people who are gluten intolerant or gluten sensitive, and thus need to be avoided. However, it isn't always easy to identify which particular type of protein is causing the problem; some sufferers may react to all gluten proteins, others to just one, and sensitivity can vary, too. The issue isn't isolated to the proteins listed above, either: oats, for instance, are gluten free, but they contain a very similar protein called **avenin**, which can cause a reaction in some people. For this reason, it is very important that sufferers seek medical advice and undergo allergy testing, and follow the advice they are given by their medical practitioner.

THE LINK BETWEEN COELIAC DISEASE AND GLUTEN

Modern diets have become increasingly high in refined wheat products, and thus gluten. The Western diet, for instance, is today packed with wheat-based products, such as bread, pasta, pastries, biscuits and cookies, and it is thought that this, alongside better awareness and diagnosis, has resulted in the dramatic rise in recorded numbers of people with coeliac disease. This is backed up by the fact that there has also been a notable increase in diagnosed coeliac cases in India and China as these once mostly rice-based cultures have adopted a more Westernized, wheat-heavy diet.

The story of wheat and bread

When early man first started to grow grains, the hardy grasses contained small, hard seeds bearing only traces of gluten. After removing the inedible outer husks, these grains, which were mostly ancient relatives of barley and oats, could be ground between two stones to make flour. This was mixed with water to form a paste or gruel that was left to dry in the sun or perhaps baked on a hot stone – sometimes leavened by wild yeasts that had combined with the flour and water – forming a type of prototype flatbread. Wheat, however, wasn't cultivated until about 10,000 years ago, and even then the varieties that were grown were low-gluten types, such as spelt and einkorn.

The cultivation of these types of wheat slowly spread throughout Asia, being refined along the way, and it is estimated from DNA evidence that the first wheat suitable for making yeasted bread was cultivated around 3,500 years ago. It then spread to Europe, and the rest, as they say, is history.

Through much of Europe and the Western world, bread was originally made by the 'sourdough' method, whereby natural yeasts from the atmosphere and on the grains would be used to make a fermented starter. When the flour was mixed with water, the yeast would start to digest the starch and lactic bacteria would digest the various anti-nutrients that can interfere with absorption and digestion within the gut. All European breads were made in this way until the late 19th century, when baker's yeast, *Saccharomyces cerevisiae*, was discovered and used to make white, much lighter breads that took less time to ferment and rise. Prior to this, most bread was dark, dense and flat; white flours could be made by sifting out the bran, but these were much more expensive and therefore only enjoyed by those who could afford it, meaning whiter breads quickly became a sign of higher social status.

The Industrial Revolution moved the process of bread forwards with the advent of factory-milled flour and wheat that had been grown on the North American prairies, which was widely exported. Unlike its European counterpart, this American wheat made a much 'stronger' bread flour as it was higher in gluten, and the

Above It is perfectly possible to make many different types of bread using gluten-free flours and additions such as xanthan gum.

texture of breads thus became even more aerated as the gluten could better hold and retain the structure of the risen dough.

The next radical change to the wheat used to make our daily bread occurred in the 1960s, when the intensification of agriculture led to high-yielding varieties being cultivated. Artificial fertilizers boosted production and a range of pesticides and fungicides protected the abundant and fast-growing crops. Today, nearly all the wheat grown in the West is *Triticum aestivum* (common wheat), which has been selectively bred to create a crop with shorter stems and grains with loose husks to make processing simpler. Notably, it also has a higher protein and gluten content than more ancient types. Another, newer, grain to watch for is *Triticale*, which has been specifically bred from wheat and rye to have a high gluten content, similar to that of wheat, while being tolerant to a variety of growing conditions, like rye.

Alongside the increased production of a new breed of wheat came changes in bread production that revolutionized commercial baking – namely the Chorleywood bread process (CBP), which was developed in 1961 and is still used to produce some 80 per cent of bread in the UK. It involves the use of high-speed machinery and factory production, alongside additives such as extra yeast, enzymes and hard fats, which together mean that bread can be made much more cheaply and quickly. Indeed, with high-gluten wheat flour, fast-working yeasts and more additives, the dough can be mixed and baked in less than 3½ hours, and result in a longer-lasting, softer loaf. Even short fermentation is rendered unnecessary, which means that proteins and gluten that previously would have been partially or wholly digested by the fermentation process remain in the bread in much higher quantities.

Little wonder, then, that some people's bodies have not been able to keep up with the rapid pace of change and can't handle the high levels of gluten found in so many wheat-based products. Partially in response to this realisation, we are slowly seeing a return to wholegrain breads made with a mixture of cereal flours and seeds, sold alongside cheaper white sliced loaves. Sourdough, too, is gradually returning in popularity, with buyers and bakers choosing it not only for flavour but for its beneficial health properties, which we discuss in more detail on page 41.

Coeliac disease & wheat allergy

Coeliac disease is a digestive condition that causes the small intestine to become inflamed and less able to absorb nutrients. It is caused by an adverse reaction to gluten, a protein found in certain cereals. Other conditions are also linked to gluten, while not being coeliac disease.

What is coeliac disease?

Coeliac disease is widely misunderstood, often being regarded as an allergy or food intolerance. It is, in fact, a lifelong autoimmune disease caused by the body reacting to gluten, and affects the gut and other parts of the body as the immune system (the body's defence against infection) mistakenly attacks healthy tissue.

In a person with a healthy digestive system, food that has been broken down in the stomach and duodenum passes through the small intestine, which is lined with small finger-like projections called villi. These increase the surface area of the small intestine and allow essential nutrients to be absorbed into the bloodstream. For those with coeliac disease, when gluten reaches the villi, the immune system responds by attacking the gluten as if it were a threat, causing damage to the villi and flattening them. Symptoms can range from feeling very unwell with a stomach upset to weight loss and joint pain.

There is currently no cure for the condition, but it can be managed well by changing to a diet that omits all gluten products. Provided that the diet is followed, the damaged villi in the lining of the small intestine will eventually recover and return to normal and all symptoms should subside. Gluten can never be reintroduced, however, as once the body has become sensitized to it, it will always be affected by it.

SYMPTOMS OF COELIAC DISEASE

Gut-related symptoms may include:

- abdominal pain, bloating, flatulence and regular bouts of diarrhoea
- nausea
- constipation

Nutrition-related symptoms may include:

- fatigue (due to anaemia caused by iron or folate deficiency)
- weight loss (due to nutrients not being absorbed)
- loss of dental enamel and low bone density (due to poor calcium absorption)

General symptoms may include:

- frequent mouth ulcers
- hair loss
- blistering itchy skin rash, mostly on elbows and knees (dermatitis herpetiformis)

Getting diagnosed

Almost one in a hundred people are affected by coeliac disease, but it is thought that there are a great many more who remain undiagnosed. Any one at any age can develop coeliac disease, though it is most commonly discovered in middle age, with nearly a quarter of cases first being diagnosed in people over the age of 60. The condition is known to be hereditary, with a one in 10 chance of either having or developing coeliac disease if a close family member has it.

It can take time for an accurate diagnosis to be made. The first step is to consult your doctor, who will carry out a blood test to look for the antibodies that the body makes in response to eating gluten. It's important not to cut gluten out of your diet prior to testing as this may give a negative result. As a guideline, you should aim to eat some gluten in more than one meal a day for at least six weeks before your blood test. Some people with coeliac disease do not make the usual coeliac antibodies. This is known as IgA (immunoglobulin A) deficiency.

If the test is positive, you will be referred to a specialist, who will carry out a biopsy of the lining of the small intestine to check for damage that would indicate coeliac disease. This involves passing a small camera called an endoscope through your mouth and stomach and into the gut; it is a simple procedure and anaesthetic spray will be used to numb your throat, or a sedative will be offered. In children, this is usually performed under a general anaesthetic.

Although it can take time for an accurate diagnosis to be made, it is vital to make sure that your symptoms are not due to another medical condition, such as IBS (irritable bowel syndrome) or non-coeliac gluten sensitivity. Should you have coeliac disease, it's important to minimize the risk of associated health issues such as osteoporosis, small bowel cancer and other autoimmune diseases. Sometimes, coeliac disease is coupled with other allergies or food intolerances, such as dairy intolerance (see page 36). If you live in the UK, you may also be entitled to gluten-free food on prescription, such as bread and mixes. You can also ask your doctor to refer you to a dietitian, who will be able to give individual advice and help with any problems you have following a gluten-free diet.

What is wheat allergy?

A wheat allergy (or intolerance) is an immune reaction to any of the hundreds of proteins found in wheat, which is triggered by the immune system and usually occurs within minutes of eating. White blood cells send out immunoglobulin E (IgE) antibodies to 'attack' the wheat. At the same time, chemical messengers alert the rest of the body. People who suffer from an allergy or intolerance to wheat will also benefit from a gluten-free diet, as will those who have dermatitis herpetiformis. Diagnosis is generally done through skin-prick testing by a professional allergist. Products labelled as gluten free may still contain wheat starch, so it's important to read packaging carefully.

What is non-coeliac gluten sensitivity?

Normally shortened to NCGS, this is often called a gluten intolerance. It is not an autoimmune reaction since there are no associated antibodies and no damage to the lining of the gut (as with coeliac disease), nor is IgE released by the body (as with wheat allergy), but a diagnosis will be required in order to rule out both. Sufferers may have symptoms that are identical to those of coeliac disease, and these are improved when gluten is removed from the diet.

SYMPTOMS OF WHEAT ALLERGY

Wheat allergy triggers a wide range of symptoms. As these may be indicative of all sorts of ailments, it is important to seek medical advice before concluding that wheat is the culprit. Symptoms may include:

- swelling of the lips and tongue and difficulty in swallowing
- sneezing and runny nose
- itchy and watery eyes
- skin rashes and eczema
- muscular aches and pains
- nausea or an upset stomach
- anaphylaxis (a life-threatening reaction)

What is dermatitis herpetiformis?

Dermatitis herpetiformis is a rare skin condition linked to coeliac disease. It is caused by a sensitivity to gluten and manifests as raised blisters and an itchy rash, usually on the elbows and knees but sometimes on other parts of the body as well. Statistics vary quite a bit, but it affects more males than females and it is rare in children. A gluten-free diet will alleviate symptoms and, for many, will clear it up. Although the name suggests otherwise, it is unrelated to the herpes virus.

Below Triticum aestivum is the most common variety of wheat that is grown for producing bread flour.

A healthy diet

If you have been diagnosed with coeliac disease or have recently discovered that you are gluten intolerant, you will most likely be making significant dietary changes, which means that this is a good time to reassess how you can achieve a healthy diet.

From flattened intestinal villi and nutrient deficiencies to low energy and a weakened immune system, being gluten sensitive or intolerant plays havoc with your body, and it's therefore important to get your diet on track as soon as you receive your diagnosis.

To function properly, your body needs a daily intake of a full range of essential nutrients in the right proportions, including plenty of complex carbohydrates (for coeliacs, these can include potatoes, rice, gluten-free grains such as millet and quinoa, gluten-free bread and gluten-free pasta); protein providers such as meat, poultry, fish or a vegetarian or vegan source; low-fat milk and dairy foods or dairy alternatives (see pages 36–9) for essential fatty acids, vitamins and minerals; and a minimum of five portions of fruit and vegetables.

Once they have switched to a gluten-free diet, some people find that they put on weight more easily as the lining of the gut starts to heal and the absorption of nutrients returns to normal. Appetite quickly returns as you start to enjoy food without discomfort afterwards, and you may start to eat more than before. Try to ensure your diet is nutrient-dense and contains plenty of whole foods. Although there is a wide range of gluten-free products available, they may not be as high in fibre, iron and B-vitamins as their gluten-containing counterparts, so check labelling and avoid overindulging in foods that are high in saturated fats or sugar.

Water-soluble vitamins such as B-vitamins and vitamin C are absorbed as they travel out of the stomach and enter the small intestine. Deficiencies in these and other vitamins and minerals are therefore more common in coeliacs, and something that can lengthen the time your gut takes to heal. It is best to obtain these nutrients from your diet as the body absorbs them most easily from food, though a general multivitamin and mineral supplement may be helpful, as long as the contents are at the recommended daily amount (RDA) levels; some can be harmful if taken in excess. A food diary may be useful so that you can make sure you are getting adequate nutrients, and to flag up other food intolerances.

Below Different foods contain different amounts of essential vitamins and minerals, such as potassium, folate and iron.

Vitamin C

Also known as ascorbic acid, vitamin C is important for the formation of collagen, a protein that strengthens bones and anchors teeth into the gums and – vital for coeliacs – assists tissue repair and speedy healing. It should be eaten daily as the body is unable to store it, so make sure you eat plenty of fruit and vegetables.
Good sources include: citrus and soft fruits, broccoli, bell peppers and tomatoes.

B-vitamins

This is a large group of vitamins, but those especially important for coeliacs are B1, B2, B6, folate and vitamin B12. Wheat products such as bread and breakfast cereals are high in these vitamins and are often fortified with extra amounts, so make sure that the gluten-free equivalents that you buy are also fortified.

Vitamin B1 (thiamin) This helps the body to convert carbohydrates and fats into energy. It is essential for growth, and for maintaining the functions of the heart and the digestive system.
Good sources include: peas, spinach, liver, beef, pork, nuts and soya beans.

NON-DAIRY SOURCES OF CALCIUM

Because of the possibility of secondary lactose intolerance (see page 36), newly diagnosed coeliacs are often advised to reduce the amount of dairy products they eat in the first few weeks after diagnosis. It's therefore really important to eat plenty of calcium from other, non-dairy, sources during this time. These include:

- eggs
- calcium-enriched soya and other non-dairy milks
- tinned salmon and sardines (finely mash in any bones as well)
- seafood such as prawns/shrimp, crab, cockles and mussels
- nuts, especially almonds
- seeds, especially sesame seeds
- pulses such as chickpeas, beans and lentils and products made from them, like tofu

Vitamin B2 (riboflavin) Necessary for the release of energy from carbohydrates, this vitamin also helps the body to digest fats.
Good sources include: asparagus, milk, yogurt, meat, fish and eggs.

Vitamin B6 (pyridoxine) This is involved in the production and digestion of amino acids. It helps the body manufacture insulin, histamine – which is involved in allergic reactions – and antibodies that fight infection. It also plays a key role in the production of haemoglobin, the oxygen-carrying molecule in red blood cells.
Good sources include: potatoes, sweet potatoes, bananas, chicken, turkey, salmon, mackerel, trout and tuna.

Folate (folic acid) Playing a vital role in making DNA and RNA (a substance needed to make protein), folate is key in growth and development and in the production of new cells. It works with vitamin B12 to form haemoglobin for red blood cells. It is essential during the first trimester of pregnancy as it greatly reduces the risk of the baby developing a neural tube defect such as spina bifida, and all prospective mothers are advised to take a supplement for a few months before they conceive and throughout pregnancy.
Good sources include: green vegetables such as cabbage and peas, oranges, pulses and lentils.

Vitamin B12 This is necessary for growth and repair and, together with folate, in the production of red blood cells.
Good sources include: meat, fish and seafood, although many other foods, such as breakfast cereals and some breads, are fortified with it. Vegetarians and especially vegans should take a supplement.

The importance of calcium

Calcium is the most abundant mineral in the body, with 90 per cent of it in the bones and teeth. Adequate intake throughout life is essential to ensure peak bone mass and to prevent osteoporosis in later life. It is also needed for the absorption of vitamin B12.

Vitamin D is essential for the absorption of calcium. It is produced by the action of sunlight on the skin, so make sure that your skin is regularly exposed (about 10 minutes a day, avoiding the hottest times in the summer) and consider taking a supplement in winter.
Good sources include: oily fish, liver, butter, margarine, cheese and eggs, so check your diet carefully for vitamin D-fortified foods if you follow a vegan diet. Various non-dairy sources of calcium are listed in the box, while details of how to make your own non-dairy milks and other products are provided on pages 36–9.

The importance of iron

Iron deficiency is frequently caused by a poor intake or poor absorption of iron and is very common in newly-diagnosed coeliacs. Anaemia reduces the red blood cell count and thus the amount of oxygen carried to the tissues. Signs of iron-deficiency anaemia include fatigue and faintness, lack of concentration, coldness in the fingers and toes due to bad circulation, and soft or brittle nails. Vitamin C is needed for the absorption of iron and for it to be used effectively, so make sure that you eat iron-rich foods along with some fresh fruit or vegetables or a small glass of fruit juice.

GOOD SOURCES OF IRON

Foods that contain at least 2mg of iron per 100g/3½oz include:

- dried fruit, especially prunes and apricots
- red meat and offal/variety meats (liver, kidneys etc)
- poultry
- egg yolks
- sardines, tuna, prawns/shrimp
- pulses such as soya, kidney beans and chickpeas

Managing a gluten-free diet

While it is easy to identify many foods that contain gluten, such as bread and pasta, there's a wide range of products that contain traces of gluten, some of which are not immediately obvious. Check the ingredients list on product packaging carefully to ensure it is gluten free and create your own 'safe' foods list. There are also apps available to help you.

Food labelling

By law, manufacturers must list all the ingredients in food products, and provide allergen information on the packet. Gluten-containing cereals are one of the 14 listed allergens (others include eggs, milk, nuts and soya) that have to be emphasized – in larger or bold letters – no matter how little of the allergen the product contains.

The term 'gluten free' can only be used on foods that contain 20 parts per million or less of gluten. Many have additional wording – 'suitable for coeliacs' – so that you can see at a glance that it is safe.

Some products contain ingredients that are inherently gluten free, but the manufacturer cannot guarantee this as the food may be produced or packaged in an area where gluten-containing foods are present. These will have labelling such as 'may contain traces of gluten' or 'made in a factory also handling wheat'.

The Coeliac UK website has a directory (only members can access it) and a mobile app with a barcode scanner, so that you can check products in the supermarket before you buy. Or try scanglutenfree.com.

FOODS THAT ARE NATURALLY GLUTEN FREE

- fresh meat, poultry and fish
- fresh fruit and vegetables, including potatoes
- eggs
- dairy products
- soya and plain tofu
- plain nuts and seeds
- rice
- pulses and lentils
- sugar, honey, golden/light corn syrup, maple syrup, date syrup, molasses, treacle
- jams, jellies and marmalades
- flavourings, such as fresh herbs and spices, vanilla extract
- pure fats, such as butter and oils

Below Fresh fruit and vegetables are all gluten free, and are therefore always safe food choices, as well as being beneficial for your health.

FOODS AND DRINKS THAT MAY INCLUDE GLUTEN

Food type	Definitely contains gluten	May contain gluten
Meat and poultry	Scotch eggs, corned beef, breaded ham, meat-based stuffings, crumb-coated pieces such as gougons, chicken nuggets	Cooked poultry, sausages, sausagemeat, burgers, meatballs, salami, pâté
Fish	Breaded fish, battered fish, any food that has been deep-fried with other-gluten-coated food, eg from fish and chip shops	Crab sticks
Dairy	Yogurt with whole grains	Low-fat yogurt, blue cheeses, sour cream, ice cream, mousse
Vegetarian products	Seitan	Quorn, veggie burgers and sausages, vegetable suet (often coated with flour)
Grains and grain products	Wheat, barley, rye, spelt, triticale, kamut, farro, emmer, einkorn, durum, farina, orzo, bulghur wheat, semolina, couscous	Buckwheat, oats, flours such as gram, sorghum and sweet rice (gluten free but may be cross-contaminated during production)
Sauces, condiments and cooking ingredients	Chinese soy sauce	Mustards, curry powder, malt vinegar, tamari, miso, stock/bouillon cubes or powder, seasoning, stuffing and batter mixes, white pepper, marinades, brown sauce, tomato sauce, salad cream, dressings, packet and jarred sauces and mixes, soups, pickles, baking powder, icing/confectioners' sugar, dried yeast
Snacks	Dry-roasted nuts, Japanese rice crackers, pretzels, bread sticks, ice cream cones and wafers	Corn tortillas, flavoured crisps/potato chips, popcorn and rice cakes, Bombay mix, wasabi peas
Confectionery	Liquorice, wafer chocolate bars (and communion wafers), bars with malted fillings	Caramels, marshmallows, marzipan, chocolates, muesli bars, boiled sweets/candies* (* ones containing glucose syrup are gluten free, but may affect people with a wheat allergy)
Drinks	Malted milk drinks, barley water	Beer, lager, stout, ale, instant coffees (some contain wheat as a bulking agent)

Above Store ingredients in sealed jars and label them clearly to help reduce the risk of cross-contamination.

A DOZEN DINING QUESTIONS

If the restaurant doesn't have specific gluten-free options or if you are attending a catered event, explain your dietary needs to the waiting staff and don't be afraid to ask them to speak to the chef. Be assertive but polite and don't forget to smile!

1. Are there croutons on the salad/soup?
2. Is the soup thickened with flour and does it contain pearl barley or pasta?
3. Does the salad dressing contain wheat or flour?
4. Are the 'bacon bits' and 'crab' real or artificial substitutes such as crab sticks?
5. Has the food been marinated in anything before cooking and does it include Chinese soy sauce or teriyaki sauce?
6. Are the chips dusted in flour/spicy coating?
7. Are the mashed potatoes made from scratch or from a ready-made mix?
8. Has the food been dusted with flour before being fried/grilled/broiled/baked?
9. Has the oil been previously used to cook other breaded foods?
10. Is the ice cream served with a wafer garnish?
11. Is there a separate preparation area for gluten-free food?
12. Do you use separate cookware and utensils for gluten-free dishes?

Avoiding cross-contamination

Even the smallest amount of gluten can make someone with coeliac disease ill, so if you have a member of the family who is coeliac or gluten intolerant (and total removal of all gluten-containing products from the house is not a practical solution for you), it's important to prevent cross-contamination:

- Keep gluten-free food in sealed containers, in a separate cupboard if at all possible, and label everything clearly.
- Wipe down surfaces immediately after use.
- Keep separate bowls, pans, strainers, colanders, cooling racks and utensils for gluten-free cooking.
- Make sure that butter, spreads and preserves aren't contaminated with bread or cracker crumbs (or have separate ones).
- Use a separate toaster or toaster bags.
- Do not reuse oil after frying crumb or batter-coated foods.

Eating out

It's important to do your research before dining out. The easiest way is to choose a restaurant that has specific gluten-free options on their menu in the first place. If the restaurant choice isn't up to you, check the menu online before you go, or call them during non-busy hours to discuss the menu choices. Once you arrive, make sure that your waiter is aware of your dietary requirements before you start to order your meal.

In the UK, look for Coeliac UK's symbol on menus, which shows that the dish is both gluten-free and that the caterer meets the requirements of gluten-free preparation. Allergen information must be provided by law and if a dish contains wheat, rye, barley or oats in the ingredients, this must be stated (this can be provided orally rather than in writing, so do ask if you don't see this information). Other countries use other symbols and systems, so it is worth checking what these are before you dine out or go shopping so you know what to look for. If in doubt, ask.

Managing coeliac disease in children

Children who have been diagnosed with coeliac disease will be no different from their peers, except that they will need to avoid all foods containing gluten. While this may seem daunting at first, an early diagnosis will help your child to adapt to a new diet from a young age.

Coeliac disease may be present from birth, or it can develop at any time through childhood or adulthood. During the first few months, breast or formula milk provides all the nutrients babies need to grow and develop. A baby's digestive system is not fully matured during this period and there is evidence that giving solids too early increases the chances of allergies and food intolerances later on. Babies should not be weaned (given solid food) before the age of four months and should not be fed foods containing gluten until they are at least six months old. If you have coeliac disease, or close family members do, you should watch for any symptoms when introducing gluten to your baby's diet.

When you first discover your child has coeliac disease the way you handle the diagnosis is important. Treat the situation calmly to avoid making your child feel anxious. If your child is old enough, explain in a matter-of-fact way why there are some foods he or she cannot eat. You will also need to inform family, friends and anyone else who cares for your child, so that they do not inadvertently give your child food containing gluten.

Tips to help children with coeliac disease

Children usually respond well to treatment with a gluten-free diet and most feel significantly better after just two weeks, and will attain normal height, weight and bone health by the time they are adults. There are many ways you can help them:

- Involve your child in identifying foods that do and don't contain gluten. Use a sticker system in your pantry that the whole family can understand.
- Cook gluten-free meals for the whole family when possible; it saves time and effort on your part and will make your child feel less isolated and excluded.
- If your child attends pre-school or playgroup, rolling out and shaping play dough is a popular activity. This contains wheat flour, so care needs to be taken that your child does not put this into his or her mouth during play, and that they wash their hands afterwards, especially before eating. Gluten-free play dough can be made with white rice flour.
- When your child starts school or moves on to another school, arrange a meeting with the appropriate staff to explain your child's needs and to find out what provisions are made. It is likely that there will be other children in the school who are also coeliac or gluten-intolerant. Talk to your child about not swapping or sharing lunches or snacks with others.
- At parties, explain to the organizer in advance that your child cannot eat food containing gluten. Ask about the food they are planning to provide, so that you can bring something similar for your child, or some gluten-free food to share. Parties are hectic events, so don't expect the host to provide a special gluten-free menu.
- There are bound to be times when your child accidently eats a food containing gluten. This will cause a minor upset, but symptoms should pass in a few days. Don't assume, however, that every stomach upset is due to gluten; your child will pick up tummy bugs and illnesses like any other child.

Left It is often easiest to make your child a gluten-free packed lunch for school and outings. Make them aware that they shouldn't share their food.

Gluten-free baking

The key to successful gluten-free cooking and particularly baking is to understand the ingredients you are using and their properties. Initially, this may seem daunting, but you will soon discover a whole range of new and different ingredients and creative bakes.

Although in some recipes it may be possible to just substitute gluten-free flour for wheat flour and add a little xanthan gum, it isn't usually so straightforward. Generally, gluten-free bakes require a lot more liquid than wheat-based ones to avoid ending up with a bake that is heavy, dry or undesirably crumbly. You will find that adding ingredients such as oil, eggs, yogurt, buttermilk, crème fraiche or sour cream can help achieve a softer and moister texture and hold everything together. Ground nuts, seeds and grated fruit and vegetables such as apples, bananas and sweet potatoes can also help bind the mixture together, as well as adding flavour and nutrients.

Gluten-free batters can look and behave very differently from wheat-based ones. Typically, they are wetter and thinner. They also tend to stiffen after standing and may soak up more moisture than you'd expect. This is especially the case if you've added ingredients such as xanthan gum, ultratex or ground psyllium husk, so after mixing, spoon the batter into the tin or pan, or shape the dough, right away.

This may all sound a little difficult and confusing, but you will soon get into the habit of using a variety of ingredients and some alternative starches to wheat flours for baking, thickening and binding, and in the process come across delicious if less familiar grains.

Gluten alternatives

It is gluten that gives elasticity to the doughs from which breads, pastas and pastries are made. Gluten-free flours lack this elasticity and most do not have enough binding ingredients to hold mixtures together, so bakes such

HOW TO MAKE AND USE GLUTEN-FREE BREADCRUMBS

Gluten-free breadcrumbs can be fresh or dried, fine or coarse and are a great way to use up gluten-free bread that is past its prime – it tends to stale more quickly than wheat bread. The crumbs can be used in all sorts of gluten-free dishes to provide bulk or texture.

Fresh breadcrumbs

These are absorbent and swell when soaked in liquid. They are useful to bulk out other ingredients in recipes such as treacle tart, or as a binder in meatballs and meat and veggie loaves, where they will also soak up the juices and make the dish firmer. They can also be used to make crunchy toppings such as pangrattato (a mixture of breadcrumbs fried in oil, mixed with parsley and gluten-free Pecorino or Parmesan cheese).

The quickest way to make fresh breadcrumbs is in a food processor. Tear sliced bread into pieces (remove the crusts only if the bread is white and you want pure white crumbs) and process in a dedicated gluten-free food processor until as coarse or fine as you like. Alternatively, grate using a coarse box grater. Use or store in sealed bags in the fridge for up to a week or in the freezer for several months.

Dried breadcrumbs

Crisp, dried breadcrumbs are useful for crumb-coating fish and thin meat slices such as chicken fillets, flattened by gently bashing with a rolling pin, and chicken, turkey or fish gougons, before they are shallow- or deep-fried or baked. They can also be used to coat foods such as potato croquettes and Scotch eggs to provide a crunchy outer shell.

To make dried breadcrumbs, cut off the crusts and cut or break some stale bread into smaller pieces. Spread these out on a baking sheet in a single layer and bake at 120°C/250°F/Gas ½ for 15–20 minutes, or until crunchy and dry and just beginning to turn golden. Keep an eye on them to prevent them from burning. Remove from the oven and leave to cool.

Place the toasted bread in a strong plastic bag (you may need to do this in batches) and use a rolling pin to crush into crumbs. Do this carefully, so that you don't tear the bag.

Dry breadcrumbs can be stored in dry glass jars or food containers for up to four months. If you like, add seasonings such as dried oregano, thyme, rosemary or parsley flakes.

as cakes can be slightly crumbly. This can be solved by adding ingredients like flaxseed/linseed (see page 32), xanthan gum, ground psyllium husk or ultratex.

Xanthan gum A white, flavourless powder with a similar texture to cornflour/starch, xanthan gum acts as a substitute for gluten, and binds, thickens and stabilizes ingredients. It is useful when making breads, pastries and pasta. Grown from fermented plant bacteria, it's important to measure it carefully; it reduces crumbling in foods such as cakes, but too much can create a tough texture.

Ground psyllium husk The psyllium plant is a type of plantain from the banana family and has seeds with fibrous outer husks that are able to hold a lot of water. When hydrated, these create a gel that helps to stabilize gluten-free doughs and mixtures. Psyllium is a concentrated source of dietary fibre and the husks are not digested in the small intestine, instead being partially broken down in the colon where they promote the growth of 'good' bacteria. Ground psyllium husk can be mixed to make an egg substitute, and as a substitute for xanthan gum, though you should use a slightly higher amount. You will need to add a little more water to your recipe as psyllium is highly absorbent.

Ultratex A modified tapioca starch, ultratex is a fine white powder that thickens in the same way as a cooking starch, but also swells and thickens cold liquids, so doesn't need heating. Tasteless and colourless, it is widely used in catering to thicken sauces, but can also be used as a binding ingredient in cooking when making mixtures such as gluten-free filo pastry, as it makes the dough flexible and allows it to stretch with less risk of tearing when rolling out.

STORING GLUTEN-FREE BAKES

Gluten-free bakes generally do not keep well and should be eaten when freshly made, or frozen when cool, and defrosted as you need them. Most will freeze successfully and will keep for many weeks in the freezer. Pack in portions so that you can remove exactly what you need for breakfast or packed lunches. When defrosted, bakes such as scones and muffins can be refreshed by microwaving them for just a few seconds.

Below left Ultratex is especially useful for making gluten-free filo pastry.
Below right Xanthan gum is added to many gluten-free flour blends.

Gluten-free flours

Whether you want to avoid gluten or just want to experiment, there is a vast choice of inherently gluten-free flours that are increasingly readily available. Each has its own personality and uses, and can be blended with other gluten-free flours to suit your needs.

Different flours have different qualities, but no single grain or seed can replicate wheat flour, so for every type of recipe you should use a blend of gluten-free flours to meet your requirements, selecting for flavour, texture, properties such as binding, and nutritional content.

If you are converting a wheat flour-based recipe to gluten-free yourself, you need to know what qualities you are looking for in the flour mix. This is straightforward if you are making cakes or cookies that don't rely on gluten for the structure, but it is more difficult for bread, pasta and pastry. For this reason, it is better to follow recipes devised specifically for these.

Ready-mixed gluten-free flours are the easiest types of flour to start with, and will give good results. In the UK, four types of gluten-free flour are generally available: plain, self-raising, white bread flour, and brown bread flour. It is also possible to buy larger bags of gluten-free plain flour which don't include buckwheat; this is usually a whiter flour blend with a mild flavour.

Almost all brands of gluten-free self-raising/self-rising flour contain xanthan gum. The recipes in this book are intended for use with this type of flour, or your own flour blend containing xanthan gum. If you happen to use a brand that doesn't contain xanthan gum (this is more likely in the USA), as a rough guide, for every 115g/4oz/1 cup gluten-free flour, add 5ml/1 tsp xanthan gum for cakes and cookies and 10ml/2 tsp for breads. Sometimes, even when you use a blend that contains xanthan gum, you will need to add more; follow the recipe carefully.

Once you're accustomed to gluten-free cooking, making your own flour blends is easy and allows you to create a mixture most suited to your recipe. For recipes for bread flour blends, turn to pages 42 and 45. When blending your own flours, mix them thoroughly, especially if you are adding xanthan gum; it's a good idea to sift them together several times. Choose fine-milled versions as they will blend better, and double-check that

READY-MADE GLUTEN-FREE BLENDED FLOUR MIXES

Flour blend	Typical content	Uses
Gluten-free plain/all-purpose blend	White rice flour, potato flour, tapioca flour, maize flour, white buckwheat flour	Pastry, cookies, pasta, crackers
Gluten-free self-raising/self-rising blend	Rice flour, potato flour, tapioca flour, maize flour, white buckwheat flour, raising agents (monocalcium phosphate, sodium bicarbonate), thickener (xanthan gum)	Cakes, scones, US biscuits, some breads
Gluten-free white bread flour blend	Rice flour, tapioca flour, potato flour, thickener (xanthan gum)	White bread, some pastas, pizza bases
Gluten-free brown bread flour blend	Rice flour, tapioca flour, potato flour, buckwheat flour, carob flour, sugar beet fibre, thickener (xanthan gum)	Brown bread

each is certified as gluten free. Store the blend in a cool, dark place or in the fridge if the mixture contains flours with a high oil content, in labelled airtight containers.

Most flour blends consist of three or four components. These may be a starchy flour, a 'short' flour, a flour for flavour, and a flour for binding. For the base, start with heavier flours such as rice flour or maize flour. Next, blend with starchier ('short') flours such as tapioca flour, potato starch, cornflour/starch or arrowroot powder. For flavour, sorghum or teff flours work well. Finally, make sure there is enough 'binding' flour to hold the mixture together, such as tapioca flour. You can boost the nutrient content by adding high-protein flours such as amaranth, buckwheat or nut flours.

HOME-MADE GLUTEN-FREE BLENDED FLOUR MIXES*

Flour blend	Uses	Ingredients (each makes 500g/18oz/4½ cups)
Gluten-free white and brown rice flour blend	This can be used in any recipe that calls for gluten-free plain/all-purpose flour. Its delicate, mild flavour makes it ideal for pastries, light cakes and cookies	75g/3oz/⅔ cup white rice flour 75g/3oz/⅔ cup brown rice flour 175g/6oz/1½ cups potato starch 175g/6oz/1½ cups tapioca flour/starch
Gluten-free white flour blend	This is ideal where you want a whiter gluten-free plain/all-purpose flour, and is good for cakes, shortcrust and choux pastries, pasta, and batters	350g/12oz/3 cups white rice flour 100g/3½oz/1 cup potato starch 50g/2oz/½ cup tapioca flour/starch
Gluten-free short-textured white flour blend	This is perfect when you want a very short texture for baking, such as shortbread-type cookies, and crumble toppings	250g/9oz/2¼ cups brown rice flour 150g/5oz/1¼ cups fine maize meal 100g/3½oz/scant 1 cup cornflour/starch
Gluten-free polenta flour blend	Polenta/cornmeal makes this a slightly more textured gluten-free flour blend with a golden colour, which works well with the softness of the sorghum flour. Chestnut flour also works well here instead of some or all of the sorghum flour and gives a darker, nuttier flavour	225g/8oz/2 cups sorghum flour 175g/6oz/1½ cups fine polenta/cornmeal 100g/3½oz/scant 1 cup tapioca flour/starch
Gluten-free sorghum flour blend	A higher protein and fibre content and a sweet flavour makes this gluten-free flour blend good for soda bread, muffins, cookies and cakes where colour isn't important. It has a similar flavour and texture to a half-brown, half-white wheat-based flour	175g/6oz/1½ cups sorghum flour 175g/6oz/1½ cups potato starch 150g/5oz/1¼ cups tapioca flour/starch

* These blends are all plain/all-purpose flours. For self-raising/self-rising versions of these blends, add 20ml/4 tsp baking powder and 10ml/2 tsp xanthan gum. For home-made bread flour blends, see pages 42 and 45.

Flours for a short & crumbly texture

In many bakes, 'shortness' is a desirable quality; it describes the melt-in-the-mouth texture of baked foods such as shortcrust pastry and shortbread biscuits. This is easy to achieve with many gluten-free flours, as it is gluten developing in wheat flour that can make bakes 'tough'.

Many of the 'short-textured' gluten-free flours have a mild flavour and are often used on their own in biscuits, cookies and traybakes, or added along with starchy flour to give balance to well-flavoured flours in gluten-free flour blends. They can also be used in pancake batters or bread dough to add bulk, as the addition of liquid will reduce their shortness.

Rice flour

This is one of the most versatile of the gluten-free flours and is added in the highest proportion to most commercial flour blends. Made from ground raw rice, the most common types are white rice flour and brown rice flour, which has a slightly nutty flavour and is made from the whole grain, so is higher in fibre and nutrients.

Rice flours are used for baking and to make noodles, pasta and pancake batters. Resting mixtures such as batters and doughs is important as it gives the rice flour a chance to soak up liquid and rehydrate, which will thicken the mixture and moderate the slight sandiness of texture this flour can produce in foods. Rice flour will keep for at least a year in a cool, dry place.

Millet flour

Worthy of far more than its bird food label, these tiny seeds are a staple grain for nearly one-third of the world's population. Although many different types are grown across Africa and Asia, in the West 'pearl' millet is the most commonly available type, and has a pale cream colour and a mildly sweet flavour, similar to corn.

Millet flour is excellent for adding shortness to bakes. It should be stored in the fridge because it has a high oil content.

Maize flour and polenta/cornmeal

Maize, also known as corn, has a bright yellow colour. Although it originated in South America, it is now grown around the world. There are four types of dried, ground maize: finely ground flour (sometimes called corn flour; this is different to cornflour/cornstarch, so don't confuse the two); and ground, of which there are three types:

- Polenta/cornmeal can be coarsely or finely ground (but not as fine as maize flour) and makes excellent cornbreads and muffins with a rich flavour and moist, crumbly texture.
- Masa harina is used specifically for tortillas or tamales and is made from white corn, which has been nixtamalized (treated with an alkaline lime solution in order to make the nutrients more available). It can be difficult to get certified gluten-free masa harina, so check carefully before buying, but it is worth sourcing for its flavour and nutritive benefits.
- 'Grits' are usually made from dent corn, a starchy and less-sweet corn. After removing the hulls, the corn is ground into larger pieces than polenta/cornmeal. These can then be cooked to make a type of porridge.

Each of these have very different uses, so make sure you get the correct type for the recipe you are making.

Left Rice flour is available in white (shown here) or brown; the latter is higher in fibre and nutrients and has a more interesting flavour.
Opposite A wide range of gluten-free flours can be used in place of wheat flour, each with different properties and uses.

Flours for starch & crispness

These flours are pure starch and have a fine, powdery texture. They add crispness to bakes such as cookies and help create a light, soft structure. They may also be used for thickening sauces and desserts. Because they are virtually fat free, they have a long shelf life.

Arrowroot powder

This pure starch is made from the tuberous root of the South American maranta plant. It can be used in baking, where a light starch is needed, but should only be added in small quantities to avoid a chalky taste, and shouldn't be combined with dairy products such as yogurt or cream as this may create a slimy texture. It's often used in very plain almost fat-free bakes such as 'arrowroot biscuits', which have a mild flavour. Arrowroot is most appreciated as a thickener of liquids and makes sparkling jellies and clear sauces, where cornflour would give cloudy results.

Arrowroot powder thickens liquids and mixtures more than other starches, so use one-third less than if you were using cornflour or cornstarch. It should be mixed first with cold liquid to make a thin paste before being added to hot liquid, to prevent it from going lumpy. Remove from the heat as soon as the sauce has thickened, as further heating will thin it.

The Victorians credited it with health properties, as it is easily digested, so was often made into milk jellies for children or given as a remedy for an upset stomach. It contains few nutrients but is high in carbohydrates.

Below, left to right Arrowroot powder, cornflour/starch, and potato starch.

Cornflour/cornstarch

A fine, white, powdery starch, this is extracted from maize kernels, which are soaked and ground to separate the germ from the bran. Virtually tasteless, it is used as a thickening agent and is the main ingredient of commercial custard powder. When used in sauces it cuts out the need for fat, as unlike other flours, it blends to a smooth paste with liquid.

When making sauces, puddings and cookies, root starches such as tapioca flour and arrowroot powder (which have less effect on blood sugar levels) can be used instead of cornflour/starch, but if used in large quantities, these give a gummy texture to breads and cakes. Cornflour gives drier and harder results in baking, so can be useful when you want crispness.

Potato starch

This pure white starch has a very fine texture and is used to lighten all kinds of bakes. When mixed with liquid and heated, potato starch expands rapidly, so makes light, fluffy cakes and breads. It is produced by extracting and processing only the starchy component of potatoes, so is made from high starch or 'floury' potatoes; it is not the same thing as potato flour (see opposite) and has little nutritional value.

Flours for binding

When making a flour mix for bread, pastry or pasta, it's useful to add flours that will bind the mixture together and help to either hold the structure as it expands (when making bread) or make it more pliable and flexible (when making pastry and pasta).

Above, clockwise from top left Oat flour, potato flour, glutinous rice flour, tapioca flour/starch.

Oat flour

Oats contain avenin, which is a protein similar to gluten. While most coeliacs and those who are gluten-intolerant or gluten-sensitive have no problem eating gluten-free oats, a very small number may still be sensitive to them. It is vital that you find a gluten-free source as many oats are contaminated with other grains since they are often processed in the same place as wheat, barley and rye (this can also occur in the fields where the oats are grown). If you are one of the minority of people who cannot eat oats, quinoa flour and flakes make an excellent alternative in most recipes. If you can tolerate them, though, oats are a great source of soluble fibre, which helps to maintain a healthy gut, reduce cholesterol levels, and keep blood sugars stable.

Oats are an excellent binding flour and are an inexpensive addition to flour blends. They help bread dough to stretch as it rises, retain moisture in cakes, and give scones and cookies a more substantial texture. You can also use oat flour as an alternative to ground almonds in some recipes (add a little extra liquid as well, but not too early or the texture will become sticky and difficult to mix).

It's simple to make oat flour yourself by grinding rolled oats in a dedicated electric coffee grinder (with blades) or a food processor, to a fine consistency.

Potato flour

This is different to potato starch and is made by dehydrating cooked potatoes, then crushing and grinding to a flour. Heavy and a creamy yellow colour, it has a strong potato flavour and is useful for bakes as it binds them, helps keep them moist, and prolongs their shelf life. It's particularly good in soda breads where it produces a chewier, more bread-like consistency.

Glutinous rice flour

While white rice flour is ground from long-grain rice, glutinous rice flour, which is also known as 'sweet rice' flour (or *mochi* flour or *mochiko* in Asian stores) is ground from short-grain glutinous ('sticky' or 'sushi') rice. Despite its name, it doesn't contain gluten and is so-called because it has good binding qualities and works in a similar way to gluten.

It's not sweet either, but has a mild, almost milky taste. It is particularly good as part of the flour mix in recipes that rely on air for expanding and rising, such as choux and puff pastries, batters such as Yorkshire pudding or popovers, and steamed buns (bao buns). Glutinous rice flour is also excellent for thickening sauces.

Tapioca flour

Also known as tapioca starch, this fine, highly absorbent white powder is made from the crushed pulp of the cassava root. Excellent for lightening the consistency and binding ingredients together in bakes, it cannot be used alone as it produces an inedible chewy texture. Instead, partner it with flavoured, nutritious flours (it has few nutrients). It is a good thickening agent in soups, sauces and pie fillings (blend to a paste with cold water before adding to hot liquids) and it freezes well.

Flours for flavour

While many gluten-free flours are used for their cooking qualities, such as texture and the ability to bind and hold other ingredients together, there is also a wide range of flours that can add taste and depth to your bakes and batters.

Flours with bold flavours or that give a nutritional boost provide an opportunity to create interesting and often healthier recipes. In some dishes, they may be a main ingredient, but generally they are better used sparingly to create a more balanced taste overall. Many of these flours are more expensive, but you can mix them with more economical types, such as rice flour, or even make some yourself by grinding the grains in a dedicated gluten-free electric coffee grinder or food processor.

Amaranth flour

This tiny pseudo-grain (like quinoa) contains all nine essential amino acids, including lysine, a protein missing in most grains. It is quite high in anti-nutrients, although these can be removed by the fermentation or the sourdough process. Amaranth flour is made by grinding the buff-coloured seeds into a fine powder. It has a distinctive peppery and earthy flavour, so is better diluted with other milder-tasting flours. Too much can make baked goods dense, so use no more than 25 per cent amaranth flour in recipes. Due to its high oil content, it should be stored in the fridge.

Buckwheat flour

Although it sounds as if it is a relative of wheat, buckwheat is actually a cold-climate plant from the same family as rhubarb, sorrel and dock. The pointed triangular seeds resemble cereal grains and are ground into a fine-textured, greyish flour. Used alone, buckwheat flour has a distinctive, slightly sour, almost musty taste, but this is mellowed by mixing it with other flours. It is often used in pancakes, especially blinis, and is a good addition to breads as it gives them a chewy texture and can help to bind the dough, allowing it to hold its structure as it rises. You can also make a nutritious bread from the sprouted grains.

Carob flour

This is made from the roasted and ground pods of the carob tree, native to the Middle East. The pods look very similar to broad/fava bean pods and ripen from green to brown. Inside is a sweet pulp and hard, brown seeds. Often considered a healthy alternative to chocolate, carob only has half the fat content of cocoa and is caffeine-free. However, it is high in sugar, so if you are using carob flour instead of cocoa in a recipe that already contains sugar, try to reduce the sugar a little.

Chestnut flour

Made from ground roasted sweet chestnuts, usually from Italy or southern France, this dark-cream or pale-brown flour has a unique nutty, warm and slightly earthy sweet flavour with a hint of caramel, and is especially suited to sweet bakes. It's often used in autumnal and winter recipes as it tends to be seasonal and is not readily available all year round, especially in certified gluten-free versions. It features in French crêpes and Tuscan cuisine, and is good in breads and soda breads, where it creates a dense crumb that allows it to be thinly sliced. Although the flour feels heavy, it produces surprisingly light and moist cakes and can be used on its own or blended with other flours. Because it is higher in fat than many flours, it should be stored in the fridge.

Gram flour and other pulse flours

Milled from channa dal, which is a variety of chickpea, gram flour often features in Indian cookery. Besan flour is similar, but is a mixture of ground yellow split peas and channa dal. Both are a pale yellow colour with an earthy flavour and can be used to make various flatbreads as well as pakoras and bhajis. Italian farini di ceci is a pure chickpea flour and can be used instead of gram or besan flour. Ondhwa flour is another Indian flour made from ground rice and lentils. There are many other flours made from pulses, such as adzuki beans, mung beans, red lentils and soya beans.

Hemp flour

This is made by milling whole hemp seeds. High in protein and essential fatty acids, it is green in colour, with a distinct earthy and grassy flavour, and care needs to be taken so that it isn't overpowering. When used in small quantities – no more than 15 per cent of the total amount of flour – the taste mellows to a delicious nuttiness. Store in the freezer as it has a high oil content.

Opposite, clockwise from top left Amaranth flour, buckwheat flour, carob flour, chestnut flour, gram flour and hemp flour.

Above Quinoa flour is extremely nutritious and very versatile in cooking and baking.

Above Sorghum flour lends a lovely malt flavour to breads and pastries.

Above Teff flour is the main constituent of injera – an Ethiopian fermented pancake.

Quinoa flour and flakes

Made from ground quinoa seeds, quinoa flour is a great source of protein. A 'pseudo grain', this pale cream-coloured flour is easily digestible and has a mild, slightly grassy, nutty flavour. It can be added to all sorts of bakes, both sweet and savoury, and can also be used to thicken soups and casseroles.

You can buy quinoa flour or make it yourself by grinding raw pearl quinoa in a dedicated gluten-free electric coffee grinder or food processor. Ideally, it should be stored in the fridge.

Quinoa flakes have similar properties to rolled oats, swelling and releasing soluble fibre that gives porridge its texture. They are especially useful for those who are intolerant to oats, even the gluten-free varieties. Made by flattening and rolling quinoa seeds in the same way as oats, they can be used instead of rolled oats in all types of baking (simply substitute the same weight of quinoa flakes for rolled oats). Quinoa flakes do have a slightly stronger flavour than oats, but this can be balanced by the addition of extra flavourings in your recipe, such as vanilla extract in sweet recipes and nutritional yeast flakes in savoury ones.

Sorghum flour

One of the major cereal crops in the world, sorghum has a mild, malty flavour and a texture somewhat like a very fine and smooth wholemeal wheat flour. It works well in both sweet and savoury recipes and has good binding properties so is ideal for both pastry and breads. Traditionally, sorghum flour is used to create pancakes and flatbreads such as jowar roti in Indian cuisine. You will therefore find it in Asian food stores as jowar or juwar flour, although this is rarely certified gluten-free, so will only be acceptable if you are wheat-intolerant rather than coeliac. Sorghum is one of the more expensive types of gluten-free flour but can be blended with cheaper varieties, such as rice flour.

Teff flour

A staple in Ethiopia, where it is used to make a naturally fermented pancake-like flatbread with a spongy texture know as injera, teff grains are harvested from a grass, also known as 'lovegrass', which is one of the world's earliest cultivated plants. The tiny round grains are roughly the size of poppy seeds and come in many colours, including creamy white, khaki, dark brown and red. The grass thrives in difficult climates where there are long hot periods without any rain. The grains may be cooked as a porridge or ground into a fine flour with a faintly smoky and malty flour.

Teff flour comes in several different varieties, but is mostly available as wholegrain 'white' flour (sometimes labelled 'ivory teff'), which has a mild and sweet taste, and a darker brown teff flour, which has a richer, deeper flavour. The darker flour is excellent in pancakes and well-flavoured rich fruit and chocolate cakes. In gluten-free breads, it creates a rich, intense flavour and dark colour, or you can blend it with starchy flours and some creamy millet flour for a lighter result.

Coconut flour

This is a very dense, coarse-textured flour with a mild but distinctive coconut taste, and has multiple uses, though primarily it is used for bulk and flavour. A by-product of coconut milk, the leftover flesh is dried at low temperature, then ground to a fine flour-like powder – see below. You can also make coconut flour by grinding gluten-free desiccated/dry unsweetened shredded coconut in a dedicated gluten-free electric coffee grinder or food processor.

Coconut flour contains almost twice the fibre of wheat flour and as it is low in digestible carbohydrates and helps to maintain blood sugar levels, is ideal for those watching their carbohydrate intake, diabetics and pre-diabetics. It is a good source of protein, containing about 19g/¾oz protein per 100g/3½oz, as well as lauric acid – a fat that helps support the immune system.

Unlike other gluten-free flours, coconut flour isn't easy to incorporate into regular recipes without making other adaptions, so it is best to stick to recipes specifically created for coconut flour, rather than simply swapping it in. It absorbs a huge amount of liquid, so you will probably need to add at least the equivalent volume of liquid to the amount of coconut flour. You will also need to add extra binding ingredients such as eggs, and sticky sweeteners such as maple syrup or honey.

Above Coconut flour has many uses, and is high in protein and fibre.

HOW TO MAKE COCONUT FLOUR

1 Preheat the oven to 110°C/220°F/Gas ¼. Line a baking sheet with baking parchment (don't use foil as the metal may taint the flavour of the coconut). Spread the leftover pulp from making coconut milk (see page 38) over the parchment in a thin, even layer, using a fork to break up any lumps.

2 Bake the pulp for 15 minutes, then remove from the oven and stir with a fork. Spread out again into an even layer and bake for a further 15–20 minutes, or until it is completely dry and golden in colour. Coconut can burn even at a low temperature, so check it often towards the end of the cooking time.

3 Remove the coconut from the oven and leave until completely cool. Tip into a dedicated gluten-free food processor and process for 4–5 minutes or until it is very finely ground. Store the flour in an airtight container in the fridge or freezer (due to its high oil content) and use within one year.

Nut & seed flours

Nuts and seeds can be ground to make flavoursome and nutritious flours. Useful in gluten-free cooking, they can be used to enhance the taste and texture of bakes when mixed with another flour, and on some occasions can stand alone in place of other gluten-free flours.

Nut and seed flours are low in carbohydrates and high in fat and protein. The easiest way of using nut flours in baking is to combine them with a ready-made gluten-free flour blend. The nut or seed flour provides texture and moistness, and the gluten-free flour blend will give the bake lightness and bind the ingredients together. Most cakes and muffins (and other baking recipes that involve rising agents such as baking powder) can be converted in this way, replacing up to 25 per cent of the flour in the recipe with nut or seed flour.

All kinds of nuts

From the warm and humid Amazon rainforests to the cooler deciduous woods of Europe, nuts grow around the world and have been a cooking ingredient for centuries. While all nuts can be made into gluten-free flours and nut meals, some are more suitable for baking than others.

Almonds These have a delicate flavour and are the most easily available and versatile of all nuts for baking. Almonds belong to the same family of trees as the apricot, plum and peach, which is why they have such an affinity with these fruits. Ground, they are used for recipes such as macaroons, Bakewell tart and frangipane and go well with fragrant spices including cinnamon, cardamom and ginger. When buying ready-ground almonds, check the ingredients carefully as some include a bulking agent that may contain gluten.

Chestnuts These have a much lower fat and calorie content than most other nuts, and are high in starch. Chestnuts are always cooked before grinding into a fine flour, and are not sold ground or as nut meal. The flour (also see page 26) is often associated with Christmas baking and goes well with oranges, caramel, chocolate, pears, and spices such as vanilla, cinnamon and cloves.

HOW TO MAKE NUT FLOUR

1 Lightly toast your choice of nuts in a single layer on a baking tray at 160°C/325°F/Gas 3 for 10–12 minutes, until they smell nutty and are just starting to turn golden. Remove from the oven. Alternatively, dry-fry over a medium heat, stirring often so that they colour evenly. Leave to cool.

2 Grind the nuts in small batches of no more than 115g/4oz/¾ cup at a time, in a dedicated gluten-free coffee grinder or a food processor. Grind in 10-second bursts, until they are the desired consistency. Take care not to over-blend or the oils will come out and they will clump together.

3 Scrape down the sides with a spatula to check all the nuts have been processed, then sift the nuts, using a coarse sieve or strainer to remove any larger pieces. Return the large pieces to the blender and process again. Use straight away or store in the fridge in an airtight container for up to one week.

Hazelnuts Usually sold as shelled whole nuts, often with their papery brown skins still on, these make a very distinctive light brown flour with a rich taste. Lightly roasting them before grinding intensifies their flavour and will allow you to rub off the skins easily. Hazelnuts go well with soft fruits such as raspberries and blueberries, pears, coffee, maple syrup and spices such as cinnamon.

Peanuts One of the least expensive nuts, peanuts are an excellent way of adding extra protein to dishes. Buy them ready-shelled with the red papery skins removed, then lightly roast until pale golden, before grinding. They have a distinctive taste and work well in breads, muffins and cookie-style biscuits on their own or mixed with strong chocolate or toffee flavours.

Pecans The pecan tree grows naturally in North America, predominantly in the southern states, and the name originates from the native-American word *paccan* used to describe any nut which needed to be cracked open with a stone. They have a softer, slightly sweeter flavour than walnuts, but are very oily, so don't grind them too finely or the oil will come out and the nuts will clump together. Pecans go well with apples, pears, bananas, coffee, caramel, cinnamon and cardamom.

Above Most nuts can be processed, either as they are or toasted, to create ground nuts of varying coarseness, from meal through to flour.

GROUND NUT PRODUCTS

Nut flour, ground nuts and nut meal are three different ingredients, but are interchangeable in most recipes, with slightly differing results:

Nut flour is milled from skinned blanched nuts into a very fine flour. It is perfect in delicate bakes or when you want light and fluffy results. It is almost impossible to make such a finely ground flour at home, but it is available online and from health food stores. Check whether the product is milled from whole nuts, as nut flour is sometimes a by-product of making nut oils; the nuts are pressed to extract the oils, then the leftover nuts are ground up into flour. This is not necessarily a problem and may suit your recipe, but be aware that this type of nut flour will be drier and contain very little fat.

Ground nuts are the most readily available (ground almonds being the commonest). They are made from skinned and blanched nuts, ground to an even consistency. The result is not quite as fine as nut flour, although you will find different consistencies between brands.

Nut meal is similar to ground nuts, but the nuts are ground with their skins on, and nuts such as almonds are unblanched to retain more flavour. It is darker in texture and colour, and higher in fibre.

Pistachios These small nuts make a green-coloured flour that adds a beautiful colour to bakes and other dishes, so don't mix with dark-coloured flours or ingredients. Ground pistachios are good in both sweet and savoury foods and often feature in Middle Eastern cooking. The flour goes well with apricots, cherries, orange, lemon, pomegranate, raspberries, tahini, honey and rose flavourings.

Walnuts Although grown in many parts of the world, most walnuts are sourced from France, Italy and California. They can be bought shelled as walnut halves or pieces; the latter tend to be cheaper and are excellent for making nut flour, although you should use sparingly as the nuts have a slightly bitter flavour. Walnut flour works particularly well in coffee bakes and brownies. It is also a well-known partner for dates, excellent with bananas, and often used in savoury cooking with cheeses such as Stilton and Cheddar.

HOW TO MAKE NUT FLOUR FROM LEFTOVER NUT PULP

After making and straining dairy-free nut milk (see page 38), there will be some damp leftover pulp in the nut bag or muslin/cheesecloth. This can be dried and made into nut flour. It will have less flavour and fat than ground nuts or nut meal, but can be used in small amounts in most recipes instead of gluten-free plain/all-purpose flour. Substitute 25g/1oz/¼ cup nut flour in every 115g/4oz/1 cup flour when making cakes and pastry. You can use a higher proportion in cookies, some cakes and muffins since they are denser and chewier, but don't overdo it.

Some nut pulps make better flour than others; blanched almonds and cashew nuts make excellent flour that is virtually white in colour. The pulp from unskinned almonds and from hazelnuts can also be used for making flour, although they will be considerably darker in colour.

1 Preheat the oven to 110°C/220°F/Gas ¼. Line a baking sheet with baking parchment. Spread the leftover pulp from making nut milk over the baking parchment in a thin, even layer, using a fork to break up the lumps.

2 Bake the nut pulp for 15 minutes, then remove it from the oven and stir with a fork. Spread it out again into an even layer and bake it for 10–15 minutes more or until it is completely dry. It can burn easily, so check it often towards the end of the cooking time. Remove from the oven and leave until completely cool.

3 Blitz in a dedicated gluten-free food processor for a few minutes, until finely ground. Store in an airtight container at room temperature for a few weeks, in the fridge for up to two months, or freeze for six months.

All kinds of seeds

You can buy numerous ready-ground seed flours and meals for cooking and baking. Amaranth, buckwheat, hemp, millet and quinoa are all seeds which are made into flour (see pages 26–28). Other seeds made into flours include sunflower, pumpkin, chia, flaxseeds/linseeds and sesame seeds.

Most seeds are too small to grind in a food processor, so use a dedicated gluten-free mini blender with a grinding blade or a coffee grinder and process in the same way as nuts in small quantities to yield a fine consistency; processing too many at a time may leave some seeds unground and some over-processed.

Chia seeds These tiny brown seeds come from the *Salvia hispanica* plant, a member of the mint family, and have a fairly neutral flavour. Rich in protein, fibre and omega-3 fatty acids, they are digested relatively slowly, providing a slow release of energy to keep blood sugar levels stable. Chia seeds can absorb up to 10 times their own weight of water due to their soluble fibre content and will form a gel if allowed to soak for a few minutes. Ground chia seeds can therefore be used as an egg substitute in recipes with small amounts of egg (this is less successful in recipes where there are more than two eggs). To make the equivalent of 1 egg, blend 15ml/1 tbsp ground chia seeds with 45ml/3 tbsp cold water. Leave the mixture for 5 minutes, until gloopy.

Flaxseeds/linseeds Linseed is the same as flaxseed (originally flax was grown as a fibrous plant to make linen and linseed grown for its seeds, but the names are now interchangeable).There are two types: golden and brown, the latter having a slightly nuttier taste. Readily available as a fine meal, and simple to grind yourself, both kinds can be used in recipes to mimic gluten and bind ingredients together. Like chia seeds, flaxseeds or linseeds are high in omega-3 fatty acids and when ground, can be mixed with water (15ml/1 tbsp flaxseeds with 45ml/3 tbsp water) and used as an egg substitute in bakes in exactly the same way.

Sesame seeds These tiny white or black seeds have a delicious mild, nutty flavour. Because they are very high in oil, it is difficult to grind them yourself to make a flour or meal. You can buy sesame seed flour made from 'fat-reduced sesame seeds'; basically the oil is squeezed out first and the flour is a by-product. The flour is excellent for Middle Eastern and Asian desserts and can be used to replace ground almonds in most recipes. It works well with flavourings such as saffron, rose and honey.

Pumpkin seeds Olive green in colour and with a pointed oval shape, pumpkin seeds are the middles of the large white seeds found in the fibrous hearts of pumpkins. Roasted and ground into a meal, they are widely used in South American cooking for thickening sauces. Strongly-flavoured, pumpkin seed flour can be used in both sweet and savoury baking, but take care that the taste and colour doesn't overpower the dish.

Sunflower seeds As the name suggest, these are the seeds of the huge yellow sunflowers that are an important crop in many parts of the world. Lightly toasting and cooling the seeds before making flour or meal dries them a little and renders them easier to grind. Mildly sweet and nutty, yet neutral enough to be used for most recipes, sunflower seed meal can be swapped in place of ground almonds, particularly if you have a nut intolerance or allergy. When using sunflower seed meal in recipes with bicarbonate of soda/baking soda, you may find tiny green specks in the bake after cooking. This is simply a chemical reaction and perfectly safe to eat; it won't affect the flavour.

OTHER WAYS TO USE NUT AND SEED FLOURS AND MEALS

While gluten-free baking is the most common use of nut and seed flours and meals, there are many other ways you can use them to add taste, texture and extra protein to your gluten-free cooking:

- Use coarser nut and seed meals as a binding ingredient instead of gluten-free breadcrumbs in home-made sausages, sausage rolls, meatballs and meat loaves.
- Add as a thickener and flavour-enhancer in saucy spiced dishes such as kormas.
- Use drier, finely ground flours as a gluten-free coating for egg-dipped strips of chicken and fish, and bakes or fries, to form a crispy crust.
- Replace small amounts of flour when making crumble toppings. Almond flour or meal is lovely with fruit such as peaches and apricots, while hazelnut flour is especially good with apples, plums and pears.
- Use finely ground nuts or seeds in lieu of some of the flour in pancakes and batter mixtures to make more nutritious blends.

Above Pumpkin, sunflower and sesame seeds are cheap, nutritious and readily available, and can all be made into flours for baking.

Above Finely ground flaxseed is extremely useful in gluten-free cooking since it helps to bind foods as well as providing bulk and nutrients.

Sugar & sweeteners

Many types of sugar can be used in gluten-free cooking and baking. At one end of the spectrum there is unrefined molasses sugar, a moist dark sugar with a raw treacly taste, and at the other is icing or confectioners' sugar, which is pure white and ultra-refined.

Sugars add more to baking than just a sweet taste – they also affect the colour, texture and keeping qualities. In cakes, the light and airy texture is created by tiny air bubbles trapped around the edges of sugar crystals, which expand as they cook, and the golden-brown colour is mainly due to the sugar caramelizing. Sugar also helps cakes stay moist after baking and keeps them fresh-tasting for longer.

Sugar alternatives

If you want to reduce your sugar intake in bakes and desserts, you can make cakes with grated fruit and vegetables or ground almonds to lend natural sweetness, or try adding sweet ingredients such as dried fruit. You can also use alternatives to traditional sugar, of which there are four main types: natural sugars, sweet extracts, artificial sweeteners, and sugar alcohols.

Natural sugars

Products such as honey or maple syrup and coconut sugar are still essentially sugar but they do contain small amounts of vitamins, minerals and beneficial enzymes and have distinctive flavours.

Below Maple syrup and maple sugar are flavoursome natural sugar alternatives. The colour of the syrup varies, from pale golden to amber.

Honey The original sweetener, honey has long been used to naturally sweeten foods. It comes in a huge array of flavours, and either set or runny. Unless adding at the end, when the flavour will be retained, you can use cheaper blended honey in cakes and bakes.

Maple syrup and sugar This delicious golden syrup is harvested from the rising sap of maple trees, native to north-east America, mainly in Canada but also in parts of the USA such as Vermont. Boiled to reduce and thicken, it usually has a slightly thinner consistency than other syrups and honeys. Avoid maple-flavoured syrup in baking since it is vastly inferior to the real deal; if you want a cheaper alternative to maple syrup, it is better to use a blended honey. Maple sugar is made by reducing maple syrup even further until it crystallizes. It is expensive and best reserved for sprinkling on foods.

Brown rice malt syrup Also known as rice syrup or rice malt, this is made by enzymic action on brown rice, which is then reduced to thicken. Its major components are forms of glucose rather than fructose, but it has almost twice the calories of the equivalent amount of sugar.

Below Coconut sugar has delicious toffee-ish overtones and has a lower GI than regular brown sugar.

HOW TO MAKE DATE SYRUP

This easy-to-make syrup has a rich, very dark brown colour and a sweet sticky consistency. A natural healthy sweetener, it's great in small quantities for baking as well as drizzling over desserts. It will keep in the fridge for up to three weeks.

MAKES ABOUT 350ML/12FL OZ/1½ CUPS

175g/6oz/1 cup pitted dates, roughly chopped
250ml/8fl oz/1 cup boiling water
5ml/1 tsp lemon or lime juice

1 Put the dates into a blender, pour over the water, cover and leave for 1 hour.

2 Add the lemon or lime juice. Blend until very smooth.

3 Pour into sterilized glass jars. Store in the fridge for up to a month.

Carob molasses Found online and in health food stores, this has a rich chocolatey flavour. It is made by soaking milled carob pods in water, then reducing the extracted liquid to a thick syrup.

Coconut sugar, crystals and syrup Sometimes labelled 'crystallized coconut nectar', coconut sugar is subtly sweet and similar to brown sugar in appearance and taste but with a hint of caramel. It is produced from the sap of the flower buds and blossoms of the coconut tree and is boiled to evaporate most of the moisture to make coconut syrup. To make sugar, it is further boiled until crystals form. It has a lower glycemic index (GI) than ordinary sugar, so will not spike blood sugar levels in the same way. It also contains small amounts of minerals including iron, zinc, potassium and magnesium.

Date syrup and sugar The syrup is made by simmering dates in water until pulpy, then blending until smooth. A dark brown colour, it has a rich, treacly depth and is used in Middle Eastern cuisine in sweet and savoury dishes. Date sugar is made from dried pulverized dates.

Sweet extracts

These extracts come from natural sources and are usually exceptionally sweet. They are often highly processed and can cause spikes in blood sugar levels.

Stevia Made from a leaf of a South-American herb, stevia is at least 150 times sweeter than sugar but contains zero calories. It comes in powder form or may be mixed with aloe syrup to make a pourable liquid. It can be used in cooking where the role is to add sweetness, but not as a direct substitute in recipes where sugar is an integral part of the structure or texture.

Agave syrup This is derived from the sap of the agave plant (a cactus, native to Mexico). After the juice is extracted, it is concentrated into a syrup. It tastes similar to mild molasses, and as a rule, the darker the colour, the deeper the flavour. It is about one-and-a-half times as sweet as sugar, meaning that the same level of sweetness can be achieved by using less. It can be subsituted for syrups such as golden/light corn syrup, but you should cook at a slightly lower temperature as it burns quite easily.

Agave powder This can be used as a sweetener or for sprinkling and dusting, as you would icing/confectioners' sugar. It has a neutral, mild flavour, and also acts as a prebiotic to support intestinal health, so is particularly valuable to those with coeliac disease. As an inulin it has a very low impact on blood sugar levels and also supports bone health by increasing the body's absorption of calcium.

Artificial sweeteners

Created in laboratories, artificial sweeteners include **sucralose** and **aspartame**. They are at least 200 times sweeter than table sugar and either very low-calorie or calorie-free and may have a slightly bitter aftertaste. Some are specifically made for baking and can be swapped for table sugar.

Sugar alcohols

These alcohols are found naturally in fruit and vegetables. The most commonly used one in baking is **erythritol**, which is found in fruits such as apples and pears. It has about 70 per cent of the sweetness of table sugar but only about 5 per cent of the calories. It is not absorbed into the blood stream, so doesn't affect blood sugar levels, which means that it is diabetic-friendly. It is usually readily available online and in most major supermarkets, and is used in a couple of recipes in this book, so it's worth stocking up on some.

Date syrup Energy 473kcal/2016kJ; Protein 5.8g; Carbohydrate 119.1g, of which sugars 119.1g; Fat 0.3g, of which saturates 0.2g; Cholesterol 0mg; Calcium 79mg; Fibre 9.3g; Sodium 18mg.

Dairy alternatives

Many people who have adverse symptoms to gluten also have problems with other foods, such as a dairy intolerance. For some, this is because their bodies are more prone to allergies and intolerances, but 'secondary lactose intolerance' is a common occurrence in coeliac disease.

Lactose, a milk sugar from dairy products, is broken down by an enzyme called lactase, which is found in the lining of the gut. Lactose intolerance causes symptoms such as bloating, diarrhoea and abdominal discomfort. When first diagnosed with coeliac disease, the lining of the gut will have considerable damage caused by eating gluten. Since lactase is found in the small intestine, the damage may mean that that insufficient lactase is being produced. Once the sufferer is on a gluten-free diet, the gut is able to heal and lactose digestion should return to normal, though this can take up to two years.

Lactose intolerance can be effectively treated by avoiding all foods and drinks that contain lactose and replacing them with lactose-free alternatives. A major source of lactose in our diet is milk, including cows' milk, goats' milk and sheep's milk (some who are mildly lactose intolerant find the latter two easier to digest).

Other products such as cream, cheese, yogurt and butter also contain lactose and may need to be avoided if you're lactose intolerant. The level of lactose in these varies and is sometimes quite low; some people find they can tolerate small amounts of lactose in their diet without any problems, while others experience symptoms after consuming food containing only a tiny amount. A food diary can help you monitor the reactions you have to different products and quantities.

Unexpected foods and drinks that may contain lactose include salad cream and mayonnaise, cookies, chocolate, cakes, breakfast cereals, instant potatoes, packet soups and processed meats such as ham.

DAIRY ALLERGY

A dairy allergy is different from lactose intolerance and involves the immune system. In people with an allergy, the body reacts to the proteins in milk and other dairy products as if they were undesirable invaders, and releases substances that cause allergy symptoms. While some, such as rashes, may be relatively mild, others may be more severe and include difficulty swallowing and breathing, both of which may need immediate medical attention.

Check the ingredients on packets carefully; the word 'lactose' will not necessarily be listed on the food label, so you need to look for words such as 'milk' and 'whey'. Some ingredients sound like they contain lactose when they don't, such as lactic acid, sodium lactate and cocoa butter; these are all fine to eat.

Dairy-free foods

For those who need to exclude dairy from their diet, there are plenty of alternatives. The range of commercially made products continues to increase and some, such as nut milks, can easily be made at home.

Lacto-free milk This product is available as skimmed, semi-skimmed and whole milk, all of which are widely available in supermarkets, both in fresh and long-life UHT form. Both are pre-treated with the enzyme lactase to remove the lactose.

Nut, seed and grain milks and creams Most nuts can be made into 'milks' with a subtle nutty flavour and silky-smooth texture; ideal for drinking on their own, in shakes, on breakfast cereals or to use in cooking.

The most popular are soya, almond and oat milks, all of which come in both sweetened and unsweetened varieties. Hazelnut, cashew nut and rice milks are also all readily available, as are more distinctive-tasting ones, such as hemp milk, which has a grassy aftertaste, and some seed milks. To match the demands of barista coffees, you can now buy 'barista' non-dairy milks to create frothy coffees and hot chocolate.

There are also soya and oat-based alternatives to replace dairy cream and crème fraîche. Read the descriptions on the side of the packets and cartons; while some are suitable for cooking, others are intended only for serving chilled.

For all of the above, make sure you check the ingredients carefully as some contain thickeners and may not be gluten free. If you intend to use them habitually, it is well worth making your own so that you know exactly what has gone into them.

Opposite A wide range of non-dairy milks is now available to buy, from simple soya and nutty hazelnut to grassy hemp and creamy oat.

HOW TO MAKE COCONUT MILK AND COCONUT CREAM

Coconut cream is the thick part of the coconut milk that rises to the top; it can be used in place of dairy cream in many recipes, but can't be 'whipped'. You can either scoop it from the top of a chilled can of coconut milk, or you can make your own. Use the leftover coconut pulp to make coconut flour (see page 29).

MAKES ABOUT 250ML/9FL OZ/1 CUP MILK

flesh from 1 mature coconut
150ml/¼ pint/⅔ cup near-boiling water

1 Carefully remove the brown skin from the coconut flesh with a sharp knife, then chop it into pieces and place it in a food processor.

2 Pour over the water. Blend until fairly smooth, leave for 5 minutes, then blend again for a few seconds, until smooth.

3 Pour the mixture into a strainer lined with muslin or cheesecloth positioned over a glass or stainless-steel bowl and leave it to drain.

4 Bring the corners of the cloth together, then squeeze to extract the milk.

5 Set the coconut milk aside for about 30 minutes. The coconut cream will float to the top of the milk and can be spooned off the surface, leaving the milk.

HOW TO MAKE ALMOND MILK

This recipe makes a medium-thickness unsweetened almond milk. It will keep for up to four days in the fridge and may separate slightly, so give it a stir before using. The leftover nut pulp can be made into nut flour (see page 30).

MAKES ABOUT 750ML/1¼ PINTS/3 CUPS

175g/6oz/1 cup unsalted blanched almonds
750ml/1¼ pints/3 cups filtered water, plus soaking water

1 Put the almonds in a large glass, ceramic or stainless-steel bowl (plastic may taint the flavour of the milk). Pour over enough water to cover by about 2.5cm/1in. Leave to soak at room temperature for at least 8 hours or place in the fridge and soak for up to 24 hours.

2 Drain and rinse the almonds, then tip them into a blender and add a third of the filtered water. Pulse a few times to break up the nuts, then blend continuously for 1 minute.

3 Add a further 250ml/8fl oz/1 cup water and blend for 2–3 minutes or until the mixture is smooth.

4 Pour the mixture through a nut bag or a muslin/cheesecloth-lined strainer over a jug or pitcher and leave to drain for a few minutes.

5 Slowly pour in the remaining measured water and leave to drain again. Gently squeeze the bag to extract all of the milk.

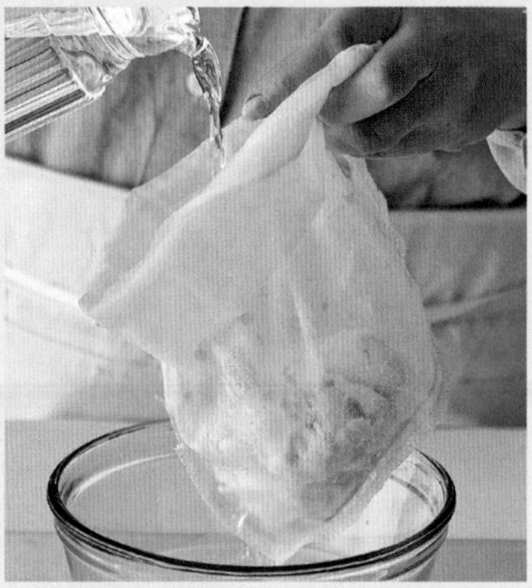

Above Coconuts can be used to make all sorts of dairy- and gluten-free foods, from milk, cream, oil and butter to flour and even vinegar.

Butter alternatives There are lots of dairy-free spreads and margarines, but not all are suitable for cooking, so you may need to buy one for spreading and one for cooking. Even if you can eat butter, hard margarines often produce better results in gluten-free baking.

Coconut oil is an excellent substitute for butter in baking (you may need to chill it first on a warm day to solidify it) and for frying, as it can be heated to high temperatures. The taste may be distinctly nutty and aromatic or completely flavourless, so choose a product that suits your needs; try to buy cold-pressed coconut oil rather than a refined one. Note that coconut butter is not the same as coconut oil and is made from crushed dried coconut flesh, rather than being extracted. It can be used in baking but is not interchangeable with butter.

Yogurt Soya yogurts and coconut-milk based yogurts are readily available in many supermarkets, but do check they are gluten free. You can also make yogurt yourself from any non-dairy milk with a reasonably high protein content; almond, soya and coconut all work well, using a yogurt starter culture. Make sure you buy one that is dairy and gluten free, as some contain dried milk powders.

Cheese Soya-based cheeses have been on the market for many years and are usually more suited to eating chilled than for cooking. More recently, coconut oil based cheeses have become available as an alternative to 'cream' cheese, and in grated and sliced form (similar to processed cheese slices). These can be eaten cold but are intended for use in cooking and are similar in taste and texture to a creamy mild Cheddar. Nut cheeses are also increasingly available, especially cashew cheese.

Breads & doughs

There's nothing quite like the aroma and flavour of freshly baked bread and here you'll discover a wide choice of gluten-free recipes that ensure you don't miss out on this favourite staple food, from straightforward and quick white and brown loaves made with ready-blended bread flours, and costing a fraction of the store-bought equivalent, to more elaborate creations that make use of the vast range of gluten-free grains and flours available. You can enjoy breads from all around the world, too, with gluten-free versions of Naans, Bagels and Steamed Buns. There are also recipes to cater for those who enjoy sweet breads, such as Teacakes, Rich Fruit Teabread, and a chocolatey brioche.

Traditional bread relies on gluten to give elasticity to the dough. Gluten-free doughs need alternatives such as xanthan gum or ground psyllium husk to compensate for the lack of gluten, and eggs might also be added as a natural leavener, and to add moistness and flavour. Gluten-free flours often require a lot more liquid than their traditional wheat-flour counterparts, so don't be surprised if your bread 'dough' looks more like a creamed cake mixture and needs to be spooned into the tin or pan. As a bonus, you won't need to knead the mixture (which is how gluten is developed in wheat bread dough), so you'll find making gluten-free bread a lot easier. If you prefer to make your own bread flour rather than using a commercial ready-blended one, try the blends on pages 42 and 45.

If you want to make gluten-free bread in a bread machine, make sure you follow the recipe provided by the manufacturer, since the ingredients and setting will be different from that for regular bread. Also, take care to avoid cross-contamination. Given how easy it is to make gluten-free bread by hand, it is probably simplest to avoid using a machine.

These recipes use easy-blend/rapid rise dried yeast, which is often sold in 7g/¼oz sachets to keep it fresh. It is sprinkled on to the dried ingredients and mixed before liquid is added. If you prefer to bake with fresh yeast, double the quantity, e.g. 7g/¼oz (10ml/2 tsp) easy-blend dried yeast is the same as 15g/½oz fresh baker's yeast. Sourdough breads, by contrast, are made with a flour-and-water paste that is left to ferment by wild airborne yeast for several days. Although this requires advance planning because additional time is needed for the sourdough starter to ferment and the dough to rise, it's well worth giving it a go as it results in a bread with a more open, airy texture and a delicious, distinctive flavour. Many people who have a gluten intolerance or allergies often find this slowly fermented bread easier to digest.

Simple white loaf

This everyday gluten-free white loaf is perfect for sandwiches or toast. If you prefer a dairy-free version, use extra water instead of the milk. Use within two days of making, or cut it into slices as soon as the loaf is cool enough and then freeze.

MAKES 1 LARGE OR 2 SMALL LOAVES

1 egg (or 15g/½oz/2 tbsp chickpea flour blended with 45ml/3 tbsp water)
60ml/4 tbsp sunflower oil
5ml/1 tsp cider vinegar or lemon juice
15ml/1 tbsp caster/superfine sugar
5ml/1 tsp salt
150ml/¼ pint/⅔ cup lukewarm milk
150ml/¼ pint/⅔ cup lukewarm water
400g/14oz/3½ cups bought gluten-free white bread flour blend or home-made white bread flour blend (see box)
10ml/2 tsp easy-blend/rapid-rise dried yeast

HOME-MADE WHITE BREAD FLOUR BLEND

This can be used as an alternative to store-bought ready-blended gluten-free white bread flour. You can double the quantities and store in a large airtight jar.

MAKES 400G/14OZ/3½ CUPS

150g/5oz/1¼ cups white rice flour (or a mixture of brown and white rice flour)
150g/5oz/1¼ cups potato flour
50g/2oz/½ cup tapioca flour
50g/2oz/½ cup cornflour/starch
10ml/2 tsp xanthan gum

Sift all the ingredients and mix thoroughly in a bowl.

1 Grease a 900g/2lb or two 450g/1lb loaf tins/pans. Put the egg or blended chickpea flour paste, oil, vinegar or lemon juice, sugar, salt, milk and water into a large mixing bowl and whisk together with a fork until blended.

2 Sift over the flour, then sprinkle over the yeast. Mix the flour and liquid to make a thick, smooth batter.

3 Pour and scrape the mixture into the prepared tin or tins and level the top with a spatula or the back of a wet (so it doesn't stick) spoon. The batter should come about halfway up.

4 Loosely cover with oiled clear film or plastic wrap and leave to rise in a warm place for 20–30 minutes or until the batter has risen just up to the rim of the tin; don't leave it for any longer than this or the bread won't hold its shape when it is baked.

5 While the bread is rising, preheat the oven to 200°C/400°F/Gas 6. Remove the clear film and bake the smaller loaves for 35–40 minutes and the larger loaf for about 45 minutes, until well browned on the top.

6 Carefully remove the loaf or loaves from the tins to test whether the bread is baked; it should sound 'hollow' when the base is tapped. Transfer to a wire rack and leave to cool completely before slicing.

Loaf: Energy 1022kcal/4265kJ; Protein 18.1g; Carbohydrate 171.4g, of which sugars 11.8g; Fat 29.3g, of which saturates 5g; Cholesterol 120mg; Calcium 114mg; Fibre 2.2g; Sodium 77mg.
Blend: Energy 1398kcal/5913kJ; Protein 23.8g; Carbohydrate 327.1g, of which sugars 3.9g; Fat 3g, of which saturates 0.3g; Cholesterol 0mg; Calcium 80mg; Fibre 15.7g; Sodium 82mg.

Simple brown loaf

This wholesome gluten-free brown bread has a moist, close-textured interior and can be thinly sliced for sandwich making. Gluten-free brown loaves tend to be denser than white ones but folding a whisked egg white into the dough will aerate it and stop the bread sinking as it bakes.

MAKES 1 LARGE OR 2 SMALL LOAVES

400g/14oz/3½ cups bought gluten-free brown bread flour blend or home-made wholegrain bread flour blend (see box)
2.5ml/½ tsp salt
15ml/1 tbsp easy-blend/rapid-rise dried yeast
1 egg, plus 1 egg white
75ml/5 tbsp olive oil
30ml/2 tbsp honey
300ml/½ pint/1¼ cups warm water

1 Line the base and sides of a 900g/2lb or two 450g/1lb loaf tins/pans with baking parchment or lightly oiled greaseproof paper.

2 Sift the flour and salt into a large mixing bowl, adding any bran left in the sieve or strainer. Add the yeast and stir to mix. Make a small well in the middle.

3 Lightly whisk the whole egg in a jug or pitcher. Add the olive oil and honey, then pour the liquid mixture into the dry ingredients. Add the water and gradually stir together to make a smooth, thick batter.

4 Cover the bowl with clear film or plastic wrap and leave in a warm place for 30 minutes. The mixture should be puffy and have risen by about one-third.

5 Whisk the egg white until fairly stiff, but not dry. Gently fold into the yeasted batter, then pour and scrape the mixture into the prepared tin or tins. Cover with clear film and leave in a warm place to rise for 30–45 minutes. The mixture should come to just below the rim of the tin(s). Remove the clear film if necessary near the end of the rising time, so it doesn't stick to the top. Preheat the oven to 190°C/375°F/Gas 5.

6 Bake the bread for 30–35 minutes if making two 450g/1lb loaves or 40–45 minutes if making one 900g/2lb loaf, or until the top is firm. Remove from the tin, remove the paper and place on a baking sheet. Return to the oven for a further 5 minutes to crisp the bottom and sides. The bread should sound 'hollow' when tapped on the base.Transfer to a wire rack to cool completely before slicing.

Variations

- For a vegan version, substitute 30ml/2 tbsp chickpea flour blended with 60ml/4 tbsp water for the egg and egg white, and use maple syrup or agave syrup in place of the honey. The bread will be a little heavier in texture without the aeration from the whisked egg white, but will still be delicious.
- You can add seeds to the mixture if you like – sesame and poppy are especially good since they are small and light. Add them when you shake any bran from the sieve or strainer into the bowl, so they are well incorporated.

HOME-MADE WHOLEGRAIN BREAD FLOUR BLEND

This flour blend produces a nutty, wholesome loaf. It can be used as an alternative to store-bought gluten-free bread flour. You can double the quantities and store what you don't use immediately in a large airtight jar, ready for when you next bake bread.

MAKES 400G/14OZ/3½ CUPS

150g/5oz/1¼ cups buckwheat or teff flour
115g/4oz/1 cup sorghum or brown rice flour
65g/2½oz/⅔ cup tapioca or cornflour/starch
65g/2½oz/⅔ cup quinoa flour
10ml/2 tsp xanthan gum

Sift all the ingredients and mix thoroughly in a bowl.

Energy: 2108kcal/8794kJ; Protein 38.2g; Carbohydrate 327.8g, of which sugars 24.9g; Fat 68.7g, of which saturates 11.4g; Cholesterol 231mg; Calcium 49mg; Fibre 22.4g; Sodium 156mg.
Blend: Energy 1401kcal/5891kJ; Protein 28.7g; Carbohydrate 317.4g, of which sugars 4.6g; Fat 6.5g, of which saturates 0.3g; Cholesterol 0mg; Calcium 102mg; Fibre 7.6g; Sodium 50mg.

Sourdough starter

Mild-flavoured brown rice flour is perfect for making a gluten-free sourdough starter. You can use a mixture of white and brown rice flour if you want a whiter loaf, but don't use white alone. Adding grapes will introduce more wild yeasts and produce a more vigorous starter.

MAKES 600ML/1 PINT

Day one

115g/4oz/1 cup brown rice flour
150ml/¼ pint/⅔ cup mineral or filtered water
small bunch of unwashed organic grapes (about 12 grapes) or 1 unwashed organic apple

Day two

40g/1½oz/⅓ cup brown rice flour
60ml/4 tbsp mineral or filtered water

Day three

40g/1½oz/⅓ cup brown rice flour
60ml/4 tbsp mineral or filtered water

Day four

75g/3oz/⅔ cup brown rice flour
120ml/4fl oz/½ cup mineral or filtered water

1 On day one, combine the flour and water in a mixing bowl to make a smooth paste, then put the grapes, still on their stalks, in the middle. Cover the bowl with a plate and leave in a warm place for 24 hours.

2 On day two, lift out the grapes and discard. Stir the mixture, then add the next batch of flour and water and stir again. Re-cover and leave for another 24 hours.

3 On day three, stir, add the flour and water and stir again. The starter should smell slightly yeasty and have a few bubbles. Re-cover and leave for another 24 hours.

4 On day four, stir, add the flour and water and stir again. Re-cover and leave for another 24 hours.

5 The starter should now be fairly bubbly (if not, feed it again as on day two and leave for another 24 hours). It can now be used to make bread or you can transfer it to a bowl and cover with clear film/plastic wrap, or into a clip-top jar without the rubber seal. Do not put it into a tight glass jar as the build-up of gas may cause it to crack. It can be kept in the fridge for up to 10 days, but check daily and lift the lid or film to allow the gases to escape.

6 When you are ready to bake, remove the starter from the fridge and leave it at room temperature for an hour. If it has been more than two days since you last 'fed' it, stir in 75g/3oz/⅔ cup brown rice flour and 120ml/4fl oz/½ cup mineral or filtered water and leave it for at least 2 hours before using.

Cook's tips

- When you have used some of your starter, you will need to 'feed' and replenish it; provided that you do this, it should keep indefinitely.
- Replenish the starter by the amount you have removed (you need to do this at least every two weeks, even if you haven't made any bread). For example, if you have used 300ml/½ pint/1¼ cups, you will need to add 150ml/¼ pint/⅔ cup water and 150g/5oz/1¼ cups flour and stir it really well to combine everything. Let this ferment at room temperature for 24 hours, then store it in the fridge.

Energy 988kcal/4134kJ; Protein 17.3g; Carbohydrate 216.3g, of which sugars 0g; Fat 2.2g, of which saturates 0g; Cholesterol 0mg; Calcium 65mg; Fibre 7.2g; Sodium 14mg.

Classic sourdough

Sourdough bread has a distinctive, slightly acidic flavour and a more aerated texture than wheat-based leavened bread. This gluten-free version is made in the traditional way without commercial yeast, relying instead on natural yeasts present in brown rice flour and in the air.

MAKES 1 LOAF

1 large egg, lightly beaten
75g/3oz/⅔ cup potato flour
50g/2oz/½ cup sweet rice flour or millet flour, plus extra for dusting
7g/¼oz salt
10ml/2 tsp ground psyllium husk

For the bread base

150ml/¼ pint/⅔ cup sourdough starter (see opposite)
150g/5oz/1¼ cups white rice flour
75g/3oz/⅔ cup sorghum flour
300ml/½ pint/1¼ cups lukewarm water

1 For the bread base, mix the ingredients together in a large bowl, cover with clear film or plastic wrap and leave in a warm place for 3–4 hours, or overnight in a cool place, until the mixture has risen a little.

2 Line a 20cm/8in deep round cake tin/pan or a 900g/2lb loaf tin with baking parchment, or generously flour a banneton or proving basket.

3 Stir the beaten egg into the bread base mixture. Mix the potato flour, sweet rice or millet flour, salt and ground psyllium husk together, then sift into the bowl. Stir everything together to make a thick, smooth batter.

4 Spoon and scrape the mixture into the tin or banneton. Smooth the surface. Leave to rise, uncovered, in a warm place for 2–4 hours (the time will depend on the sourdough starter). It is ready when it has risen by about a third and it has a puffy top with one or two small cracks on the surface. Don't overprove, or the loaf may collapse when baking.

5 When the loaf is almost ready, place a roasting tray of hot water on the bottom shelf of the oven and preheat to 230°C/450°F/Gas 8.

6 If using a banneton, carefully tip the loaf on to a floured baking sheet before baking. Put the sheet or the tin in the oven and bake for 5 minutes. Reduce the temperature to 200°C/400°F/Gas 6 and bake for 25–30 minutes more.

7 Check the loaf is cooked by squeezing the sides with a clean dish towel; it should feel fairly firm. If not, return to a low oven and cook for a few more minutes. Transfer to a wire rack and leave to cool before slicing.

Energy 814kcal/3415kJ; Protein 18.6g; Carbohydrate 169.8g, of which sugars 1.3g; Fat 5.6g, of which saturates 1.2g; Cholesterol 116mg; Calcium 64mg; Fibre 9.4g; Sodium 62mg.

Sourdough baguette

French bread is made from a high-gluten flour known as 'type 55' and is cooked in special steam ovens. These gluten-free sourdough baguettes come quite close to the real thing, with crisp crusts and soft-crumb centres. They are best eaten on the day of making.

MAKES 2–3 LOAVES

40g/1½oz/3 tbsp unsalted butter, plus extra for greasing
275g/10oz/2½ cups potato flour
75g/3oz/⅔ cup tapioca flour, plus extra for dusting
10ml/2 tsp caster/superfine sugar
5ml/1 tsp salt
5ml/1 tsp xanthan gum
5ml/1 tsp ground psyllium husk
3 large egg whites, whisked
5ml/1 tsp white wine vinegar

For the bread base

150ml/¼ pint/⅔ cup sourdough starter (see page 46)
175ml/6fl oz/¾ cup lukewarm water
75g/3oz/⅔ cup sorghum flour
300ml/½ pint/1¼ cups lukewarm water

1 For the bread base, pour the starter into a mixing bowl and stir in the water. Sift over the sorghum flour, then mix. Cover with clear film or plastic wrap and leave in a warm place for 2–4 hours, until risen and very bubbly.

2 Melt the butter and leave to cool until tepid. Combine the flours, sugar, salt, xanthan and psyllium husk. Sift this over the bread base mixture. Combine the egg whites and vinegar, then add to the mix with the butter.

3 Beat the mixture for about 2 minutes, until smooth and thick. It should look like a spoonable cake mixture rather than a bread dough. If the mixture isn't thick enough to hold its shape when dropped from a spoon (this depends on the sourdough starter and the flours), stir in a further 15–30ml/1–2 tbsp sorghum flour.

4 Generously grease a baguette pan with butter and sprinkle with rice flour. Place scoops of the mixture along the individual baguette moulds and form into baguette shapes, leaving a 2cm/¾in space at the ends to allow for expansion. Let the dough rise in a warm place for 1–2 hours or until almost doubled in size.

5 When the baguettes are nearly ready, preheat the oven to 230°C/450°F/Gas 8, then put a roasting tray of very hot water on the bottom shelf of the oven. Leave the oven to heat for a further 5 minutes.

6 Dust a little tapioca flour over the tops of the baguettes, then put them in the oven. Bake for 10 minutes, then lower the oven temperature to 200°C/400°F/Gas 6.

7 Bake for a further 20–25 minutes or until the baguettes are dark golden and crisp. Cover them loosely with foil if they are browning too much. Check the baguettes are cooked by gently squeezing them underneath; they should feel firm. Transfer to a wire rack, cover with a dish towel and leave to cool.

Variation

If you don't have any sourdough starter, combine 150g/5oz/1¼ cups sorghum flour with 7g/¼oz easy-blend/rapid-rise dried yeast, then whisk in 250ml/8fl oz/1 cup lukewarm water. Combine this mixture with all the remaining bread base ingredients.

Energy 1040kcal/4402kJ; Protein 21.7g; Carbohydrate 205.5g, of which sugars 9g; Fat 17.9g, of which saturates 10.4g; Cholesterol 43mg; Calcium 49mg; Fibre 13.3g; Sodium 1121mg.

Brown sourdough loaf

Like Classic Sourdough, this tangy gluten-free brown loaf is made from a sourdough starter, which relies on yeasts that occur naturally in the atmosphere. It has a chewy crust and a close texture. Its dark colour comes from a combination of brown-coloured flours and molasses.

MAKES 1 LARGE OR 2 SMALL LOAVES

1 large egg, lightly beaten
15ml/1 tbsp lukewarm water
2.5ml/½ tsp molasses or black treacle
175g/6oz/1½ cups bought gluten-free brown bread flour blend or home-made wholegrain bread flour blend (see page 45)
5ml/1 tsp ground psyllium husk
5ml/1 tsp salt

For the bread base

150ml/¼ pint/⅔ cup sourdough starter (see page 46)
200g/7oz/1⅔ cups brown rice flour
50g/2oz/½ cup teff flour
300ml/½ pint/1¼ cups lukewarm water

1 For the bread base, combine the ingredients in a large bowl, cover with clear film or plastic wrap and leave in a warm place for 3–4 hours, or overnight in a cool place, until slightly risen, spongy and bubbly. Line a 900g/2lb or two 450g/1lb loaf tins/pans with baking parchment.

2 Whisk the egg, water and molasses and stir into the bread base mixture. Sift the brown or wholegrain bread flour, psyllium husk and salt over the top, adding any bran left in the sieve or strainer. Stir to make a batter.

3 Spoon and scrape the mixture into the tin or tins. Smooth the surface with the back of a wet spoon. Leave to rise, uncovered, in a warm place for 2–4 hours (the time will depend on the sourdough starter). It is ready when it has risen to almost double the original size, with a puffy top and one or two small cracks on the surface. Don't overprove or the bread may collapse when baking.

4 When the bread is almost ready, preheat the oven to 230°C/450°F/Gas 8, then put a roasting tray of very hot water on the bottom shelf of the oven. Allow the oven to steam up for a few minutes then bake the bread at the high temperature for 5 minutes. Reduce the oven to 200°C/400°F/Gas 6 and bake for 25–35 minutes more.

5 Remove the bread from the tin(s) and check it is cooked by gently squeezing the sides with a clean dish towel; it should feel fairly firm. If not quite cooked, return to a low oven and cook for a few more minutes. Cool on a wire rack before slicing and serving.

Energy 1874kcal/7849kJ; Protein 39.4g; Carbohydrate 391.2g, of which sugars 2.2g; Fat 12.3g, of which saturates 2.7g; Cholesterol 231mg; Calcium 111mg; Fibre 20.9g; Sodium 113mg.

Sorghum & millet loaf

Sorghum flour's malty flavour and binding properties work especially well with mild-tasting millet flour. This simple loaf is both gluten free and yeast free, so you don't need to wait for it to rise before you bake it. An added bonus is that it will stay fresh for a couple of days.

MAKES 1 LARGE OR 2 SMALL LOAVES

30ml/2 tbsp sesame seeds
175g/6oz/1½ cups sorghum flour
175g/6oz/1½ cups millet flour
115g/4oz/1 cup millet flakes
15ml/1 tbsp gluten-free baking powder
5ml/1 tsp salt
5ml/1 tsp soft light brown sugar
15ml/1 tbsp sunflower oil
5ml/1 tsp white wine vinegar
450ml/¾ pint/scant 2 cups lager or sparkling water

1 Preheat the oven to 180°C/350°F/Gas 4. Line a 900g/2lb or two 450g/1lb loaf tins/pans with baking parchment. Sprinkle 15ml/1 tbsp of the sesame seeds over the base.

2 Place the flours, millet flakes, baking powder, salt and sugar in a large mixing bowl and stir to combine. Make a small well in the middle of the mixture.

3 In a jug or pitcher, whisk together the oil and vinegar, then add the lager or water. Pour into the dry ingredients and mix together to make a thick batter.

4 Pour the mixture into the prepared tin or tins. Sprinkle with the remaining sesame seeds. Bake for 5 minutes, then reduce the oven temperature to 200°C/400°F/Gas 6 and bake for a further 35–45 minutes or until the bread is risen and a skewer comes out clean.

5 Cool in the tin for 5–10 minutes under a clean dish towel, then carefully knock out the bread on to a wire rack. Cover with a dish towel and leave until completely cold before cutting.

Cook's tip

For a softer crust, dust the top of the loaf with 5ml/1 tsp millet flour instead of sesame seeds before baking, and give it a second very light dusting of flour when the loaf is removed from the oven and before it cools.

Energy 1940kcal/8101kJ; Protein 32.5g; Carbohydrate 355.1g, of which sugars 4.3g; Fat 36.3g, of which saturates 4.5g; Cholesterol 0mg; Calcium 389mg; Fibre 3.2g; Sodium 2069mg.

Seeded quinoa bread

A mixture of quinoa flour and gluten-free brown bread flour is used to make this nutty-textured loaf. Serve for breakfast with butter and a good-quality conserve, or cut it into generous slices to accompany soup or a hearty salad for a satisfying lunch.

MAKES 1 LOAF

225g/8oz/2 cups quinoa flour
225g/8oz/2 cups bought gluten-free brown bread flour blend or home-made wholegrain bread flour blend (see page 45)
10ml/2 tsp easy-blend/rapid-rise dried yeast
10ml/2 tsp salt
60ml/4 tbsp sugar
25g/1oz/¼ cup mixed seeds, plus 15ml/1 tbsp extra for sprinkling
25g/1oz/¼ cup roughly chopped nuts (such as walnuts or hazelnuts)
350ml/12fl oz/1½ cups lukewarm water
oil, for greasing
nut milk, to glaze

1 Sift the flours into a large mixing bowl, add the yeast, salt, sugar, mixed seeds and nuts, and stir to combine. Make a well in the middle.

2 Pour the lukewarm water into the well in the dry ingredients, then stir, mixing in the flour gradually, to form a pliable dough.

3 Knead the dough on a lightly floured surface for a few seconds just until smooth, then place in a clean mixing bowl, cover with a damp dish towel and leave in a warm place for 1–1½ hours, until the dough is nearly doubled in size.

4 Knock back/punch down the dough and knead for a couple of seconds. Re-cover with the dish towel and set aside to prove for another 30 minutes, until doubled in size. Preheat the oven to 220°C/425°F/Gas 7.

5 Oil a 450g/1lb loaf tin/pan. Shape the dough to neatly fill the tin. Score the top of the loaf with a sharp knife lengthways and across, to help the dough rise. Brush the top with milk and sprinkle with seeds.

6 Bake for 35–40 minutes, until the loaf is risen and golden, and sounds hollow on the base when tapped. Remove from the tin and cool on a wire rack for at least 20 minutes before slicing and serving.

Variations

• You can also cook this loaf in a 20cm/8in deep round cake tin/pan, scoring the top into eight wedges in step 5.

• For Cheese and Onion Quinoa Bread, sauté 1 finely chopped onion in 15g/½oz butter in a frying pan for 7–8 minutes, until tender. Allow the onion to cool, then knead it into the dough in step 4 with 50g/2oz/½ cup grated strong Cheddar cheese.

Energy 2130kcal/8952kJ; Protein 54.9g; Carbohydrate 360.4g, of which sugars 78.4g; Fat 55.4g, of which saturates 8.1g; Cholesterol 0mg; Calcium 488mg; Fibre 18g; Sodium 4080mg.

Sprouted buckwheat loaf

While buckwheat flour, with its earthy, slightly musty flavour, can be a bit of an acquired taste, buckwheat sprouts are much milder and have a subtle sweetness. Sprouting the seeds makes their nutrients more available during digestion, a positive for many with gluten intolerance.

MAKES 1 LARGE OR 2 SMALL LOAVES

400g/14oz/2 cups raw buckwheat
350ml/12fl oz/1½ cups water
30ml/2 tbsp mixed dried herbs
5ml/1 tsp salt
100g/3½oz/⅔ cup mixed seeds (such as sunflower, pumpkin, shelled hemp)
oil, for greasing

1 Soak the buckwheat for 7 hours, changing the water at least once. Discard the water and rinse the buckwheat. The water coming out will be slightly pink and slimy; you need to keep rinsing until this disappears.

2 Return the buckwheat to the bowl and sprout for 24 hours, rinsing them as often as you can. If you can see little tails grow out before 24 hours are up, they are ready, so check them regularly. Rinse very thoroughly.

3 Put the sprouted buckwheat in a blender or food processor. Add the measured water, the herbs and the salt, then process to a dough-like consistency.

4 Transfer the dough to a glass bowl, cover and leave at room temperature for 7 hours. When ready, it should have risen a little and when you stir it should be bubbly and smell sour. If no bubbles have formed, let it ferment for another couple of hours. Once ready, stir in the seeds.

5 Grease a 900g/2lb or two 450g/1lb loaf tins/pans with oil and line the base with baking parchment. Pour the dough into the tin or tins, cover with clear film or plastic wrap, and leave it to ferment for a further hour or two.

6 Preheat the oven to 180°C/350°F/Gas 4. Remove the clear film from the dough, then bake for 60 minutes. Remove from the oven and let it cool for at least 30 minutes before you slice it. It is best eaten while it is fresh, but it will keep in the fridge for a week.

Cook's tip

Instead of part of the water you could also use kefir water and/or kombucha. These contain beneficial bacteria, which help the dough to ferment, in turn helping it to rise and producing a more developed 'sourdough' flavour.

Energy 2083kcal/8693kJ; Protein 55.6g; Carbohydrate 362.9g, of which sugars 8g; Fat 55.2g, of which saturates 7.7g; Cholesterol 6mg; Calcium 278mg; Fibre 19.2g; Sodium 2015mg.

Soda bread

This bread is easy to make and doesn't contain yeast, so can be ready to eat in less than an hour. The recipe contains hemp flour, but you can swap it for extra oat flour if you prefer. Cutting the cross on top of the loaf is important as it ensures that the bread cooks through.

MAKES 1 LOAF

225g/8oz/2 cups bought gluten-free brown bread flour blend or home-made wholegrain bread flour blend (see page 45), plus extra for dusting
50g/2oz/½ cup gluten-free oat flour
25g/1oz/¼ cup hemp flour
2.5ml/½ tsp xanthan gum
5ml/1 tsp salt
5ml/1 tsp bicarbonate of soda/ baking soda
5ml/1 tsp dried herbs (optional)
2.5ml/½ tsp soft light brown sugar (optional)
275ml/10fl oz/generous 1 cup buttermilk (see Cook's tip)
30ml/2 tbsp milk

1 Preheat the oven to 190°C/375°F/Gas 5. Line a heavy baking tray with baking parchment.

2 Sift together the flours, xanthan gum, salt, bicarbonate of soda, and herbs and sugar (if using) into a bowl. Make a well in the middle and pour in the buttermilk and milk. Mix with your hands or a spoon to form a soft dough – this should be slack but not too wet.

3 Sprinkle a little flour on your hands and a work surface, then tip out the bread on to the surface and knead it briefly until smooth.

4 Sprinkle the surface of the dough with flour, then lightly roll it into a 20cm/8in round, shaping it with your hands. Slash a deep cross into the top of the loaf using a large, sharp knife, cutting about three-quarters of the way through the dough.

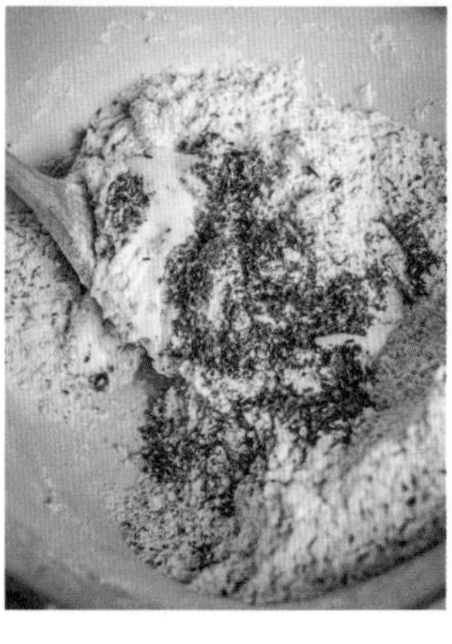

5 Transfer the loaf to the baking tray and bake it for 35–40 minutes, until risen and lightly browned. When the loaf is cooked, it should sound hollow when the bottom is tapped and feel light when you pick it up.

6 Remove the bread from the oven and transfer it to a wire rack to cool. You can slice it while it is just warm.

Cook's tip

You can create a substitute for buttermilk by whisking together 300ml/½ pint/1¼ cups full-fat/whole milk and a good squeeze of lemon juice, then leaving it to stand for 15–20 minutes at room temperature until it starts to curdle (include the curdled bits).

Energy 1230kcal/5166kJ; Protein 34.6g; Carbohydrate 231.9g, of which sugars 16.8g; Fat 17.8g, of which saturates 2.8g; Cholesterol 7mg; Calcium 394mg; Fibre 27.1g; Sodium 2223mg.

Polenta bread

A combination of polenta and golden olive oil makes this gluten-free bread a beautiful sunny colour. It is best eaten while still slightly warm, with a little butter or a drizzle of olive oil to moisten. It's especially good served with soups or chunky vegetable and bean casseroles.

MAKES 1 LOAF

250g/9oz/2¼ cups fine polenta/cornmeal
75g/3oz/⅔ cup gluten-free self-raising/self-rising flour blend
2.5ml/½ tsp gluten-free baking powder
5ml/1 tsp salt
15ml/1 tbsp caster/superfine sugar
1 egg
400ml/14fl oz/1⅔ cups milk
30ml/2 tbsp olive oil, plus extra for greasing

1 Preheat the oven to 200°C/400°F/Gas 6. Grease the sides and line the base of a 450g/1lb loaf tin/pan with baking parchment.

2 Put the fine polenta in a large mixing bowl. Sift over the flour, baking powder, salt and sugar and stir to combine. Make a small well in the middle.

3 Whisk the egg with the milk and oil. Pour into the dry ingredients and mix together. Pour into the prepared tin.

4 Bake for 30 minutes or until a skewer inserted into the middle comes out clean. Turn out on to a wire rack, remove the lining paper and leave to cool.

5 Slice and serve buttered or drizzled with olive oil.

Energy 1716kcal/7180kJ; Protein 48.4g; Carbohydrate 277.2g, of which sugars 34.6g; Fat 44.7g, of which saturates 9.5g; Cholesterol 255mg; Calcium 527mg; Fibre 8.1g; Sodium 2222mg.

Cheesy cornbread

This moist, buttery cornbread is so rich and flavoursome that it can easily be eaten on its own, but is also great served in still-warm slices with guacamole or spicy chilli dishes. It has a lovely light texture from whisked egg whites, which are folded into the mixture before baking.

MAKES 1 LOAF

75g/3oz/6 tbsp butter
1 large onion, finely chopped
400ml/14fl oz/1⅔ cups milk
225g/8oz/2 cups fine polenta/cornmeal
175g/6oz mozzarella cheese, roughly grated
2 large eggs, separated
salt and ground black pepper, to taste

1 Preheat the oven to 200°C/400°F/Gas 6. Use a little of the butter to grease a 450g/1lb loaf tin/pan.

2 Melt 25g/1oz/2 tbsp of the butter in a pan, add the chopped onion and sauté for 10 minutes, until softened.

3 Pour in the milk and stir until heated, without allowing it to boil. Still stirring, add the polenta in a steady stream. Continue, until the mixture is smooth, then remove from the heat and stir in the cheese and remaining butter. When both have melted, season.

4 Whisk the egg whites to stiff peaks. Stir the egg yolks into the polenta mixture, then fold in the egg whites. Tip the mixture into the tin and smooth the top.

5 Bake for 35–40 minutes, until a skewer comes out clean. Turn out on to a wire rack to cool a little.

Energy 252kcal/1060kJ; Protein 5.6g; Carbohydrate 35.6g, of which sugars 8.8g; Fat 10.7g, of which saturates 1.6g; Cholesterol 57mg; Calcium 73mg; Fibre 1.3g; Sodium 82mg.

Focaccia

This gluten-free focaccia recipe is simple to make and easy to adapt. Try adding Mediterranean flavours such as chopped fresh rosemary, oregano or thyme, some halved black or green olives, or a large pinch of dried red chilli flakes.

MAKES 1 FOCACCIA

450g/1lb/3½ cups bought gluten-free white bread flour blend or home-made white bread flour blend (see page 42)
15ml/1 tbsp caster/superfine sugar
5ml/1 tsp salt
10ml/2 tsp easy-blend/rapid-rise dried yeast
2 eggs, lightly beaten
5ml/1 tsp balsamic vinegar
30ml/2 tbsp olive oil, plus extra for greasing and drizzling
300ml/½ pint/1¼ cups warm water
coarse sea salt, for sprinkling

1 Sift the flour, sugar and salt into a large mixing bowl. Sprinkle over the yeast and stir in, then make a small well in the middle.

2 Mix together the eggs, balsamic vinegar and the 30ml/2 tbsp of olive oil in a jug or pitcher. Pour the mixture into the well, then pour in the warm water and mix together to make a very soft dough.

3 Cover the bowl with a damp dish towel or clear film/plastic wrap and leave to rise in a warm place for about 1 hour or until doubled in size.

4 Brush the base of a 33 x 23cm/13 x 9in shallow-sided baking tin/pan with a generous coating of olive oil.

5 Knock back/punch down the dough.Tip and scrape the soft dough into the prepared tin and level out to cover the base completely and smooth the top.

6 Using your fingers, splash the surface of the dough with some water (or spray using an atomizer), then sprinkle over some coarse sea salt and drizzle with lots of olive oil – be generous with the oil. Using floured fingertips, make lots of dimples all over the surface of the dough.

7 Leave the dough to rise in a warm, draught-free place for 1–1½ hours or until it has doubled in volume. Near the end of the rising time, preheat the oven to 200°C/400°F/Gas 6.

8 Bake the focaccia for 10 minutes in the preheated oven, during which time it will absorb all the olive oil on the surface. Drizzle over a little more olive oil, then bake for a further 20–25 minutes or until the focaccia is golden in colour.

9 Immediately remove from the tin and allow it to cool slightly on a wire rack. Serve while still warm.

Variations

• For Onion Focaccia, finely chop ½ red onion and add to the mixture in step 2. Very finely slice the remaining ½ red onion and sprinkle over the top of the focaccia during the last 10–15 minutes of the cooking time.

• For Rosemary Focaccia, sprinkle a few sprigs of fresh rosemary over the top of the dough when you add the coarse salt and oil.

Energy 2027kcal/8466kJ; Protein 37.6g; Carbohydrate 375.2g, of which sugars 16.6g; Fat 41.3g, of which saturates 8.3g; Cholesterol 462mg; Calcium 73mg; Fibre 4.8g; Sodium 2134mg.

Pittas

These gluten-free pittas are great for serving warm with dips such as hummus and for using as pockets for falafals and kebabs. Both ground psyllium husk and an egg are used in the dough to make it pliable enough to roll out and shape into ovals.

MAKES 6

10ml/2 tsp ground psyllium husk
120ml/4fl oz/½ cup warm water
375g/13oz/3¾ cups gluten-free plain/all-purpose flour blend, plus extra for dusting
5ml/1 tsp caster/superfine sugar
2.5ml/½ tsp salt
10ml/2 tsp easy-blend/rapid-rise dried yeast
1 large egg, lightly beaten
5ml/1 tsp white wine vinegar
45ml/3 tbsp vegetable oil, plus extra for greasing

1 Put the ground psyllium husk in a jug or pitcher and add the water. Whisk together and leave the mixture for a few minutes to thicken.

2 Sift the flour, sugar and salt into a large mixing bowl. Add the yeast and stir together with a fork to mix. Make a small well in the middle.

3 Whisk the egg together with the vinegar and oil. Pour into the well, then pour in most of the psyllium husk mixture. Stir together, adding more of the liquid if needed; the dough should be soft and slightly sticky.

4 Turn out on to a floured surface and gently knead just until smooth. Return the dough to the cleaned-out bowl, cover with a damp dish towel and leave in a warm place to rise for about 2 hours or until doubled in size.

5 Knock back/punch down the dough and knead lightly. Divide into tangerine-sized balls and flatten with the palm of your hand. Dust a clean cloth with flour and place the flattened rounds of dough on it, leaving space to expand between them. Sprinkle with flour and lay another cloth on top. Leave to prove for 1–2 hours.

6 Preheat the oven to 230°C/450°F/Gas 8. Place several baking sheets in the oven to heat, then lightly oil them and place the pittas on them, well spaced out. Sprinkle with a little water and bake for 6–8 minutes – they should be lightly browned but not too firm, and slightly hollow inside.

7 Place the pittas on a wire rack to cool a little before eating, or wrap them in a clean, dry dish towel to keep them soft for eating later.

Energy 289kcal/1204kJ; Protein 4.6g; Carbohydrate 50.4g, of which sugars 0.2g; Fat 7.5g, of which saturates 1.2g; Cholesterol 39mg; Calcium 8mg; Fibre 1.5g; Sodium 15mg.

Naans

Naans are one of the main types of bread served at most meals in India. These gluten-free ones can be varied by adding toppings, such as seeds, herbs and dried chilli flakes. They are the perfect accompaniment for curries and other liquid dishes, and also make a filling snack.

MAKES 8

500g/18oz/4½ cups gluten-free plain/all-purpose flour blend, plus extra for dusting
2.5ml/½ tsp xanthan gum
5ml/1 tsp gluten-free baking powder
5ml/1 tsp salt
5ml/1 tsp caster/superfine sugar
50g/2oz/¼ cup softened butter, plus extra for glazing
about 250ml/8fl oz/1 cup lukewarm milk
oil, for greasing

1 Sift the flour, xanthan gum, baking powder, salt and sugar into a large mixing bowl. Mix well, then rub in the butter using your fingertips. Add enough of the milk to make a soft dough – the quantity will vary according to the specific flour you use.

2 Transfer the dough to a lightly floured pastry board and knead for a few seconds, until smooth and pliable. Shape the dough into a ball, cover with a damp dish towel and leave to rest for 30 minutes.

3 Set the grill or broiler to its highest setting and preheat it for 8–10 minutes, then line a grill pan with a piece of foil and brush it with a little dab of oil.

4 Divide the dough into eight equal-sized portions, then form into balls.

5 Roll each ball into a circle measuring 13cm/5in in diameter, then gently pull the lower end to form it into a traditional teardrop shape. Roll it out again, maintaining the teardrop shape, to form a 23cm/9in naan.

6 Place a naan in the prepared grill pan and cook it 13cm/5in below the heat source for about 1½ minutes until it puffs up. Keep an eye on it as it can burn easily. Turn it over and grill for a further minute or until brown patches appear.

7 Place the cooked naan on a clean dish towel and brush the surface with a little melted butter. Wrap it in the towel to keep it hot and soft while you finish cooking the other naans. Serve warm.

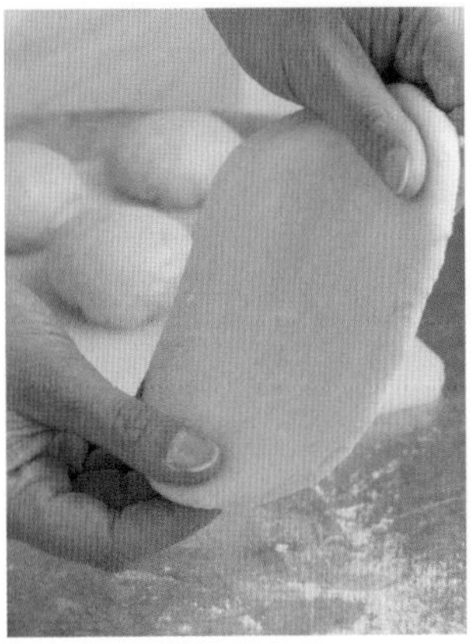

Energy 282kcal/1176kJ; Protein 4.2g; Carbohydrate 51.5g, of which sugars 1.6g; Fat 6.5g, of which saturates 3.8g; Cholesterol 15mg; Calcium 39mg; Fibre 0.7g; Sodium 297mg.

Pizza

This thin and crispy gluten-free pizza base is made with a mixture of flours. Here it is topped with smoky grilled vegetables and mozzarella, but you can top with ingredients of your choice. The result is much more tasty than buying mass-produced gluten-free pizza bases.

SERVES 2–4

115g/4oz/1 cup fine polenta/ cornmeal
50g/2oz/½ cup potato flour
50g/2oz/½ cup soya flour
5ml/1 tsp gluten-free baking powder
2.5ml/½ tsp salt
50g/2oz/4 tbsp soft margarine
about 105ml/7 tbsp milk

For the topping

2 baby or 1 small aubergines/ eggplants, sliced
1 courgette/zucchini, sliced
30ml/2 tbsp olive oil
1 yellow bell pepper, seeded and thickly sliced
4 plum tomatoes, skinned and chopped
30ml/2 tbsp chopped fresh basil, plus whole sprigs to garnish
115g/4oz mozzarella cheese, sliced
salt and ground black pepper, to taste

1 Preheat the grill or boiler to high. Brush the aubergine and courgette slices with a little oil and place on a grill rack with the pepper slices. Cook under the grill until lightly browned, turning once. Remove and set aside.

2 Preheat the oven to 200°C/400°F/Gas 6. Place the fine polenta, potato flour, soya flour, baking powder and salt in a mixing bowl and stir to combine.

3 Lightly rub in the margarine until the mixture resembles coarse breadcrumbs, then stir in enough of the milk to make a soft but not sticky dough.

4 Place the dough on a sheet of baking parchment on a baking sheet, and roll it out to form a 25cm/10in round, making the edges slightly thicker than the middle.

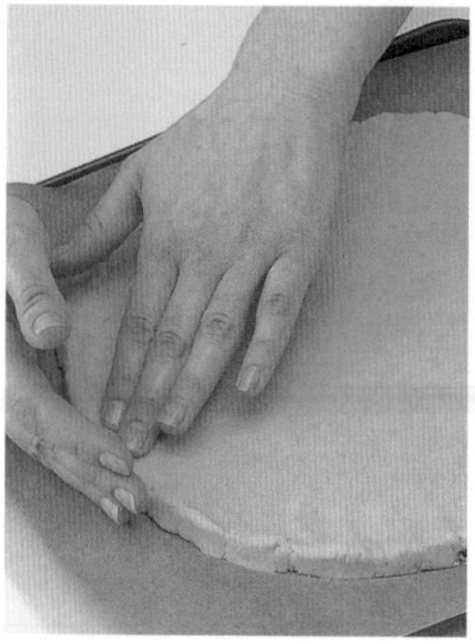

5 Brush the pizza dough with any remaining olive oil, then spread the chopped tomatoes over the surface. Sprinkle with the chopped basil, and arrange the grilled vegetables and mozzarella slices over the tomato. Season to taste.

6 Bake for 25–30 minutes, until crisp and golden brown. Garnish the pizza with fresh basil sprigs and serve immediately, cut into slices.

Cook's tip

You can top this pizza base with anything you fancy, but avoid anything that is too wet or it will make it soggy.

Energy 459kcal/1906kJ; Protein 13.3g; Carbohydrate 48.2g, of which sugars 8.7g; Fat 23.9g, of which saturates 5.25g; Cholesterol 18mg; Calcium 166.5mg; Fibre 6.5g; Sodium 243mg.

Calzoni

Calzoni are essentially folded breads that encase a flavoursome filling. This gluten-free version is made with a simple yeasted dough enriched with eggs and olive oil. It is filled here with tomato, ricotta and salami, but you can vary the filling to suit – just ensure it isn't too wet.

MAKES 4

450g/1lb/4 cups bought gluten-free white bread flour blend or home-made white bread flour blend (see page 42), plus extra for dusting
5ml/1 tsp xanthan gum
2.5ml/½ tsp salt
10ml/2 tsp caster/superfine sugar
5ml/1 tsp easy-blend/rapid-rise dried yeast
2 eggs
90ml/6 tbsp olive oil, plus extra for greasing and drizzling
200ml/7fl oz/scant 1 cup warm water

For the filling

30ml/2 tbsp fresh ricotta cheese
3 slices salami, coarsely chopped
2 sun-dried tomatoes in olive oil, drained and chopped
15ml/1 tbsp chopped fresh parsley
salt and ground black pepper, to taste

For the tomato sauce

30ml/2 tbsp extra virgin olive oil
2 garlic cloves, finely chopped
400g/14oz can chopped tomatoes
30ml/2 tbsp chopped fresh parsley
salt and ground black pepper, to taste

1 Sift the flour, xanthan gum, salt and sugar into a mixing bowl. Stir in the yeast, then make a well in the middle. Whisk together the eggs and oil and pour into the well with most of the water. Mix to a soft sticky dough. Knead the dough on a lightly floured surface until smooth, then return to the cleaned bowl, cover with a damp dish towel and leave to rise for 30 minutes.

2 Meanwhile, make the tomato sauce. Heat the oil in a pan over a low heat and fry the garlic for 2 minutes without browning. Add the tomatoes and stir together. Bring to the boil and simmer for 15 minutes. Add salt and pepper to taste, then stir in the chopped parsley.

3 Preheat the oven to 200°C/400°C/Gas 6. Oil a heavy baking sheet. Cut the dough into four equal pieces, then roll each into a circle measuring 20cm/8in in diameter between two pieces of floured baking parchment.

4 Spread the ricotta over one half of each circle, keeping the edges clear. Sprinkle over the salami, tomato and parsley, drizzle with oil and season. Lift each on to the baking sheet, fold in half and seal with the back of a fork.

5 Bake for 15 minutes or until the calzoni are golden, then serve with the tomato sauce offered separately.

Energy 745kcal/3101kJ; Protein 12.3g; Carbohydrate 93.7g, of which sugars 3.6g; Fat 35.6g, of which saturates 6.3g; Cholesterol 122mg; Calcium 52mg; Fibre 2.2g; Sodium 281mg.

Thin potato breads

A cross between a bread and a pancake, these are made with a combination of mashed potato and gluten-free flour. Bear in mind that the potatoes need to cool and the dough must be chilled for half an hour, so allow time for this.

MAKES 16

500g/18oz floury potatoes, peeled
25g/1oz/2 tbsp butter
60ml/4 tbsp double/heavy cream
5ml/1 tsp salt
175–225g/6–8oz/1½–2 cups bought gluten-free white bread flour blend or home-made white bread flour blend (see page 42)

1 Cut the potatoes into same-size, smallish chunks. Put them in a pan and pour over just enough boiling water to cover, then bring to the boil and simmer, uncovered, for 15–20 minutes, until tender.

2 Drain the potatoes well, then return them to the pan and dry them over a low heat for a few seconds to drive off any residual steam.

3 Push the potatoes through a ricer, masher or sieve into a large mixing bowl. Add the butter, cream and salt and beat together. Leave to cool.

4 When the potatoes are just cool, stir in 115g/4oz/1 cup of the flour. Add more flour, a spoonful at a time, allowing it to absorb the moisture, until you have a fairly firm dough (it will firm a little more as it chills).

5 On a lightly floured surface, knead the dough until it is smooth. Divide the dough into pieces about the size of a large egg, roll into balls and put on a baking tray. Chill in the fridge for 30 minutes.

6 Roll out each ball of dough very thinly. Heat a large ungreased frying pan or griddle and cook each bread over a medium heat, until brown spots appear on the surface, turning once.

7 Put the cooked breads between two clean dish towels to stop them from drying out. Once they are all cooked, serve immediately.

Energy 91kcal/379kJ; Protein 1.2g; Carbohydrate 13.8g, of which sugars 0.5g; Fat 3.5g, of which saturates 2.1g; Cholesterol 19mg; Calcium 4mg; Fibre 0.5g; Sodium 137mg.

Chickpea flour flatbreads

Chickpea flour is commonly used in Asia for making bread, and is nutritious as well as being gluten free. Here, it is used in simple crispy flatbreads, easy to make and much nicer than any shop-bought version. They are best served warm.

MAKES 6

130g/4½oz/generous 1 cup chickpea flour, plus extra for dusting
5ml/1 tsp olive oil
230ml/7½fl oz/scant 1 cup water

1 Preheat the oven to 180°C/350°F/Gas 4. Line a baking tray with baking parchment.

2 In a large mixing bowl, rub together the chickpea flour and olive oil using your fingertips, until all the oil has been incorporated.

3 Pour in the water and stir until thoroughly mixed. The mixture will have a solid 'dough' consistency, but because there's no yeast, it does not need kneading.

4 Transfer the dough to a lightly floured work surface and cut it into six pieces. Roll each into a ball.

5 Using a well-floured rolling pin, roll out each ball into a circle 5mm/¼in thick. Transfer these to the prepared baking tray.

6 Bake for 15–20 minutes, until the edges are slightly crispy, then remove from the oven and serve warm.

Cook's tip

These flatbreads can also be used as bases for pizzas. Simply prepare and bake as above, then add your chosen toppings, such as tomato sauce, roasted veg and cheese, and bake again for a couple of minutes.

Energy 215kcal/902kJ; Protein 4.3g; Carbohydrate 24.1g, of which sugars 10.5g; Fat 12g, of which saturates 5.3g; Cholesterol 44mg; Calcium 59mg; Fibre 1.4g; Sodium 79mg.

Oat & cinnamon rolls

The combination of oats and warm spicy cinnamon is perfect at breakfast. Even better, you can make this gluten-free bread dough the night before and leave it in the fridge, ready for shaping and baking the next morning. For a plain roll, just omit the cinnamon and sugar topping.

MAKES 12

350g/12oz/3 cups bought gluten-free white bread flour blend or home-made white bread flour blend (see page 42)
10ml/2 tsp xanthan gum
5ml/1 tsp salt
10ml/2 tsp ground cinnamon
50g/2oz/scant ½ cup gluten-free rolled oats
15ml/1 tbsp soft light brown sugar, plus 10ml/2 tsp to glaze
7g/¼oz easy-blend/rapid-rise dried yeast
150ml/¼ pint/⅔ cup hot water
150ml/¼ pint/⅔ cup milk, plus a little to glaze
10ml/2 tsp white wine vinegar
45ml/3 tbsp sunflower oil, plus extra for greasing
2 eggs, lightly beaten

1 Lightly oil a large baking sheet or line it with a sheet of baking parchment.

2 Sift the flour, xanthan gum, salt and cinnamon into a large mixing bowl. Stir in the oats, the 15ml/1 tbsp brown sugar, and the yeast. Make a well in the middle.

3 Mix the water and milk together, then stir in the vinegar and the sunflower oil. Add the eggs to the dry ingredients, then pour in the milk mixture. Stir together to make a soft dough. It will look more like a thick cake mixture than a regular bread dough.

4 Cover the bowl with a damp dish towel and leave in a warm place for an hour or until the dough has nearly doubled in size.

5 Knock back/punch down the dough with a wooden spoon, then shape the dough into 12 even-sized balls and place them on the prepared baking sheet, spacing them well apart.

6 Gently brush the tops of the rolls with milk and sprinkle with a little light brown sugar.

7 Leave the rolls to prove in a warm place for 15–20 minutes until puffy and slightly risen, but don't let the rolls overprove or they may collapse when they are baked. Meanwhile, preheat the oven to 200°C/400°F/Gas 6.

8 Place the risen rolls in the preheated oven and bake for 12–15 minutes, until they are risen and golden and sound 'hollow' when tapped.

9 Remove the rolls from the tray and allow to cool on a wire rack for 15 minutes. Serve warm with butter and honey or fruit preserves, as you prefer.

Variations

- Add a mashed ripe banana and 30ml/2 tbsp finely chopped walnuts with the liquid to make Banana and Walnut Rolls.
- For Half-and-Half Rolls, use 175g/6oz/1½ cups each of gluten-free white bread flour and gluten-free brown bread flour. Add an extra 15ml/1 tbsp milk to the dough.

Energy 173kcal/725kJ; Protein 3.7g; Carbohydrate 29.1g, of which sugars 2.8g; Fat 4.8g, of which saturates 0.9g; Cholesterol 39mg; Calcium 24mg; Fibre 0.7g; Sodium 185mg.

Potato buns

The addition of mashed potatoes in these buns makes them moist and light. Like many gluten-free breads, the dough is very soft and would spread too much if it were baked on a tray. Instead the mixture rises and is baked in a muffin tin for support, to make individual buns.

MAKES 12

7g/¼oz easy-blend/rapid-rise dried yeast
5ml/1 tsp caster/superfine sugar
75ml/5 tbsp warm milk
15ml/1 tbsp vegetable oil, plus extra for greasing
175g/6oz potatoes, peeled, boiled and mashed
1 egg, beaten
5ml/1 tsp salt
about 175g/6oz/1½ cups bought gluten-free white bread flour blend or home-made white bread flour blend (see page 42), plus extra for dusting

1 Put the yeast, sugar, milk and vegetable oil in a large mixing bowl and whisk together well. Add the mashed potato, beaten egg and salt to the bowl and stir well with a sturdy spoon to combine all the ingredients thoroughly.

2 Gradually sift the flour over the mixture and work it in with the spoon. You may not need all of the flour, so add it in batches and stop when the mixture resembles a thick cake batter.

3 Cover the bowl with clear film or plastic wrap and leave in a warm place for 20 minutes, until the mixture is slightly puffy, to allow the yeast to start working. Lightly oil and flour a 12-cup muffin tin/pan.

4 Gently stir the dough to knock out the air, then divide it between the muffin cups and spread using the back of a spoon dipped in water, to smooth the tops. The cups should be about two-thirds full.

5 Let the dough rise for about 20 minutes, until it has risen to the top of the muffin cups. When nearly ready to bake, preheat the oven to 190°C/375°F/Gas 5.

6 Put the buns in the preheated oven and bake them for 20–25 minutes, until the tops are nicely browned and the buns are cooked through; if you take one of the buns out of the tin and tap the bottom it should sound 'hollow' and feel quite firm.

7 Remove from the oven and leave the buns to cool in the tin for 5–10 minutes, before removing to a wire rack to cool further. They are best served warm.

Energy 81kcal/340kJ; Protein 1.8g; Carbohydrate 14.5g, of which sugars 0.5g; Fat 1.8g, of which saturates 0.4g; Cholesterol 20mg; Calcium 11mg; Fibre 0.4g; Sodium 14mg.

Steamed buns

These soft, fluffy, gluten-free steamed buns are popular throughout China and make a satisfying alternative to rice. They are especially good served with slow-cooked pork or crispy duck, or as an accompaniment to all sorts of curries, soups and stews.

MAKES 20

175g/6oz/1½ cups cornflour/starch, plus extra for dusting
75g/3oz/⅔ cup potato flour
115g/4oz/1 cup glutinous rice flour
115g/4oz/1 cup white rice flour
2.5ml/½ tsp salt
15ml/1 tbsp caster/superfine sugar
15ml/1 tbsp easy-blend/rapid-rise dried yeast
about 300ml/½ pint/1¼ cups warm water

1 Sift the cornflour, potato flour, glutinous rice flour, white rice flour, salt and sugar into a large mixing bowl. Add the yeast and stir until well blended.

2 Make a small well in the middle of the dry ingredients and pour in the water. Stir to make a stiff dough that just comes together. If it is very dry, add a little more water, a teaspoon at a time.

3 Cover the bowl with a clean damp dish towel or clear film/plastic wrap and leave to rise in a warm place for about 1 hour or until doubled in size.

4 Knock back/punch down the dough to its original size, then leave for a further 30 minutes to rise again.

5 Divide the dough into two pieces. On a large piece of baking parchment lightly dusted with cornflour, roll out one of the pieces into a sausage shape, then press it out into a flat rectangle about 5mm/¼in thick. Lift up the long side and roll it up tightly into a tube. Cut into 2cm/¾in rounds.

6 Cut a circle of baking parchment that will fit inside your steamer and make a few small holes in it to allow the steam to come through and circulate. Arrange the buns on the paper circle, spacing them at least 2cm/¾in apart to give them room to rise. Leave for a further 15 minutes to rise a little.

7 Pour boiling water into the base of the steamer and steam the buns over heat for about 10 minutes or until well risen and cooked through. Remove and keep warm while you repeat the process with the remaining piece of dough. If you have a very large or layered steamer, you can cook all the buns in one go. Serve warm.

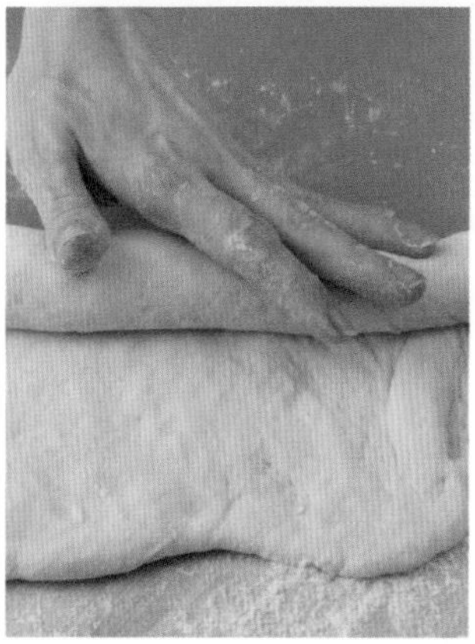

Energy 88kcal/373kJ; Protein 1.1g; Carbohydrate 20.9g, of which sugars 0.9g; Fat 0.2g, of which saturates 0g; Cholesterol 0mg; Calcium 5mg; Fibre 0.6g; Sodium 6mg.

Bagels

These little bread rings are made with two types of flour and two raising agents: yeast and baking powder. This, combined with the double-cooking method – brief poaching in boiling water, then oven-baking – gives them their unique, slightly chewy crust.

MAKES 8

20ml/4 tsp clear honey
400ml/14fl oz/1⅔ cups lukewarm water
15ml/1 tbsp easy-blend/rapid-rise dried yeast
350g/12oz/3 cups gluten-free plain/all-purpose flour blend
50g/2oz/½ cup gluten-free oat flour
7.5ml/1½ tsp ground psyllium husk
2.5ml/½ tsp xanthan gum
10ml/2 tsp gluten-free baking powder
7.5ml/1½ tsp salt
40g/1½oz/3 tbsp butter, melted
about 75g/3oz/⅔ cup white rice flour, plus extra for dusting
2.5ml/½ tsp molasses (optional)
fine polenta/cornmeal, for dusting
1 egg yolk, for glazing

1 Stir the honey into the lukewarm water in a jug or pitcher. Sprinkle over the yeast, whisk with a fork and leave to stand for a few minutes.

2 Meanwhile, sift the two flours, ground psyllium husk, xanthan gum, baking powder and 5ml/1 tsp of the salt into a large mixing bowl. Make a well in the middle.

3 Whisk the butter into the yeast liquid. Pour into the dry ingredients and mix together with a wooden spoon to make a soft, sticky batter. Cover the bowl with a clean dish towel or clear film/plastic wrap and leave in a warm place for 45 minutes–1 hour or until doubled in size.

4 Gently stir the risen dough to knock out the air, then gradually work in enough of the rice flour to make a soft but not too sticky dough.

5 Turn out the dough on to a surface lightly dusted with rice flour and divide into eight pieces. Shape each into a round ball. Poke your thumb through each one, then, working with your fingers, open the hole to form a bagel measuring 6–7.5cm/2½–3in in diameter. Place on a floured board and leave to rise for 30–45 minutes or until puffy and nearly doubled in size.

6 Preheat the oven to 200°C/400°F/Gas 6. Bring 3–4 litres/5–7 pints of water to the boil in a large pan. Add the remaining 2.5ml/½ tsp salt and the molasses, if using. Reduce the heat to a gentle boil. Dust a baking sheet with fine polenta or cornmeal.

7 Add the bagels, one at a time, to the boiling water, until you have a single layer of bagels. Poach for 20–30 seconds. Lift out with a draining spoon and place on the baking sheet. Repeat until all the bagels are poached.

8 Beat the egg yolk with 15ml/1 tbsp cold water. Lightly brush it over the bagels to glaze. Bake for 15 minutes or until well risen and dark golden-brown. Transfer to a wire rack to cool. The bagels can be kept in an airtight container for up to three days.

Cook's tip

Adding molasses to the poaching water is a traditional New York touch. Leave it out if you prefer, or add 30ml/2 tbsp sugar to the poaching water for a sweeter crust.

Energy 263kcal/1098kJ; Protein 3.5g; Carbohydrate 49.4g, of which sugars 2g; Fat 5.5g, of which saturates 3g; Cholesterol 36mg; Calcium 6mg; Fibre 0.8g; Sodium 401mg.

Teacakes

These lightly spiced gluten-free teacakes are made with a combination of flour, cornflour and ground almonds to achieve the desired crumb, and are enriched with milk, butter and an egg. They are delicious served lightly toasted and spread with a little butter or honey.

MAKES 8

225g/8oz/2 cups bought gluten-free white bread flour blend or home-made white bread flour blend (see page 42)
75g/3oz/⅔ cup cornflour/starch
5ml/1 tsp ground cinnamon
5ml/1 tsp salt
115g/4oz/1 cup ground almonds
5ml/1 tsp easy-blend/rapid-rise dried yeast
45ml/3 tbsp caster/superfine sugar
300ml/½ pint/1¼ cups warm milk, plus extra for glazing
1 egg, at room temperature, lightly beaten
40g/1½oz/3 tbsp butter, melted, plus extra for greasing
50g/2oz/¼ cup currants
50g/2oz/⅓ cup sultanas/golden raisins

1 Sift the flour, cornflour, cinnamon and salt into a large mixing bowl. Stir in the ground almonds.

2 In a jug or pitcher, mix the yeast, 5ml/1 tsp of the sugar and the milk and leave to stand for 5 minutes.

3 Add the remaining sugar to the flour and make a well in the middle. Add the egg and butter, then pour in the milk mixture. Add the fruit and stir everything to make a soft sticky dough (it will firm a little more as it rises).

4 Cover with a dampened dish towel. Leave at room temperature for 1 hour, until doubled in bulk. Grease two heavy baking sheets or line with baking parchment.

5 Gently knock back/punch down the dough with a wooden spoon. Scoop the mixture on to the baking sheets to make four buns on each. Wet your fingers and mould each bun into a round, slightly flattened shape (don't flatten too much as they will spread out as they rise). Make sure that the buns are spaced well apart.

6 Lightly brush the tops with a little milk, then leave in a warm place to prove for 30–45 minutes or until they have almost doubled in size. Don't let them over-rise or they will collapse during baking. When almost ready to bake, preheat the oven to 200°C/400°F/Gas 6.

7 Bake for 15–18 minutes or until golden. Turn out on to a wire rack to cool slightly. To serve, split while warm and spread with butter, or let the teacakes cool, then split and toast them.

Energy 342kcal/1431kJ; Protein 7.1g; Carbohydrate 48.2g, of which sugars 16.8g; Fat 14.1g, of which saturates 4g; Cholesterol 42mg; Calcium 99mg; Fibre 0.6g; Sodium 66mg.

Rich fruit teabread

This milk-enriched and gluten-free fruity loaf tastes good plain or can be lightly toasted and served with a little butter or fruit conserve. The basic dough contains an egg and saffron, which gives it a lovely golden colour.

MAKES 1 LOAF

450g/1lb/4 cups bought gluten-free white bread flour blend or home-made white bread flour blend (see page 42), plus extra for dusting
5ml/1 tsp salt
7g/¼oz easy-blend/rapid-rise dried yeast
50g/2oz/¼ cup caster/superfine sugar
pinch of ground cinnamon
pinch of ground nutmeg
pinch of powdered saffron
350ml/12floz/1½ cups lukewarm milk
1 egg, lightly beaten
50g/2oz/¼ cup butter, softened, plus extra for greasing

For the fruit filling

150g/5oz/¾ cup currants
150g/5oz/1 cup raisins
50g/2oz/⅓ cup finely diced glacé/candied citron peel
50g/2oz/⅓ cup finely diced glacé/candied orange peel

1 First poach the currants and raisins in simmering water for 10 minutes. Drain and pat dry in a cloth or kitchen paper, and put to one side.

2 Lightly grease a 900g/2lb loaf tin/pan with some butter. Sift the flour and salt into a large mixing bowl. Stir in the yeast, sugar, cinnamon, nutmeg and saffron. Make a well in the middle of the dry ingredients.

3 Pour the lukewarm milk into the well. Add the beaten egg and the butter and mix to a soft sticky batter, beating with a wooden spoon, until the butter is completely incorporated.

4 Add the poached fruit and beat into the mixture along with both types of candied fruit peel.

5 Spoon and scrape the dough into the tin. Cover with oiled clear film/plastic wrap and leave until the dough has risen level with the top of the tin (remove the clear film just before it reaches this stage).

6 Preheat the oven to 200°C/400°F/Gas 6. Bake the loaf for 35 minutes or until it sounds 'hollow' when tapped on the base. Cover the loaf with foil towards the end of the cooking time if the top is browning too much.

7 Turn out the teabread on to a wire rack to cool. Slice and serve.

Cook's tip

The teabread can be kept in an airtight container for a couple of days; just slice off what you need to prevent it from going stale. Alternatively, you can cut and freeze in individual slices, then simply remove what you need and toast it using the defrost setting on your toaster.

Variations

Try other dried fruit, such as chopped ready-to-eat dried apricots or prunes (these won't need poaching first), or you could substitute some of the fruit for chopped nuts such as toasted almonds, walnuts and hazelnuts.

Energy 1401kcal/5891kJ; Protein 28.7g; Carbohydrate 317.4g, of which sugars 4.6g; Fat 6.5g, of which saturates 0.3g; Cholesterol 0mg; Calcium 102mg; Fibre 7.6g; Sodium 50mg.

Chocolate & chestnut brioche

The softness of this bake comes from the egg and milk in the buttery brioche-type gluten-free dough. It includes chestnut flour, which has a lovely almost caramel-like flavour and is the perfect partner for chocolate. Dried apricots add both sweetness and texture.

MAKES 2 LOAVES OR 12 ROLLS

150g/5oz/1¼ cups bought gluten-free white bread flour blend or home-made white bread flour blend (see page 42), plus extra for dusting
75g/3oz/⅔ cup chestnut flour
50g/2oz/½ cup unsweetened cocoa powder
2.5ml/½ tsp xanthan gum
5ml/1 tsp salt
60ml/4 tbsp soft light brown sugar
10ml/2 tsp easy blend/rapid-rise dried yeast
3 eggs, beaten
45ml/3 tbsp warm water
45ml/3 tbsp milk
50g/2oz/¼ cup butter, melted, plus extra for greasing
5ml/1 tsp vanilla extract
50g/2oz/4 tbsp plain/semisweet chocolate, chopped into chunks
50g/2oz/¼ cup dried apricots, finely chopped
30ml/2 tbsp milk and 15ml/1 tbsp a little soft light brown sugar, to glaze

1 Sift the flours, cocoa powder, xanthan gum and salt into a large mixing bowl. Stir in the sugar, followed by the yeast. Make a small well in the middle.

2 Combine the eggs, water, milk, butter and vanilla. Pour into the dry ingredients and mix to a soft dough.

3 Transfer the dough to a lightly floured surface and knead for a few seconds, until smooth, then place the dough in a bowl, cover with a damp dish towel and leave to rise in a warm place for about 1½ hours. It may not quite double in size, but it should be soft and springy to touch.

4 Knock back/punch down the dough and flatten it slightly into a round. Sprinkle over the chopped chocolate and apricots, then fold over the sides and gently knead until these are evenly distributed.

5 Cut the dough into two halves and shape as desired; you can either form them into two traditional rounds or divide into 12 smaller brioche rolls. Place on to greased baking trays, cover with oiled clear film or plastic wrap and leave to prove for 30 minutes, until risen again. Preheat the oven to 190°C/375°F/Gas 5.

6 When ready to bake, brush the tops with milk and sprinkle with soft light brown sugar. Bake in the middle of the oven, until the brioche has a crispy top and sounds hollow when tapped on the bottom. This will take about 30 minutes for a larger loaf, but only 10–15 minutes for smaller brioche rolls.

7 Remove from the oven and place on a wire rack to cool. The loaves should be cold before you slice them, but you can enjoy the rolls while they are still warm.

Variation

For a plain brioche, add an additional 50g/2oz/½ cup gluten-free white bread flour blend instead of cocoa powder and an extra 5ml/1 tsp milk instead of the vanilla. Omit the chopped chocolate and apricots. Glaze the loaf with milk instead of a milk and sugar mixture.

Energy 178kcal/744kJ; Protein 4g; Carbohydrate 24.2g, of which sugars 10.2g; Fat 7.7g, of which saturates 4g; Cholesterol 67mg; Calcium 30mg; Fibre 1.9g; Sodium 91mg.

Pasta & noodles

Available in an amazing range of shapes and sizes, versatile pasta suits any occasion, from simple mid-week meals to sophisticated suppers. What's more, egg pasta in particular is a great starting point for a nutritious meal, being high in complex carbohydrates, a good source of protein, and low in fat, and it can be partnered with all manner of meat, seafood, cheese or vegetable sauces, too.

Fortunately, making your own gluten-free fresh egg pasta is surprisingly easy and because the dough doesn't require extensive kneading and re-rolling – unlike wheat-based ones – it's relatively quick to make. It's also simple: the only equipment you need is a long rolling pin, although a pasta machine will reduce preparation time even further and produce the very best results. You can then cut and shape the fresh egg pasta sheets to your exact requirements, whether that is fine linguine, thicker tagliatelle, or delicate sheets that can be used to make lasagne or cannelloni; you'll find recipes for all these here.

Noodles are equally easy to make, and rice ones are especially useful for vegans and anyone else who doesn't eat eggs. There are recipes here for both buckwheat and rice noodles, with their distinctive textures and tastes, plus delicious recipes that feature them, such as Spicy Buckwheat Noodles, and Tofu Soup with Rice Noodles.

For those times when you are in a hurry or too busy to make your own pasta from scratch, dried ready-made gluten-free pasta shapes and inherently gluten-free products such as rice vermicelli, dried rice noodles and cellophane noodles all make a great storecupboard standby and can be used in place of the fresh kind in many of these dishes; simply adjust the cooking time accordingly. If you are vegan, choose an egg-free dried ready-made pasta.

Fresh egg pasta

Although dried gluten-free pasta is readily available, making your own is rewarding. Xanthan gum takes the place of gluten in the dough, making it flexible and easy to handle. Try to use organic eggs as the yolks tend to be darker in colour and will make the pasta richer. Although it's best to use pasta dough fresh, you can store it in an airtight box in the fridge for 24 hours.

MAKES 450G/1LB

200g/7oz/1⅔ cups gluten-free plain/all-purpose flour blend, plus extra for dusting

5ml/1 tsp xanthan gum

3 eggs

1 Sift the flour into a large mixing bowl, add the xanthan gum and stir until well mixed. Make a well in the middle of the dry ingredients.

2 Lightly beat the eggs, just enough to blend the yolks and whites together, then pour into the well. Using a fork, gradually work in the flour to form a soft but not sticky dough.

3 Transfer the dough to a lightly floured surface and gently knead for 2–3 minutes. There's no gluten in the flour to develop, but light kneading will ensure that the xanthan gum is evenly distributed and make the dough smooth.

4 Cut the dough into four even-sized pieces, form each into a flattish ball, then wrap them in clear film or plastic wrap so they don't dry out. Chill for 30 minutes before using.

Rolling out using a pasta machine

1 If using a pasta machine, unwrap one of the dough balls, flatten a little more – so that it will pass through the pasta machine – and lightly flour on both sides.

2 Pass the flattened dough through the pasta machine on the widest setting. Fold the strip of dough in three, turn the piece by 90 degrees (so that the smooth edges are positioned left to right, not top to bottom) and feed it through again. The dough should now be smooth and of an even thickness.

3 Continue to pass the pasta through the machine in this way, narrowing the roller setting by one notch each time and rolling the dough twice on each setting. Lightly sprinkle the dough with more flour if it starts to feel sticky, but try not to add too much.

4 Lay the sheet of pasta on to a floured surface. If you are planning to make filled pasta such as ravioli (see page 89), or cannelloni (see page 86), use it immediately. If you are going to make ribbons, such as linguine (see page 82) or tagliatelle, let the sheet dry out on baking parchment for 5–10 minutes before cutting it.

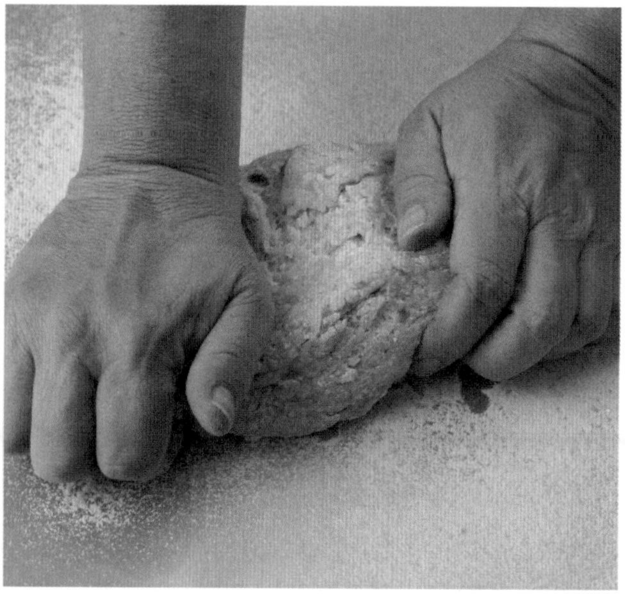

Energy 978kcal/4084kJ; Protein 32.5g; Carbohydrate 159.8g, of which sugars 0.4g; Fat 22.8g, of which saturates 6.3g; Cholesterol 693mg; Calcium 103mg; Fibre 2.1g; Sodium 252mg.

Rolling out by hand

1 If rolling by hand, unwrap one of the balls of dough and roll it out on a clean, lightly floured surface with a long rolling pin until it is about 5mm/¼in thick.

2 Lift the dough from the surface and rotate it by 45 degrees. Don't overflour the surface as this will dry out the dough; it should cling slightly, as this helps the stretching process, but not stick to the surface.

3 Continue rolling, lifting and rotating the dough until it is very thin. It is important to work quickly, although you can keep the dough pliable by covering it with a slightly moist clean dish towel when you are not working with it.

4 Use the pasta sheet immediately if you are going to make filled pasta or let it dry out slightly if you are going to make ribbons. Repeat with the remaining three pieces of pasta dough.

Cutting pasta

You can cut your pasta into the desired shape as soon as it is dry enough to roll up without it sticking to itself, either by hand using a sharp knife or pasta wheel, or by using the cutter on a pasta machine.

For lasagne, simply trim the pasta sheets to neaten the edges, then cut it into the lengths required, depending on the shape and size of your lasagne dish.

For ribbons, if using a pasta machine, fit the tagliatelle or linguine cutters as required. Pass the sheets of dough through the cutters, then hang the strands over a wooden pole suspended between two objects of even height to air dry, or carefully place them on a floured cooling rack suspended over a tray.

To cut pasta ribbons by hand, lightly flour the dough and roll it up loosely like a Swiss roll or jelly roll. Using a sharp knife, cut the roll into slices, to the thickness you require. For linguine, cut 5mm/¼in slices; for tagliatelle, cut 8mm/½in slices. Unroll the ribbons and leave them to hang over a wooden pole or place on a wire cooling rack until slightly dried, then twist into nests on a floured dish towel and leave on a wire rack to dry a little more.

Flavouring pasta

Fresh pasta can be flavoured in many different ways. For Tomato Pasta, beat the eggs with about 30ml/2 tbsp sun-dried tomato paste; for Fresh Herb Pasta, add 45ml/3 tbsp chopped mixed herbs such as fresh basil, parsley, coriander/cilantro or marjoram; and for Lemon Pasta, add the finely grated rind of 2 unwaxed lemons.

Buckwheat noodles

Buckwheat is a high-protein grain-like seed that's gluten free and, despite its name, unrelated to wheat. Also known as soba, these noodles are popular in Japanese cuisine where they are typically served in a hot clear broth. They are delicious tossed in a little dressing and added to a salad.

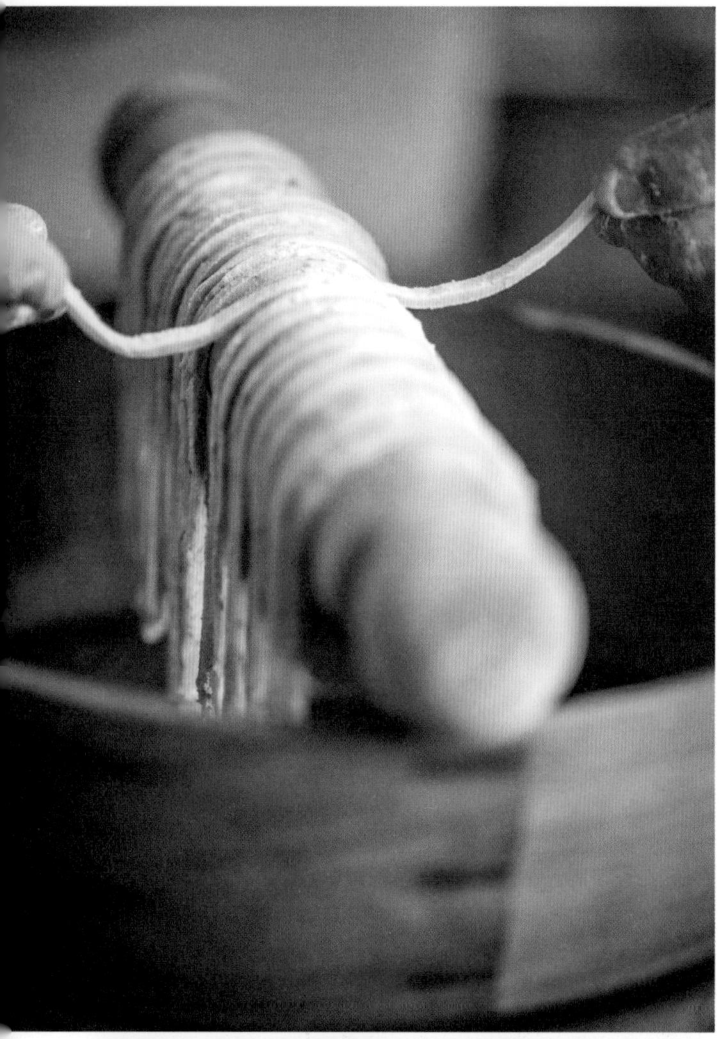

SERVES 4

115g/4oz/1 cup buckwheat flour, plus extra for dusting
15ml/1 tbsp dried herbs or ground sea greens (optional)
1 egg
5ml/1 tsp olive oil
15ml/1 tbsp water, if necessary

1 Combine the flour and herbs or sea greens, if using, in a mixing bowl and make a well in the middle. Crack the egg into the well, add the olive oil and combine. Add a small amount of water if necessary to make a soft dough.

2 Knead the dough on a lightly floured surface for 5–10 minutes, or until it stops sticking to your hands so much. If time allows, wrap it in clear film or plastic wrap and rest it in the fridge for several hours, or overnight if possible. This makes it easier to handle.

3 Cut the dough in half and re-wrap one piece in clear film or plastic wrap.

4 Lightly flour the surface of the unwrapped piece of dough, flatten it and roll it out in a pasta machine following the steps on page 78. Alternatively, place the floured dough ball between two sheets of clear film or on a lightly floured surface, and roll out the dough as thinly as possible with a rolling pin.

5 Cut the rolled-out dough into fine strips, either using a pasta machine or with a long sharp knife.

6 Hang the noodles on skewers or a rolling pin suspended between two items of a similar height (or over a container such as a bread bin) and leave them to dry for at least 15 minutes. Repeat the process with the second piece of dough.

Cook's tip

Buckwheat noodles take a little longer to cook than fresh egg pasta noodles. Add the noodles to a large pan of rapidly boiling salted water (use a little less salt if you made the noodles with the addition of sea greens as they will be fairly salty already) and cook for 5 minutes or until just tender. Drain, then use immediately or they may stick together as they cool.

Energy 134kcal/559kJ; Protein 4.2g; Carbohydrate 24.4g, of which sugars 0.1g; Fat 2.9g, of which saturates 0.6g; Cholesterol 58mg; Calcium 12mg; Fibre 0.8g; Sodium 21mg.

Rice noodles

These slightly translucent gluten-free noodles are easy and inexpensive to make. Although rice flour has a 'sandy' texture, it becomes smooth when it is soaked in water and the resulting batter can be spread over the surface of a cloth and steamed, before being sliced into noodles.

SERVES 4

225g/8oz/2 cups rice flour
600ml/1 pint/2½ cups water
a pinch of salt
15ml/1 tbsp vegetable oil, plus extra for brushing

1 Place the flour in a mixing bowl and stir in some of the water to form a paste. Pour in the rest of the water, beating it to make a lump-free batter. Add the salt and oil and leave the mixture to stand for 15 minutes.

2 Meanwhile, fill a wide pan with water. Cut a piece of smooth cotton cloth a little larger than the diameter of the pan (you are making slits in the cloth, so use one you are happy to cut). Stretch it over the top of the pan, pulling the edges tautly down over the sides, then wind a piece of string around the edge, to secure. Using a sharp knife, make three small slits, about 2.5cm/1in from the edge of the cloth, at regular intervals.

3 Bring the water to the boil. Stir the batter and ladle 30–45ml/2–3 tbsp on to the cloth, swirling it to form a 13–15cm/5–6in circle. Cover with a domed lid, such as a wok lid, and steam for 1 minute, or until the noodle sheet is translucent.

4 Carefully insert a spatula or knife under the noodle sheet and prise it off the cloth. (If it doesn't peel off easily, you may need to steam it a little longer.)

5 Transfer the noodle sheet to a lightly oiled baking tray, brush lightly with oil, and cook the remaining batter in the same way. From time to time, you may need to top up the water through one of the slits and tighten the cloth again.

6 Carefully cut the cooked noodle sheets into wide strips using a long thin knife, and gently stir-fry or poach them as required.

Cook's tip

You can store these noodles in the fridge for a day or two, so it's worth making double the quantity of the batter. Keep the cut noodles in a glass or stainless-steel bowl covered with clear film or plastic wrap.

Energy 251Kcal/1046kJ; Protein 4g; Carbohydrate 45g, of which sugars 0g; Fat 5g, of which saturates 1g; Cholesterol 0mg; Calcium 24mg; Fibre 1.1g; Sodium 0.2g.

Linguine with minty courgettes

Sweet, mild courgettes and refreshing mint are a great combination and are delicious with pasta for a light lunch or quick supper. Home-made gluten-free fresh egg linguine has been used here, but you could use bought gluten-free dried pasta, if you prefer.

SERVES 4

450g/1lb gluten-free fresh egg linguine (see page 78) or 250g/9oz gluten-free dried linguine or other pasta
75ml/5 tbsp garlic-infused oil
4 courgettes/zucchini, sliced
1 small bunch of fresh mint, roughly chopped
salt and ground black pepper, to taste

1 Cook the linguine in salted, boiling water, until al dente: 2–3 minutes for fresh, 10 minutes for dried.

2 Meanwhile, heat 45ml/3 tbsp of the oil in a large frying pan and add the courgettes. Fry for 2–3 minutes, stirring occasionally, until they are tender and golden.

3 Drain the pasta well and toss with the courgettes and chopped mint.

4 Season to taste with salt and pepper, drizzle over the remaining oil and serve immediately.

Energy 618kcal/2586kJ; Protein 19.1g; Carbohydrate 90g, of which sugars 4.7g; Fat 21.3g, of which saturates 3.8g; Cholesterol 173mg; Calcium 121mg; Fibre 4.8g; Sodium 70mg.

Chargrilled pepper & pasta salad

Gluten-free vegetable rice pasta is made with brown rice flour and is coloured with spinach and beetroot. It looks stunning in this vibrant salad, which has a real Mediterranean feel and flavour. Serve as a meal in its own right or as an accompaniment to grilled chicken or fish.

SERVES 4

2 large bell peppers (red and green)
250g/9oz/2¼ cups gluten-free dried vegetable rice pasta spirals
1 handful of fresh basil leaves
1 handful of fresh coriander/cilantro leaves
1 garlic clove
salt and ground black pepper

For the dressing

30ml/2 tbsp gluten-free pesto
juice of ½ lemon
60ml/4 tbsp extra virgin olive oil

1 Put the peppers under a hot grill or broiler and cook them for 10 minutes, turning them frequently, until they are charred on all sides.

2 Put the hot peppers in a plastic bag, seal the bag and set aside until the peppers are cool. Meanwhile, cook the pasta according to the instructions on the packet.

3 Whisk all the dressing ingredients together in a large mixing bowl. Drain the pasta well and transfer it into the bowl of dressing. Toss to mix, then set aside to cool.

4 Remove the peppers from the bag and hold them one at a time under cold running water. Peel off the charred skins with your fingers, split the peppers open and pull out the cores. Rub off all the seeds under the running water, then pat the peppers dry and chop them.

5 Roughly chop the basil, coriander and garlic, add to the pasta and toss to mix. Season and serve.

Variation

If you can't find vegetable rice pasta, make this with gluten-free red lentil fusilli instead; it has a lovely slightly sweet flavour that works well with the bell peppers.

Energy 386kcal/1623kJ; Protein 10.4g; Carbohydrate 53.1g, of which sugars 7.4g; Fat 16.1g, of which saturates 1.8g; Cholesterol 3mg; Calcium 109mg; Fibre 4.3g; Sodium 32mg.

Pasta & chickpeas

Here, protein-rich chickpeas are cooked with rosemary and vegetables, then blended to make a smooth, creamy sauce. Combined with gluten-free pasta and tossed together with more whole chickpeas, this is a hearty and healthy meal.

SERVES 6

675g/1½lb/3 cups dried chickpeas, soaked overnight and drained
2 celery sticks
2 carrots
2 onions, halved
4 garlic cloves
2 fresh rosemary sprigs
450g/1lb gluten-free dried ditalini or other pasta
salt and ground black pepper
extra virgin olive oil, to serve

1 Rinse the soaked chickpeas. Put them in a large pan and cover with cold water. Bring to the boil, then boil hard for 5 minutes. Drain and rinse under cold water.

2 Return the chickpeas to the pan, cover with fresh water and add the vegetables and rosemary sprigs. Bring to the boil and simmer gently for 45 minutes. Remove and discard the vegetables and rosemary.

3 Drain the chickpeas over a bowl, reserving the cooking liquid. Put one-third of the chickpeas in a blender with 150ml/¼ pint/⅔ cup of the cooking liquid. Process to a smooth sauce.

4 Pour the sauce back into the pan, add the remaining whole chickpeas, season and simmer for 10 minutes, stirring occasionally.

5 Meanwhile, cook the pasta in a pan of salted boiling water until just tender, about 10–12 minutes. Drain well, then stir into the chickpeas and sauce. Boil for about 1 minute, stirring gently to prevent sticking.

6 Taste, adjust the seasoning as required and serve with olive oil for drizzling.

Energy 638kcal/2707kJ; Protein 33.6g; Carbohydrate 116.1g, of which sugars 9.2g; Fat 7.6g, of which saturates 0.7g; Cholesterol 0mg; Calcium 219mg; Fibre 20.6g; Sodium 61mg.

Orecchiette with garlic & chilli

Orecchiette, literally meaning 'little ears' in Italian, are small pasta discs with little dimples, perfect for catching this simple garlic and chilli-spiced sauce. Use a good-quality, fragrant extra virgin olive oil and heat it gently to retain all the flavour.

SERVES 4

400g/14oz gluten-free dried orecchiette or other pasta
150ml/¼ pint/⅔ cup olive oil
3 garlic cloves
4 whole dried red chillies
60ml/4 tbsp tomato paste

1 Bring a large pan of salted water to the boil. Add the pasta and cook for 10–12 minutes, until just tender.

2 Heat the oil in a different very large pan. Add the garlic and chillies and fry over low–medium heat for 3–4 minutes, until the garlic is soft and golden brown and the chillies are very shiny and swollen.

3 Scoop the garlic and chillies out of the oil with a slotted spoon and transfer to a food processor or blender. Add the tomato paste, then process until smooth. Stir back into the oil remaining in the pan.

4 Drain the pasta and add it to the pan containing the garlic and chilli mixture. Toss over the heat until the pasta is coated with the sauce, then serve.

Cook's tip

This is a hot and spicy dish, so if you prefer less heat, reduce the amount to just 2 or 3 chillies.

Energy 591kcal/2480kJ; Protein 13.8g; Carbohydrate 78.3g, of which sugars 5.6g; Fat 26.9g, of which saturates 3.8g; Cholesterol 0mg; Calcium 33mg; Fibre 5.1g; Sodium 40mg.

Two-cheese & mushroom cannelloni

Folding sheets of gluten-free fresh egg pasta, whether home-made or store-bought, around this tasty mushroom filling is infinitely easier than trying to spoon the mixture into tubes of dried cannelloni. It also requires less cooking, which means the mushrooms won't be overcooked.

SERVES 4

melted butter, for greasing
½ quantity gluten-free fresh pasta dough (see pages 78–9) or 250g/9oz bought lasagne sheets
45ml/3 tbsp olive oil
1 garlic clove
2 onions, roughly chopped
500g/18oz/2 cups fresh mushrooms, chopped (see Cook's tip)
115g/4oz/½ cup cream cheese

For the sauce

25g/1oz/2 tbsp butter
250g/9oz drained canned tomatoes, seeded and chopped
200ml/7fl oz/scant 1 cup single/light cream
150g/5oz/1½ cups freshly grated Parmesan cheese, plus extra to serve
8 fresh basil leaves, torn, plus extra to serve
salt and ground black pepper

1 Preheat the oven to 160°C/325°F/Gas 3. Brush the butter inside a large, shallow ovenproof dish.

2 Lightly crush the garlic clove by placing it on a board and pressing with the flat of a knife blade until it splits open. Heat the oil in a pan and add the garlic. Gently cook until the garlic is pungent and just starting to colour, then discard, leaving the flavoured oil behind.

3 Add the chopped onions and the mushrooms to the garlicky oil. Cook for about 10 minutes or until both have softened.

4 Transfer the onions and mushrooms to a mixing bowl, season with salt and pepper and gently stir in the cream cheese while the vegetables are still warm.

5 Roll out the pasta dough into a long, thin rectangle (see pages 78–9). It needs to be the same width as the dish so that the filled cannelloni will fit in neatly, and long enough that you can slice the strip into eight squares. If using bought sheets, trim to size. Place each square flat on a board and add a tablespoon or two of filling, spreading it out almost to the ends of the pasta.

6 Roll up the pasta and place it in the buttered dish. Repeat with the remaining pasta sheets and filling.

7 To make the sauce, melt the butter in a separate pan and add the tomatoes. Simmer over a low heat for about 10 minutes.

8 Add the cream, half the freshly grated Parmesan and the basil, season with salt and ground black pepper, then remove from the heat.

9 Pour the sauce over the filled cannelloni. Sprinkle with the remaining freshly grated Parmesan and bake for 25 minutes, until golden and bubbling.

10 Leave to stand for 5 minutes before serving with extra freshly grated Parmesan and basil on top.

Cook's tip

You can use any cultivated or wild mushrooms for this recipe, so long as they are flavoursome.

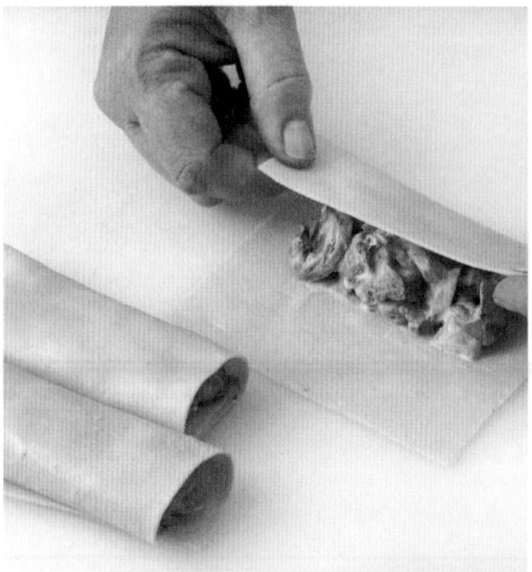

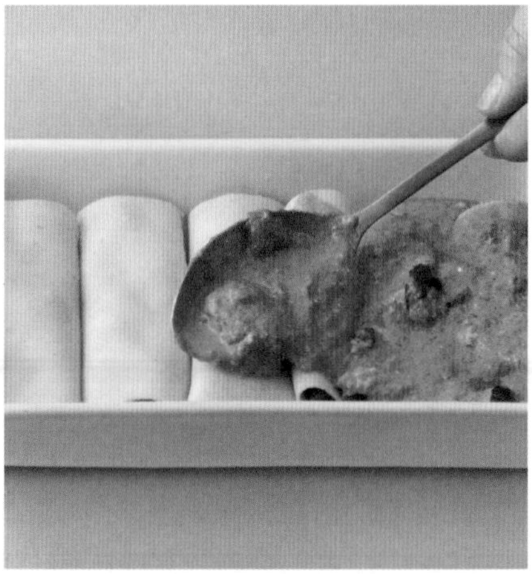

Energy 695kcal/2882kJ; Protein 23.4g; Carbohydrate 28.7g, of which sugars 7.3g; Fat 54.4g, of which saturates 29g; Cholesterol 198mg; Calcium 497mg; Fibre 3.6g; Sodium 517mg.

Spinach & ricotta ravioli

These little pasta parcels are filled with spinach and ricotta cheese and flavoured with a hint of lemon. An Italian-style tomato sauce and a scattering of grated cheese adds the finishing flourish to this tasty gluten-free dish.

SERVES 6

1 quantity of fresh gluten-free pasta dough (see pages 78–79) or 450g/1lb bought lasagne sheets
350g/12oz fresh ricotta cheese
500g/18oz spinach, cooked and finely chopped
grated rind of 1 large lemon
fine polenta/cornmeal, for dusting
salt and ground black pepper, to taste
freshly grated mild pecorino cheese, to serve

For the tomato sauce

900g/2lb fresh tomatoes, or 2 x 400g/14oz cans tomatoes
1 small onion, quartered
1 carrot, quartered
1 celery stick, quartered
1 large parsley sprig
10 fresh basil leaves
salt, to taste
45ml/3 tbsp extra virgin olive oil (optional)

1 First, make the tomato sauce. If using fresh tomatoes, skin them by plunging them into boiling water for about 30 seconds, then refreshing in cold water. Peel away the skins and cut into quarters. If using canned tomatoes, drain them and cut the tomatoes into quarters.

2 Put the tomatoes, onion, carrot, celery, parsley and basil into a large pan. Cover with a lid and bring to the boil, then simmer for 30 minutes.

3 Remove the lid and simmer for 20 minutes more, or until most of the liquid has evaporated.

4 Remove the pan from the heat and push the mixture through a food mill, sieve or strainer. Season to taste with salt, and add the oil, if using.

5 For the filling, in a mixing bowl, combine the ricotta cheese, spinach and lemon rind. Season to taste with salt and pepper.

6 Roll out the fresh pasta dough into a long, thin rectangle, as finely and as evenly as possible (see pages 78–9). If using bought lasagne sheets, just set them out on a floured surface.

7 Spoon the filling in a neat row along one half of the long side of the sheet(s), a scant tablespoon at a time, leaving 2.5cm/1in between the mounds. Fold the pasta sheet(s) over to cover the filling.

8 With your fingers, press down between the mounds of filling so that the pasta sticks together. Cut out the ravioli with a serrated pasta cutter or knife and press round the edges again to make sure each is sealed.

9 Dust a wide baking tray with fine polenta and lay the ravioli over it, taking care not to overlap them or lay them on top of one another.

10 Bring a large pan of salted water to the boil and drop in the ravioli. Cook for 3–4 minutes, in batches. They should rise to the surface when cooked. Scoop out as soon as they are cooked and transfer them to a warmed bowl. Drizzle with tomato sauce and sprinkle with some freshly grated pecorino before serving.

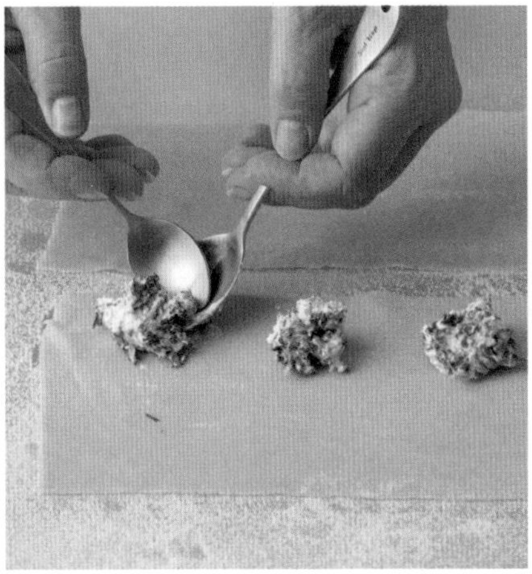

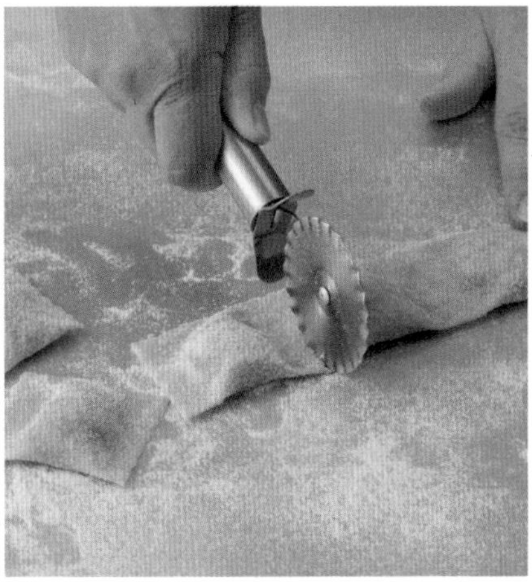

Energy 310kcal/1295kJ; Protein 14.8g; Carbohydrate 37.5g, of which sugars 10g; Fat 11.4g, of which saturates 5.3g; Cholesterol 145mg; Calcium 323mg; Fibre 5.8g; Sodium 238mg.

Lasagne with pesto & potatoes

The combination of pasta and pesto is an all-time favourite. This substantial crowd-pleaser also includes potatoes and a creamy cheese sause, and makes the perfect warming gluten-free vegetarian supper dish for wintry weather. Serve with a salad, if you like.

SERVES 4

3 medium potatoes, peeled
50g/2oz/¼ cup unsalted butter
50g/2oz/½ cup gluten-free plain/all-purpose flour blend
600ml/1 pint/2½ cups milk
60ml/4 tbsp gluten-free green pesto
115g/4oz/1¼ cups freshly grated Parmesan cheese, plus extra to serve
1 quantity of gluten-free fresh pasta dough (see pages 78–79) or 450g/1lb bought lasagne sheets
salt and ground black pepper
fresh thyme or basil, to garnish

1 Cook the potatoes in a large pan of salted boiling water for 10–15 minutes, until just soft. Drain and leave to cool slightly, then slice them thinly. Preheat the oven to 190°C/375°F/Gas 5.

2 Melt the butter in a pan over a gentle heat, stir in the flour and cook, stirring for 1 minute. Remove from the heat and gradually pour in the milk, whisking constantly. Return to the heat and cook, stirring, until the sauce is thick and smooth and coats the back of a wooden spoon. Simmer for 1 minute.

3 Stir in half the pesto and season with salt and pepper to taste. Add about half the freshly grated Parmesan cheese and stir again.

4 Roll out the pasta dough, if using freshly made, into a long rectangle, as finely and as evenly as possible (see pages 78–9). Cut into two sheets to fit a shallow ovenproof dish.

5 Spread one-quarter of the cheese sauce over the base of the dish. Cover with a layer of half of the potatoes, then add another layer of the sauce. Dot with some of the remaining pesto.

6 Cover with half of the lasagne sheets and another layer of the sauce, then a few dots of pesto. Sprinkle with half of the remaining Parmesan.

7 Repeat the layering process, finishing off with the last of the sauce. Sprinkle the remaining freshly grated Parmesan cheese on top.

8 Bake for 20–30 minutes, until golden. Serve, sprinkled with fresh herb leaves and extra freshly grated Parmesan.

Cook's tip

It is important not to boil the potatoes for too long or they will become so soft that you won't be able to slice them. They'll also taste watery.

Energy 745kcal/3124kJ; Protein 30.2g; Carbohydrate 81.5g, of which sugars 9.6g; Fat 34.2g, of which saturates 15.1g; Cholesterol 291mg; Calcium 600mg; Fibre 3.1g; Sodium 412mg.

Chicken & mushroom noodle soup

Good stock made by poaching chicken with vegetables provides the flavour base for this wholesome meal-in-a-bowl. The chicken is then shredded and added to the stock with lightly cooked fresh vegetables and gluten-free rice vermicelli noodles.

SERVES 6

1 chicken, about 1.2kg/2½lb, cut into 8 pieces
3 carrots, chopped
2 celery sticks, with leaves, chopped
1 large parsnip, chopped
1 kohlrabi, chopped
1 leek, chopped
5 green peppercorns
1 bay leaf
6–8 parsley sprigs, plus 15ml/1 tbsp finely chopped leaves
115g/4oz/1¾ cups sliced mushrooms
150g/5oz dried medium rice noodles, broken into small pieces
salt and ground black pepper, to taste

1 Put the chicken pieces into a large pan and cover with cold water. Add the carrots, celery, parsnip, kohlrabi and leek to the pan.

2 Season to taste, add the green peppercorns, bay leaf and parsley, and bring to a simmer over low heat. Cover and cook for about 1 hour, skimming occasionally.

3 Strain the soup into another pan. Remove the chicken and discard the celery, peppercorns, bay leaf and parsley.

4 Finely chop the remaining vegetables (the carrot, parsnip, kohlrabi and leek) and add them to the soup, then remove the chicken skin and meat from the bones and add the chicken shreds to the soup.

5 Add the mushrooms and rice noodles and cook for 5 minutes more. Sprinkle with parsley and serve hot.

Energy 389kcal/1618kJ; Protein 28.3g; Carbohydrate 26.7g, of which sugars 5.4g; Fat 18.6g, of which saturates 5.1g; Cholesterol 132mg; Calcium 48mg; Fibre 3.9g; Sodium 112mg.

Tofu soup with rice noodles

This light and refreshing dish is such an easy gluten-free supper solution; the aromatic spicy broth is simmered briefly and then the tofu, beansprouts and noodles are quickly added. Use firm tofu as the softer variety will disintegrate during cooking.

SERVES 4

1 quantity of fresh thick rice noodles (see page 81) or 150g/5oz dried rice noodles
1 litre/1¾ pints/4 cups vegetable stock
1 fresh red chilli, seeded and sliced
15ml/1 tbsp gluten-free light soy sauce
juice of 1 small lime
10ml/2 tsp palm sugar or light muscovado/brown sugar
5ml/1 tsp thinly sliced garlic
5ml/1 tsp grated fresh root ginger
200g/7oz firm tofu
90g/3½oz mung beansprouts
30ml/2 tbsp chopped fresh mint
15ml/1 tbsp chopped fresh coriander/cilantro
15ml/1 tbsp chopped fresh sweet basil
50g/2oz/½ cup roasted peanuts
spring onion/scallion slivers and red bell pepper slivers, to garnish (optional)

1 Place the noodles in a heatproof bowl and pour over enough boiling water to cover. Soak fresh noodles for 3 minutes and dried ones for 10–15 minutes, until soft. Drain, rinse, drain again, then set aside.

2 Place the vegetable stock, red chilli, soy sauce, lime juice, sugar, garlic and ginger in a wok or large frying pan over a high heat.

3 Bring to the boil, then cover and reduce to a low heat. Simmer for 10–12 minutes.

4 Meanwhile, cut the tofu into cubes or strips and add to the soup, along with the drained noodles and mung beansprouts. Cook gently for 2–3 minutes. Remove from the heat and stir in the fresh herbs.

5 Roughly chop the roasted peanuts. Ladle the soup into four individual serving bowls and scatter the peanuts over the top.

6 Serve immediately, garnished with spring onion and red pepper slivers, if you like.

Energy 266Kcal/1108kJ; Protein 10.5g; Carbohydrate 35.1g, of which sugars 3g; Fat 8.8g, of which saturates 1.4g; Cholesterol 0mg; Calcium 321mg; Fibre 2.4g; Sodium 115mg.

Spicy buckwheat noodles

This chilled noodle salad is ideal for a gluten-free summer lunch. The cool temperature of the noodles contrasts with the spiciness of the dressing, and pear adds a delicious sweetness.

SERVES 2

90g/3½oz dried or fresh buckwheat noodles (see page 80)
1 hard-boiled egg
½ cucumber
½ pear
ice cubes, to serve

For the sauce

30ml/2 tbsp gluten-free chilli paste
30ml/2 tbsp sugar
10ml/2 tsp sesame oil
5ml/1 tsp chilli powder
5ml/1 tsp sesame seeds
1 garlic clove, finely chopped
2.5ml/½ tsp gluten-free soy sauce

Cook's tip

Be sure to use a large pan and plenty of water when cooking dried noodles, as they contain a lot of starch so will stick to the pan if you use too little.

1 Cook the noodles in boiling water for 5 minutes or according to packet instructions. Drain, then rinse in cold water until the water runs clear. Chill for 30 minutes.

2 Slice the egg in half. Seed the cucumber and slice it into long, thin strips. Peel and core the pear and slice it into fine strips.

3 In a bowl, combine all the ingredients for the sauce.

4 Arrange the noodles in two dishes. Pour over the sauce, top with the pear and cucumber strips, add a halved egg and arrange the ice cubes round the edge.

Energy 238kcal/990kJ; Protein 9g; Carbohydrate 27.9g, of which sugars 3.4g; Fat 10.9g, of which saturates 2.2g; Cholesterol 173mg; Calcium 58mg; Fibre 1.7g; Sodium 459mg.

Chinese veggie vermicelli

Vermicelli rice noodles are quickly and easily prepared, and make a great gluten-free storecupboard staple. Here, they are combined with Asian vegetables.

SERVES 4

4 pieces of sweet dried beancurd wafers/sticks
300g/11oz dried rice vermicelli noodles
10 dried Chinese black mushrooms
45ml/3 tbsp vegetable oil
30ml/2 tbsp crushed garlic
1 large onion, thinly sliced
100g/3¾oz/½ cup beansprouts
115g/4oz drained canned bamboo shoots, sliced into strips
115g/4oz Chinese long beans or green beans, sliced into thin strips
30ml/2 tbsp gluten-free hoisin sauce
30ml/2 tbsp gluten-free vegetarian mushroom oyster sauce (optional)
30ml/2 tbsp gluten-free dark soy sauce
45ml/3 tbsp sesame oil
400ml/14fl oz/1⅔ cups vegetable stock

1 Soak the beancurd wafers in cold water until soft (some varieties take a few hours). Soak the vermicelli and mushrooms in separate bowls of boiling water for about 10 minutes and about 30 minutes respectively.

2 Drain each ingredient as soon as it has softened. Slice the beancurd wafers thinly. Cut off and discard the stems of the mushrooms and slice the caps into strips.

3 Heat the oil in a wok and fry the garlic for 40 seconds, until light brown. Add the sliced onion and stir-fry for 2 minutes, then add the beansprouts, bamboo shoots, beans and mushrooms.

4 Stir-fry for 1 minute, then stir in the hoisin sauce, oyster sauce (if using), soy sauce and sesame oil and combine. Add the beancurd wafers to the wok and stir-fry for 2 minutes more.

5 Add the noodles and pour in the stock. Toss over the heat for 4 minutes, until all the ingredients are cooked. Spoon into bowls and serve.

Energy 470kcal/1956kJ; Protein 9.8g; Carbohydrate 68.9g, of which sugars 5.5g; Fat 17.2g, of which saturates 2.3g; Cholesterol 0mg; Calcium 57mg; Fibre 3.2g; Sodium 1169mg.

Thai vegetable noodles

This noodle dish is ideal for a relaxed gluten-free lunch or supper as it can mostly be prepared ahead and contains plenty of fresh vegetables, including carrots, beansprouts and cabbage. Ginger and plum sauce give it a fruity flavour, while lime adds a zesty tang.

SERVES 4

1 quantity of fresh thick rice noodles (see page 81) or 150g/5oz dried rice noodles
30ml/2 tbsp groundnut/peanut oil
2.5cm/1in piece fresh root ginger, sliced into thin strips
1 garlic clove, crushed
115g/4oz drained canned bamboo shoots, sliced into strips
2 carrots, sliced into strips
130g/4½oz/1½ cups beansprouts
1 small white cabbage, shredded
30ml/2 tbsp gluten-free Thai fish sauce
30ml/2 tbsp gluten-free soy sauce
30ml/2 tbsp gluten-free plum sauce
10ml/2 tsp sesame oil
15ml/1 tbsp soft light brown sugar
juice of ½ lime
90g/3½oz mooli/daikon, sliced into thin strips
small bunch of fresh coriander/cilantro, chopped
60ml/4 tbsp sesame seeds, toasted

1 Place the noodles in a heatproof bowl and pour over enough boiling water to cover. Soak fresh noodles for 3 minutes and dried ones for 10–15 minutes, until soft.

2 Drain the noodles well, return to the bowl and cover with a lid to keep them warm.

3 Meanwhile, heat the oil in a wok or large frying pan and stir-fry the ginger and garlic for 2–3 minutes over a medium heat, until golden. Add the bamboo shoots, increase the heat to high and stir-fry for 5 minutes.

4 Add the carrots, beansprouts and cabbage and stir-fry for a further 5 minutes, until they are beginning to char on the edges.

5 Stir in the sauces, sesame oil, sugar and lime juice. Add the noodles, mooli and fresh coriander and combine.

6 Spoon into a bowl, sprinkle with sesame seeds and serve immediately.

Energy 304kcal/1264kJ; Protein 5.6g; Carbohydrate 37.1g, of which sugars 6.1g; Fat 14.4g, of which saturates 2.3g; Cholesterol 0mg; Calcium 133mg; Fibre 1.9g; Sodium 846mg.

Cellophane noodles with pork

Cellophane or glass noodles are usually made from mung bean starch or sometimes green pea starch and are used in many Asian dishes, especially stir-fries and spring rolls. They are both gluten free and fat free and have a lovely, slightly chewy texture.

SERVES 2

200g/7oz dried cellophane noodles
30ml/2 tbsp vegetable oil
200g/7oz minced/ground pork
1 garlic clove, crushed
1 fresh green or red chilli, seeded and finely chopped
300g/11oz/3½ cups beansprouts
bunch of spring onions/scallions, finely chopped
30ml/2 tbsp gluten-free soy sauce
30ml/2 tbsp gluten-free Thai fish sauce
30ml/2 tbsp gluten-free sweet chilli sauce
15ml/1 tbsp soft light brown sugar
30ml/2 tbsp rice vinegar
30ml/2 tbsp gluten-free roasted peanuts, chopped, to garnish
45ml/3 tbsp fresh coriander/cilantro, chopped, to garnish

1 Place the noodles in a large heatproof bowl, cover with boiling water and soak for 10 minutes, until soft. Drain and set aside until ready to use.

2 Heat the oil in a wok or large, heavy frying pan. Add the pork and stir-fry the meat, breaking it up with a wooden spatula, for 2–3 minutes, until browned all over.

3 Add the garlic and chilli to the meat and stir-fry for 3–4 seconds, then add the beansprouts and spring onions, stir-frying for a few seconds after each addition.

4 Snip the noodles into lengths and add to the wok with the soy sauce, Thai fish sauce, sweet chilli sauce, sugar and rice vinegar. Toss until well combined and the noodles have warmed through.

5 Pile on to a platter or into a large bowl. Sprinkle over the peanuts and fresh coriander and serve immediately.

Energy 826kcal/3454kJ; Protein 37.5g; Carbohydrate 104.8g, of which sugars 22.6g; Fat 29g, of which saturates 6.4g; Cholesterol 66mg; Calcium 148mg; Fibre 4.6g; Sodium 1943mg.

Savoury pastry

Eating good pastry is undeniably enjoyable and making your own can be equally satisfying. Gluten-free pastry isn't difficult if you follow a few simple rules and master the basic techniques, and you don't have to rush out and buy any fancy equipment; a bowl, a set of scales or measuring cup and a rolling pin are all you need to begin with.

You'll find gluten-free versions of all kinds of classic pastries here, from shortcrust, choux and filo to puff and flaky pastry as well as more unusual types such as coconut pastry. The texture of gluten-free pastry can be a little more crumbly without the elasticity of gluten, so you will need to add ingredients to compensate for this, such as xanthan gum, ground psyllium husk or ground flaxseeds. Eggs are also often used in gluten-free pastry to help bind all the ingredients and keep them together when baking. Vegans could use a commercial egg replacer.

Aim to make pastry doughs such as shortcrust, puff and flaky a little wetter and softer than you normally would with conventional pastry dough, as gluten-free flours soak up more water; then wrap and chill them in the fridge for a few minutes (or for the given time in the recipe) to allow the pastry to firm up before rolling. The golden rule of not overhandling pastry only applies to pastries made with wheat flour, as this develops the gluten and makes the pastry tough. The removal of this risk is one of the joys of gluten-free pastry; if it cracks or crumbles you can simply knead it all back together and start again. When rolling out large pieces, you may find it easier to place the dough between two sheets of baking parchment or clear film to prevent it from sticking and also to help you transfer it into the tin in one piece.

Once you've mastered the basics of making the different pastries, you'll be able to make lots of gluten-free pies, such as Chicken & Mushroom Pie with a crisp shortcrust, and Salmon Puff Pastry Pie with golden flaky layers of puff pastry. There are also ideas for lunches and picnics, including Courgette & Feta Pasties made with quinoa pastry, and Vegan 'Sausage' Rolls made with coconut pastry, as well as all sorts of mini tartlets, packages and parcels with a variety of tasty fillings; perfect for nibbling mid-morning or for serving with drinks.

Shortcrust pastry

This crumbly gluten-free pastry is the best known and most commonly used type, used for lining tarts and flans, topping pies or wrapping around all manner of tasty fillings. The following makes enough for a 25cm/10in flan tin/pan or ten 7.5cm/3in tartlet tins/mini quiche pans.

MAKES 375G/13OZ

225g/8oz/2 cups gluten-free plain/all-purpose flour blend, plus extra for dusting
2.5ml/½ tsp xanthan gum
pinch of salt
115g/4oz/½ cup chilled butter, diced, or half butter and half white vegetable fat
60–75ml/4–5 tbsp chilled water

1 Sift the flour, xanthan gum and salt into a large mixing bowl. Cut the fat into the flour with a pastry blender or use your fingertips to rub it in. Shake the bowl occasionally to bring any large lumps of fat to the top. Blend until all the fat is incorporated and the mixture resembles fine breadcrumbs.

2 Slowly pour 60ml/4 tbsp of the water over the mixture and mix with a round-bladed knife until the dough comes together. It should be slightly wetter and softer than standard wheat pastry dough, so add a little more water if the mixture is still too dry.

3 Gather together the dough to form a ball. Incorporate any loose pieces of the rubbed-in mixture by rubbing the ball around the bowl. Knead on a lightly floured surface for just a few seconds, until smooth, then wrap in clear film or plastic wrap and chill in the fridge for at least 1 hour before rolling out.

BAKING BLIND

This baking technique lines the pastry case with parchment or foil and fills it with baking beans to stop it from rising up. This process is used to partly cook an empty pastry case so that it does not become soggy when the filling is added; to ensure a pastry case is thoroughly baked when the filling cooks in only a short time; and when the pastry case is to contain a precooked or uncooked filling.

1 Cut out a round of baking parchment or foil 7.5cm/3in larger than the flan tin/pan. Prick the base all over with a fork. Lay the parchment or foil in the case and press it over the base and up the side.

2 Put ceramic baking beans, or dried beans or peas, in the lined pastry case, spreading them out evenly over the surface.

3 Bake the pastry case in an oven preheated to 200°C/400°F/Gas 6 for 15 minutes, or until the pastry is set and the rim is dry and golden. Some recipes may suggest you brush the case with egg wash, which seals it and keeps it crisp.

4 Remove the parchment or foil and the beans. Return the case to the oven and bake for 5 minutes more, until completely dry and pale golden brown.

Energy 1650kcal/6842kJ; Protein 11.9g; Carbohydrate 180.5g, of which sugars 1.1g; Fat 97.5g, of which saturates 60.6g; Cholesterol 245mg; Calcium 21mg; Fibre 2.4g; Sodium 697mg.

Choux pastry

Elegantly light and crisp, gluten-free choux pastry puffs up during baking to create a hollow centre, perfect for fillings. This quantity is sufficient for 20 small puffs or twelve 10cm/4in éclairs. For a dairy-free version, use coconut oil instead of the butter or hard baking margarine.

MAKES 150G/5OZ

65g/2½oz/9 tbsp gluten-free plain/all-purpose flour blend
pinch of salt
50g/2oz/¼ cup butter or hard baking margarine, diced
150ml/¼ pint/⅔ cup water
2 eggs, lightly beaten

1 Preheat the oven to 200°C/400°F/Gas 6 and line a baking sheet with baking parchment. Sift the flour and salt on to another sheet of baking parchment.

2 Put the butter and water in a large pan and heat very gently until the butter has melted. Increase the heat and bring to a rolling boil.

3 Remove the pan from the heat, tip in all the flour and beat vigorously until the flour is mixed into the liquid.

4 Return the pan to a low heat and beat until it begins to form a ball. This will take about 1 minute. Remove from the heat again and allow to cool for 2–3 minutes.

5 Add the eggs a little at a time, beating all the time, until you have a smooth shiny paste that can hold its shape. You may not need all the egg.

6 Shape or pipe the paste on to the prepared baking sheet and sprinkle with water. Bake as instructed in the recipe. If making éclairs or puffs, poke a hole in the bottom of each pastry and leave to dry on a wire rack.

Cook's tip

Sweet rice flour will help the pastry puff up due to its high amylopectin content, so if you have some, substitute 30ml/2 tbsp for the same amount of gluten-free flour.

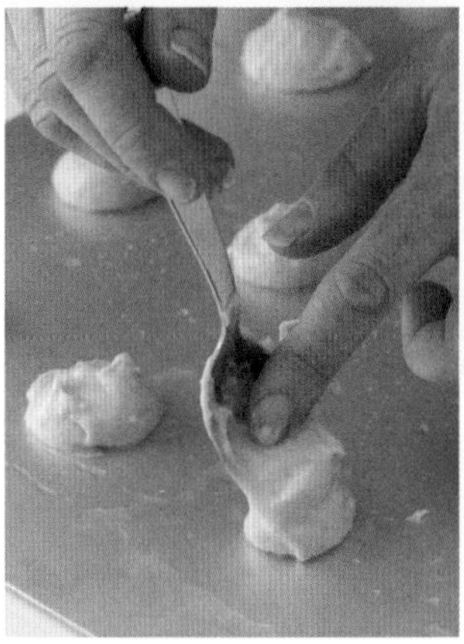

USES FOR SAVOURY CHOUX PASTRY

Choux pastry is often combined with cheese and baked to make gougères or piped into hot oil to make cheese aigrettes. All sorts of other flavourings can be added, too, such as fresh herbs, paprika, mustard, chilli, or pieces of ham or cooked bacon.

Alternatively, the choux pastry can be piped or spooned round the edge of a baking dish, before the middle is filled with any sort of pie filling, and then baked. The pastry rises up and forms a perimeter crust that is lighter than regular pastry.

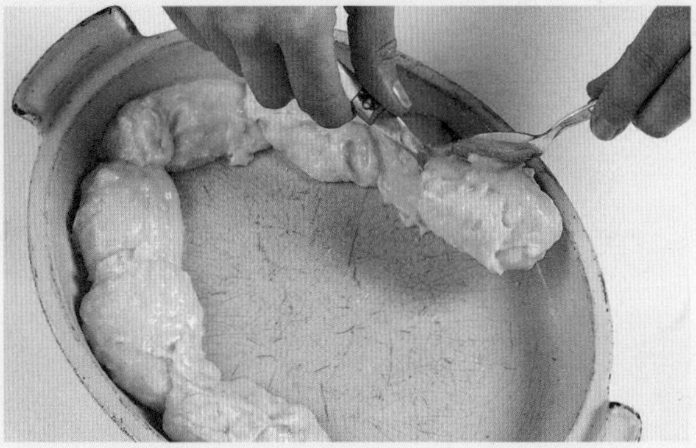

Energy 783kcal/3242kJ; Protein 18.6g; Carbohydrate 52.2g, of which sugars 0.4g; Fat 55.4g, of which saturates 30g; Cholesterol 569mg; Calcium 77mg; Fibre 0.7g; Sodium 471mg.

Puff pastry

This gluten-free pastry forms light, flaky layers. The recipe uses a mixture of half butter, for flavour, and half white vegetable fat, to give it a crisper texture. This is enough for two single crusts to fit 1.5-litre/2½-pint pie dishes.

MAKES 450G/1LB

115g/4oz/½ cup butter
115g/4oz/½ cup white vegetable fat
225g/8oz/2 cups gluten-free plain/all-purpose flour blend, plus extra for dusting
2.5ml/½ tsp xanthan gum
pinch of salt
150ml/¼ pint/⅔ cup plus 30ml/2 tbsp chilled water

1 Dice the butter and fat, then spread out on a plate and freeze for 10 minutes.

2 Sift the flour, xanthan gum and salt into a mixing bowl. Add the diced fat and stir to coat with the flour.

3 Make a well in the middle, then add the water and mix it all together with a round-bladed knife to make a dough.

4 Put the dough on to a pastry board or work surface, along with any loose flour left in the bowl. Gently shape to form a block, and seal the edges with a rolling pin.

5 Roll out the pastry to a 35 x 20cm/14 x 8in rectangle. Fold the lower third of the pastry over the middle third, then fold the top third over that.

6 Press the edges with the rolling pin to seal. Wrap in clear film or plastic wrap and chill for 10 minutes.

7 Roll out to the same size again, with the sealed edges at the top and bottom. Fold and chill as before. Repeat the rolling, folding and chilling process three more times.

8 Wrap in clear film and chill for at least 3 hours, but preferably overnight, before using as per the recipe.

Energy 2674kcal/11055kJ; Protein 11.9g; Carbohydrate 180.5g, of which sugars 1.1g; Fat 211.3g, of which saturates 106.9g; Cholesterol 352mg; Calcium 22mg; Fibre 2.4g; Sodium 699mg.

Flaky pastry

Gluten-free flaky pastry is easier to make than puff pastry. When baked, it looks and tastes very similar. The fat is incorporated by dotting it over the rolled-out dough, which creates pockets of air that separate the layers. This makes enough for two single 20cm/8in pie crusts.

MAKES 450G/1LB

225g/8oz/2 cups bought gluten-free bread flour blend or home-made bread flour blend (see page 42), plus extra for dusting
pinch of salt
175g/6oz/¾ cup chilled butter, diced, or half butter and half white vegetable fat
about 150ml/¼ pint/⅔ cup plus 15ml/1 tbsp chilled water

1 Sift the flour and salt into a large mixing bowl. Cut 40g/1½oz/3 tbsp of the fat into the flour with a pastry blender or use your fingertips to rub it in. Blend until the mixture resembles fine breadcrumbs.

2 Pour over 150ml/¼ pint/⅔ cup of water and, using a round-bladed knife, mix to a soft dough. Add more water as necessary if the mixture is too dry; it should be slightly soft but not sticky, and will get firmer after chilling.

3 Gather together the dough to form a ball. Incorporate any loose pieces of the rubbed-in mixture. Knead the dough on a lightly floured surface for just a few seconds, until smooth.

4 Wrap the dough in clear film or plastic wrap. Chill for about 15 minutes.

5 Roll the dough out to a 30 x 10cm/12 x 4in rectangle on a lightly floured surface. Cut another 40g/1½oz/3 tbsp of butter into small pieces and dot this evenly all over the top two-thirds of the pastry rectangle, leaving a 1cm/½in margin.

6 Fold the lower third of the pastry rectangle over the middle third, then fold the top third over that. Press the edges firmly with the rolling pin to seal.

7 Wrap the dough in clear film and chill for 10 minutes. Repeat the rolling and folding process once more, without adding any more fat.

8 Next, roll out the dough with the folded edges at the sides, then dot with another 40g/1½oz/3 tbsp of the fat. Fold and chill as before, then repeat the whole process one more time, to use up the last of the fat.

9 Roll out the pastry and fold it in the same way one final time (without adding any more fat), then wrap the block in clear film. Chill for at least 1 hour before using the pastry as instructed in the recipe.

Cook's tips

- When blending the fat and the flour in step 1, shake the bowl vigorously to bring any large lumps of fat to the surface; this makes it easier to ensure you blend all of the fat in properly.
- Both puff and flaky pastries freeze well, so it's a good idea to make enough for two recipes (as here) and to freeze half for later use (defrost it overnight in the fridge).
- You can also buy ready-made gluten-free puff pastry either in a block or sheets of ready-rolled pastry. Try to find one that has a high butter content as this will have a better flavour.

Energy 2096kcal/8678kJ; Protein 12.3g; Carbohydrate 180.8g, of which sugars 1.5g; Fat 146.8g, of which saturates 91.8g; Cholesterol 373mg; Calcium 32mg; Fibre 2.4g; Sodium 1060mg.

Coconut pastry

Coconut oil makes a firm, crisp pastry. You can either use raw virgin coconut oil for a mild coconut flavour or a refined coconut oil, which will be flavourless. This gluten-free vegan pastry makes enough to line a 23cm/9in flan tin/pan or eight 7.5cm/3in tartlet or mini quiche pans.

MAKES 275G/10OZ

225g/8oz/2 cups gluten-free plain/all-purpose flour blend, plus extra for dusting
2.5ml/½ tsp xanthan gum
pinch of salt
1.5ml/¼ tsp ground turmeric (optional)
90g/3¼oz/7 tbsp solid coconut oil (see Cook's tip)
90–115ml/6–7 tbsp ice-cold water

1 Sift the flour, xanthan gum, salt and turmeric, if using, into a large mixing bowl. Put the coconut oil on a plate and break it up with a knife.

2 Add the coconut oil pieces to the bowl and cut them into the flour with a fork, flat-bladed knife or pastry blender. Shake the bowl occasionally to bring any large lumps to the top. Blend until the mixture resembles coarse breadcrumbs, leaving some of the coconut oil in bigger pieces, about the size of half a pea.

3 Sprinkle 90ml/6 tbsp of the water over the mixture and mix with a round-bladed knife until the dough comes together. Add a little more water if the mixture is still too dry; it should just hold together.

4 Gather together to form a ball. Knead on a lightly floured surface for a few seconds, until smooth. Flatten the dough slightly, wrap in clear film or plastic wrap and chill for 20 minutes before using.

5 When you are ready to use the pastry, roll it out between two sheets of baking parchment.

Cook's tip

If the coconut oil is liquid at room temperature, chill it for 30 minutes until it is hard. On warm days or in warm kitchens, chill the mixing bowl and pastry board, too.

Energy 1603kcal/6651kJ; Protein 11.2g; Carbohydrate 179.8g, of which sugars 0.5g; Fat 92.8g, of which saturates 78.5g; Cholesterol 0mg; Calcium 0mg; Fibre 2.4g; Sodium 0mg.

Filo pastry

While this gluten-free filo pastry isn't as crisp as traditional filo, and though you won't be able to make it as thin, it does have the advantage that it remains pliable and doesn't dry out like the classic version. This quantity makes enough for four 30 x 20cm/12 x 8in sheets.

MAKES 500G/18OZ

250g/9oz/2¼ cups gluten-free plain/all-purpose flour blend, plus extra for dusting
30g/1oz/5 tsp ultratex
2.5ml/½ tsp salt
30ml/2 tbsp oil
20ml/4 tsp lemon juice
150ml/¼ pint/⅔ cup lukewarm water

Cook's tip

If the pastry sticks to the surface or tears beyond repair, you can simply knead the dough back together and re-roll it. You can also knead the trimmings together and re-roll them.

1 Put the flour, ultratex and salt in a bowl and stir together until well mixed. Make a well in the middle.

2 Mix the oil, lemon juice and water together. Pour into the well and mix to a soft dough (it will become pliable when kneaded, so don't be tempted to add more water).

3 Turn out on to a floured surface and gently knead for a few seconds, until smooth. Divide into four pieces and wrap in clear film or plastic wrap. Rest for 20 minutes.

4 Unwrap one of the pieces and press it out into a square in your hands roughly 12 x 12cm/5 x 5in. Lightly dust both sides with flour, then roll out on a floured surface into a rectangle about 30 x 25cm/12 x 10in. After every few rollings, carefully run a palette knife or clean thin plastic ruler underneath it. Sprinkle with a little more flour if necessary. If it tears, patch it by trimming a little off the edge and pressing into the tear.

5 Trim the edges (add these to the next piece of filo); it is now ready to use. Repeat with the remaining dough. Don't be tempted to stack the sheets or they will stick together; you need to roll and use one sheet at a time.

Energy 1186kcal/4959kJ; Protein 12.7g; Carbohydrate 227.3g, of which sugars 0.5g; Fat 25.4g, of which saturates 3.3g; Cholesterol 0mg; Calcium 4mg; Fibre 2.7g; Sodium 16mg.

Cheese choux gougères

These cheesy choux pastry puffs make an impressive gluten-free appetizer or snack, and are pleasingly quick and simple to whip up. They are best served warm.

MAKES 25

75g/3oz/⅔ cup gluten-free plain/all-purpose flour blend
50g/2oz/¼ cup butter
120ml/4fl oz/½ cup water
2 eggs, lightly beaten
75g/3oz/¾ cup grated extra mature/sharp Gouda or Cheddar cheese
freshly grated nutmeg
pinchh of salt and ground black pepper, to taste

Cook's tip

The key to good choux is to add the flour in one go and to beat well.

1 Preheat the oven to 220°C/425°F/Gas 7 and line a baking sheet with baking parchment. Sift the flour and a pinch of salt on to another sheet of baking parchment.

2 Heat the butter and water in a small covered pan over a low heat until the butter has melted. Bring to the boil, remove from the heat and add in all the flour immediately.

3 Return the pan to the heat and cook, stirring constantly, until the mixture comes away from the side of the pan and forms a ball. This may take a few minutes, but keep beating.

4 Transfer the dough to a bowl. Add the lightly beaten egg to the dough, a little at a time, beating with a wooden spoon or, preferably, with a hand-held mixer fitted with dough hooks. The mixture should just fall off a spoon when lifted; you may not need all the egg. Continue beating until the dough is smooth and glossy.

5 Add 25g/1oz/¼ cup of the cheese and season with nutmeg, salt and pepper to taste. Stir to mix.

6 Using two teaspoons, place 25 walnut-size mounds of the mixture on the prepared baking sheet, spacing them about 5cm/2in apart. Bake for about 25 minutes, or until puffed up and dark golden brown.

7 Remove from the oven and leave to cool. Cut the puffs open with scissors and fill with the remaining grated cheese. Serve within 2 hours of filling.

8 Just before serving, heat through in a hot oven for a few minutes to melt the cheese.

Energy 45kcal/187kJ; Protein 1.5g; Carbohydrate 2.4g, of which sugars 0g; Fat 3.3g, of which saturates 1.9g; Cholesterol 26mg; Calcium 25mg; Fibre 0g; Sodium 41mg.

Cheese & dill puff pastries

These little cheese pastries are best served hot so that the cheese is still soft and light and the pastry crisp from the oven. They make ideal gluten-free nibbles.

MAKES 16

225g/8oz feta cheese, drained and patted dry on kitchen paper
225g/8oz mozzarella or halloumi cheese, drained and patted dry on kitchen paper
small bunch of fresh dill, chopped
pinch of salt and ground black pepper
2 eggs, lightly beaten, plus 2 egg yolks mixed with a little water to glaze
a little plain/all-purpose gluten-free flour blend, for dusting
450g/1lb gluten-free puff pastry (see page 102), or ready-made, thawed if frozen

1 Preheat the oven to 200°C/400°F/Gas 6. In a bowl, mash the feta with a fork.

2 Grate the mozzarella or halloumi, or whizz to a paste in a blender or food processor, and add it to the feta.

3 Mix in the dill, salt and pepper and beaten eggs, then mix together. Set aside while you prepare the pastry.

4 Dust the work surface with flour and roll out the pastry thinly. Using a round pastry or cookie cutter, or the rim of a cup, cut out as many 10cm/4in rounds as you can, then gather up the trimmings, re-roll and cut out further rounds.

5 Place 10ml/2 tsp of the cheese mixture just off-centre on each pastry round. Lift the other side of the pastry round and bring it up over the filling until the edges touch each other to make a half-moon shape.

6 Use your finger to dampen the edges with a little water and pinch them together to seal. You can press along the edges with the back of a fork to make a pattern, if you like.

7 Line two baking trays with baking parchment and arrange the pastries on them, spacing them well apart. Brush the top of each pastry with a little egg yolk beaten with water, to glaze.

8 Bake for about 20 minutes, until the pastries are puffed up and golden brown. Serve immediately, while the cheese filling is still warm or, if making in advance, leave to cool and then heat them through briefly in a hot oven just before serving.

Energy 257kcal/1065kJ; Protein 6.9g; Carbohydrate 11.5g, of which sugars 0.3g; Fat 20.4g, of which saturates 11g; Cholesterol 94mg; Calcium 110mg; Fibre 0.2g; Sodium 313mg.

Potato & pea filo samosas

Most samosas are deep-fried, but these gluten-free ones are baked, making them a healthier option. They can be made in advance and then baked as and when needed, to be eaten warm.

MAKES 24

1 large potato, about 250g/9oz, peeled and diced
15ml/1 tbsp groundnut/peanut oil
2 shallots, finely chopped
1 garlic clove, finely chopped
60ml/4 tbsp coconut milk
5ml/1 tsp gluten-free Thai red or green curry paste (check it is vegan, if necessary)
75g/3oz/¾ cup peas
juice of ½ lime
250g/9 oz gluten-free filo pastry (½ quantity, see page 105)
salt and ground black pepper, to taste
oil, for brushing

1 Preheat the oven to 220°C/425°F/Gas 7 and line a baking sheet with baking parchment.

2 Bring a small pan of water to the boil, add the diced potato, cover and cook for 8–10 minutes, until tender. Drain in a colander and set aside to steam dry.

3 Meanwhile, heat the oil in a large frying pan, add the shallots and garlic and cook over a medium heat, stirring occasionally, for 4–5 minutes, until softened and golden.

4 Add the dried cooked potato, coconut milk, Thai red or green curry paste, peas and lime juice to the frying pan. Mash coarsely with a wooden spoon – you are aiming to retain some texture.

5 Season to taste and cook over a low heat for 2–3 minutes, then remove the pan from the heat and set aside until the mixture has cooled a little.

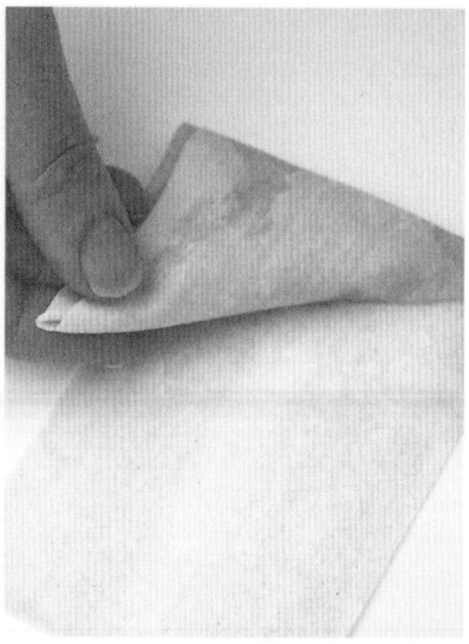

6 Roll out the filo pastry and cut into twenty-four 10 x 5cm/4 x 2in strips. Lay a strip flat on a work surface. Brush with a little oil, then place a spoonful of the mixture in the middle of one end. Turn one corner diagonally over the filling to meet the long edge. Continue folding the pastry over the filling, keeping the triangular shape as you work down the strip. Brush with a little more oil if necessary and place on the prepared baking sheet. Prepare all the other samosas in the same way, until all the filling mixture is used up.

7 Bake the samosas for about 15 minutes or until the pastry is golden and crisp. Leave to cool slightly before serving warm.

Energy 39kcal/164kJ; Protein 0.6g; Carbohydrate 6.9g, of which sugars 0.4g; Fat 1.1g, of which saturates 0.1g; Cholesterol 3mg; Calcium 3mg; Fibre 0.3g; Sodium 7mg.

Mini pork pies with hot water crust pastry

Gluten-free white bread flour, which contains xanthan gum, is used here to make hot water crust pastry for tasty little pies. Served cold, they can be made up to a day ahead – perfect for picnics.

MAKES 12

10ml/2 tsp sunflower oil
1 onion, chopped
225g/8oz pork, coarsely chopped
115g/4oz bacon, diced
45ml/3 tbsp chopped fresh herbs
6 eggs, hard-boiled and halved
20g/¾oz packet powdered aspic
300ml/½ pint/1¼ cups boiling water
salt and ground black pepper, to taste

For the pastry

450g/1lb/4 cups bought gluten-free white bread flour blend or home-made white bread flour blend (see page 42)
pinch of salt and ground black pepper
175g/6oz/¾ cup lard or white vegetable fat
1 small egg, lightly beaten, plus 1 beaten egg yolk, to glaze
300ml/½ pint/1¼ cups boiling water

1 To make the pastry, sift the flour into a large mixing bowl and add the seasoning. Add the fat and use a fork or pastry blender to work into the flour until it resembles breadcrumbs. Drizzle over the egg and stir until well mixed. Add the water, stirring constantly. Press the mixture into a ball using a spoon. Wrap in clear film or plastic wrap and chill for at least 1 hour.

2 Preheat the oven to 200°C/400°F/Gas 6. Heat the oil in a pan, add the onion and cook until soft. Stir in the pork and bacon and cook until just brown, then stir in the herbs and season to taste.

3 Roll out two-thirds of the pastry on a floured surface. Use a 12cm/4½in fluted cutter to stamp out rounds. Line 12 tartlet tins or muffin pans with the rounds and place some meat mixture in each. Add half a half-boiled egg and top with the remaining mix.

4 Roll out the remaining pastry and use a 7.5cm/3in fluted cutter to stamp out lids. Dampen the rim of each pastry base and press a lid in place. Brush with egg yolk and make a small steam hole in the top of each pie.

5 Bake for 30–35 minutes. Leave to cool for 15 minutes, then place on a wire rack to cool completely.

6 Meanwhile, stir the aspic powder into the boiling water until dissolved. Shape a piece of foil into a small funnel and use this to guide a little aspic through the hole in the top of each pie. Chill for up to 24 hours. Serve at room temperature.

Energy 360kcal/1496kJ; Protein 12.6g; Carbohydrate 30g, of which sugars 0.1g; Fat 21g, of which saturates 7.8g; Cholesterol 143mg; Calcium 23mg; Fibre 0.4g; Sodium 206mg.

Courgette & feta pasties with quinoa pastry

Quinoa flour is packed with protein and makes excellent gluten-free pastry, which is short and crisp when baked. You can use this gluten-free pastry to replace standard shortcrust pastry in most savoury and sweet pastry recipes.

MAKES 8

1 medium courgette/zucchini
1 cooking apple, about 115g/4oz in weight, peeled, cored and grated
275g/10oz/1²/₃ cups cooked red or white quinoa
300g/11oz feta cheese, crumbled
15ml/1 tbsp fresh mint, torn
ground black pepper
mint jelly, to serve (optional)

For the pastry

75g/3oz/6 tbsp butter, softened
275g/10oz/2½ cups quinoa flour
10ml/2 tsp Dijon mustard
175ml/6fl oz/¾ cup cold water
a little milk, to glaze

Variation

You could make mini pasties, if you wish, for appetizers or for nibbles to hand round with drinks. Reduce the cooking time slightly to about 15 minutes, depending on how small they are. Keep an eye on them as they will over-brown quickly; remove from the oven once they are a golden brown.

1 First, make the pastry. Cut the butter into the flour with a pastry blender or use your fingertips to rub it in. Shake the bowl occasionally to bring any large lumps of fat to the top. Blend until all the fat is incorporated and the mixture resembles fine breadcrumbs.

2 Blend the mustard with 60ml/4 tbsp of the water. Add to the bowl, then gradually add enough of the remaining cold water to make a smooth dough. Wrap in clear film or plastic wrap and chill in the fridge for 30 minutes.

3 Grate the courgette straight on to a dish towel or several pieces of kitchen paper. Roll up the towel or paper and squeeze over a sink or bowl to remove as much excess liquid as possible.

4 Transfer the grated and squeezed courgette to a large bowl and add the grated apple and quinoa. Mix in the crumbled feta cheese, mint and ground black pepper. Preheat the oven to 190°C/375°F/Gas 5.

5 Divide the chilled pastry into two even-sized pieces, roll them out and cut each into four circles measuring about 13cm/5in in diameter.

6 Divide the filling between the eight pastry rounds, positioning it on one half of each circle.

7 Fold over the other half of the circle to enclose the filling, and press the edges together to make a small pasty shape. Crimp the edges for decorative effect and make a small slit in the top of each one.

8 Place the pasties on baking sheets (no oiling needed) and brush the tops with a little milk.

9 Bake for 20–25 minutes, until the pastry is crisp and golden. Serve warm with mint jelly if you like.

Variation

For Cheese and Onion Pasties, replace the grated apple with finely chopped onion, and the feta cheese with mature/sharp Cheddar cheese.

Energy 770kcal/3230kJ; Protein 31.7g; Carbohydrate 81.2g, of which sugars 12.9g; Fat 37.7g, of which saturates 20.8g; Cholesterol 92mg; Calcium 394mg; Fibre 1.2g; Sodium 1279mg.

Leek & tofu tart with hazelnut pastry

This tart is made with a crisp hazelnut gluten-free pastry case and is filled with tender leeks and tofu baked in a nut-milk custard.

SERVES 6

350g/12oz leeks, sliced
15ml/1 tbsp olive oil
5 eggs, lightly beaten
400ml/14fl oz/1⅔ cups nut milk
15ml/1 tbsp gluten-free wholegrain mustard
250g/9oz firm silken tofu, drained and crumbled
pinch of salt and ground black pepper

For the pastry

115g/4oz/½ cup hard baking margarine, at room temperature
25ml/1½ tbsp smooth hazelnut butter
175g/6oz/1½ cups gluten-free plain/all-purpose flour blend
5ml/1 tsp xanthan gum
35ml/2½ tbsp cold water

1 For the pastry, blend the margarine and hazelnut butter in a mixing bowl until well combined. Transfer the mixture to baking parchment and chill for 30 minutes (or freeze for 10 minutes), until hardened.

2 Sift the flour and xanthan gum into a mixing bowl, add the hazelnut margarine and blend it in using a pastry cutter or rub it into the flour with your fingertips, until the mixture resembles fine breadcrumbs.

3 Sprinkle over the cold water, mix until the crumbs begin to stick together, then gather the mixture into a ball. Roll out the pastry until it is the thickness of a coin, then use it to line a 25cm/10in flan tin/pan. Chill for 10–25 minutes, or until required.

4 Put a baking sheet in the oven and preheat it to 200°C/400°F/Gas 6. Sweat the leeks in the oil in a frying pan for 10 minutes, until soft.

5 Prick the base of the pastry and line with baking parchment and dried beans. Bake for 15 minutes. Remove the paper and beans and brush the pastry with a little beaten egg. Return to the oven for 5 minutes.

6 Mix the remaining eggs with the milk, mustard and seasoning. Stir into the leeks with the tofu and pour into the pastry case. Put into the hot oven and bake for about 30 minutes, until set and golden. Remove and leave to stand for about 10 minutes before serving.

Energy 412kcal/1706kJ; Protein 12.8g; Carbohydrate 25.8g, of which sugars 1.8g; Fat 28.6g, of which saturates 10.1g; Cholesterol 195mg; Calcium 263mg; Fibre 2.4g; Sodium 260mg.

Smoked salmon quiche with potato pastry

Mashed potatoes add a short and tender texture to pastry. Here, they are mixed with gluten-free white bread flour, which contains xanthan gum, making the pastry flexible enough to line the tin.

SERVES 6

5 eggs plus 1 egg white, beaten
150ml/¼ pint/⅔ cup single/ light cream
250ml/8fl oz/1 cup full-fat/ whole milk
30–45ml/2–3 tbsp chopped fresh dill, plus extra to serve
30ml/2 tbsp capers, chopped
275g/10oz smoked salmon, chopped into bitesize pieces
ground black pepper, to taste

For the pastry

115g/4oz floury potatoes, diced
150g/5oz/1¼ cups bought gluten-free white bread flour blend or home-made white bread flour blend (see page 42), plus exta for dusting
75g/3oz/6 tbsp cold butter, diced
1 egg yolk
10ml/2 tsp chilled water, if needed

1 For the pastry, boil the potatoes for 15 minutes, until tender. Drain then mash until smooth. Leave to cool.

2 Meanwhile, in a large mixing bowl, rub together the flour and butter to form fine crumbs.

3 Stir the egg yolk into the mashed potato and add to the bowl of flour crumbs. Bring the mixture together, adding chilled water if needed. Lightly knead on a floured surface for a few seconds, until smooth.

4 Roll the pastry out on a floured surface and use to line a deep 23cm/9in round, loose-based, fluted flan tin/pan. Chill for 1 hour.

5 Preheat the oven to 200°C/400°F/Gas 6. Place a baking sheet in the oven to preheat it. Blind bake the pastry case (see page 100), then reduce the oven temperature to 160°C/325°F/Gas 3.

6 While the case is baking, beat the eggs, cream and milk together. Stir in the dill, capers and pepper, then stir in the salmon. Pour the filling into the pastry and bake for 35–45 minutes, until lightly set. Serve warm.

Energy 408kcal/1698kJ; Protein 21.5g; Carbohydrate 25.6g, of which sugars 2.8g; Fat 24.5g, of which saturates 12.6g; Cholesterol 256mg; Calcium 111mg; Fibre 0.5g; Sodium 1032mg.

Quiche Lorraine with rice flour pastry

This gluten-free pastry case is made with rice flour and polenta, flavoured with cheese, which complements the classic creamy, light egg and bacon filling. It is both indulgent and satisfying.

SERVES 4–6

6 smoked streaky/fatty bacon rashers, rinds removed
150ml/¼ pint/⅔ cup single/light cream
150ml/¼ pint/⅔ cup full-fat/whole milk
3 eggs, plus 3 yolks
salt and ground black pepper, to taste

For the pastry

150g/5oz/1¼ cups rice flour, plus extra for dusting
100g/3½oz/scant 1 cup fine polenta/cornmeal
115g/4oz/½ cup butter, diced
30ml/2 tbsp grated Parmesan cheese
1 egg yolk
30ml/2 tbsp milk

1 To make the pastry, blitz the flour, polenta, butter and Parmesan in a food processor until the mixture resembles breadcrumbs, or rub in the butter by hand.

2 Mix the egg yolk and milk together and stir into the dry ingredients to make a soft dough. Wrap in clear wrap or plastic wrap and chill for 30 minutes.

3 Lightly dust a surface with rice flour, Roll out the pastry and use it to line a deep 20cm/8in round flan tin/pan. Trim off the excess. Chill for 10 minutes.

4 Put a baking sheet in the oven and preheat to 200°C/400°F/Gas 6. Blind bake the pastry case for 10 minutes (see page 100).

5 Meanwhile, cut the bacon thinly and grill or broil until crisp. Arrange the bacon in the pastry case. Beat together the cream, milk, eggs and yolks, and seasoning. Carefully pour over the bacon in the pastry case.

6 Bake for 10 minutes, then reduce the heat to 180°C/350°F/Gas 4 and bake for a further 15–20 minutes, until the filling is puffed up and golden, and the pastry edge crisp. Remove from the oven and leave to stand and cool for a few minutes before serving.

Energy 538kcal/2232kJ; Protein 16.6g; Carbohydrate 34.3g, of which sugars 2.1g; Fat 36.8g, of which saturates 18.7g; Cholesterol 329mg; Calcium 153mg; Fibre 1.2g; Sodium 538mg.

Red onion tart with polenta pastry

Red onions are sweet when cooked, and go well with fontina and thyme in this tart. Fine polenta gives the gluten-free pastry a crumbly texture to contrast with the juiciness of the filling.

SERVES 4–6
60ml/4 tbsp olive oil
1kg/2¼lb red onions, sliced
2–3 garlic cloves, thinly sliced
5ml/1 tsp chopped fresh thyme, plus whole sprigs to garnish
5ml/1 tsp dark brown sugar
10ml/2 tsp sherry vinegar
225g/8oz fontina cheese, sliced
salt and ground black pepper, to taste

For the pastry
115g/4oz/1 cup gluten-free plain/ all-purpose flour blend
75g/3oz/¾ cup fine polenta/ cornmeal
5ml/1 tsp xanthan gum
5ml/1 tsp chopped fresh thyme
90g/3½oz/7 tbsp butter
1 egg yolk
30–45ml/2–3 tbsp iced water
salt and freshly ground black pepper, to taste

1 For the pastry, put the flour, polenta, xanthan gum, thyme and seasoning in a mixing bowl. Rub in the butter until the mixture resembles coarse breadcrumbs.

2 Beat the egg yolk with enough of the water to bind the pastry. Gather the dough into a ball, wrap in clear film or plastic wrap and chill for 30 minutes.

3 Heat 45ml/3 tbsp oil in a deep frying pan and add the onions. Cover and cook slowly, stirring occasionally, for 20–30 minutes. They should collapse but not brown.

4 Add the garlic and half the thyme, then cook, stirring occasionally, for another 10 minutes. Increase the heat slightly, then add the sugar and vinegar. Cook, uncovered, for 5–6 minutes, until the onions start to caramelize. Season to taste with salt and pepper. Cool.

5 Preheat the oven to 190°C/375°F/Gas 5. Roll out the pastry and use to line a 25cm/10in loose-based metal flan tin/pan. Prick the pastry with a fork and support the sides with foil. Bake for 12–15 minutes, until golden.

6 Remove the foil and spread the onions evenly over the base of the pastry. Add the fontina and remaining thyme. Drizzle over the remaining oil, then bake for 15–20 minutes, until the cheese is beginning to bubble. Garnish with sprigs of thyme and serve immediately.

Energy 494kcal/2054kJ; Protein 13.2g; Carbohydrate 39g, of which sugars 11.5g; Fat 32.5g, of which saturates 16g; Cholesterol 100mg; Calcium 172mg; Fibre 4.3g; Sodium 307mg.

Mince & pine nut filo pie

Gluten-free filo can be used in all manner of pies, from light and crisp scrunched pastry toppings and free-form filled parcels to this simple pie filled with minced meat, toasted pine nuts, herbs and spices, enriched with a savoury egg custard to help hold it together.

SERVES 8

1 egg
150ml/¼ pint/⅔ cup milk
75ml/5 tbsp sunflower oil, plus extra for greasing
500g/18oz gluten-free filo pastry (see page 105)
yogurt salad (see Cook's tip), to serve

For the filling

15ml/1 tbsp olive oil
15g/½oz/1 tbsp butter
1 onion, finely chopped
2–3 garlic cloves, crushed
30–45ml/2–3 tbsp pine nuts
250g/9oz lean lamb, finely minced/ground
10ml/2 tsp ground cinnamon
10ml/2 tsp dried oregano
small bunch of fresh parsley, leaves finely chopped
salt and ground black pepper, to taste

1 Preheat the oven to 200°C/400°F/Gas 6 and place a baking sheet in it to heat. Grease a shallow 22cm/8½in round ovenproof dish or tin/pan.

2 For the filling, heat the olive oil and butter in a heavy pan and stir in the onion. Cook for 1–2 minutes, until softened. Add the garlic and pine nuts.

3 Once the pine nuts begin to turn golden, add the lamb and cook for 5 minutes, until browned and most of the moisture has been driven off. Stir in the cinnamon, herbs and seasoning, then leave to cool.

4 Whisk the egg, milk and oil together in a jug or pitcher. Set aside. Divide the pastry into four pieces and roll out three pieces to form squares, slightly larger than 25 x 25cm/10 x 10in.

5 Carefully line the dish or tin with one of the pastry squares, completely covering the base and either side of the dish and allowing the corners of the pastry to overlap the edge of the dish.

6 Brush the the base and sides of the pastry with the egg mixture, then top with a second square of pastry, placed at a slight angle to the first. Brush with the egg as before, then top with the third pastry square, again at an angle to the previous sheet of pastry, so that the finished pastry case looks like a star. Brush again with the egg mixture.

7 Spoon the meat mixture into the dish, levelling the top into an even layer. Reserve 30ml/2 tbsp of the egg and milk mixture, then pour the rest over the meat.

8 Roll out the remaining piece of filo pastry to a 22cm/8½in circle, roughly the same size as the dish. Place on top of the pie.

9 Fold the dangling flaps of filo pastry over the top of the pie, sticking them down with the egg and milk mixture, which you can apply with a brush, although it may be easier and more effective to smear it on with your fingers. Make sure the very top pieces are well covered, so they crisp up.

10 Put the pie into the oven, on the baking sheet (which will help the pastry bottom to crisp, and catch any spillage), and bake for 25–30 minutes, until golden.

11 Remove the pie from the oven, leave it to stand for a few minutes, then cut it into wedges. Serve hot or at room temperature, accompanied by a yogurt dip or a yogurt-based salad.

Cook's tip

To make a cucumber and yogurt salad, combine a few tablespoons of Greek/strained plain yogurt with a little seasoning and some crushed garlic in a bowl, then add some very finely sliced cucumber and roughly chopped fresh mint. Serve soon after making.

Energy 194kcal/803kJ; Protein 9.7g; Carbohydrate 2.6g, of which sugars 2.2g; Fat 16.3g, of which saturates 3.3g; Cholesterol 52mg; Calcium 65mg; Fibre 0.5g; Sodium 51mg.

Double-crust chard pie

This tasty pie is made with Swiss chard and hard-boiled eggs encased in a tender gluten-free shortcrust pastry. Based on a Peruvian recipe, this popular pie is delicious served warm but is also good eaten cold, cut into slices.

SERVES 6

45ml/3 tbsp vegetable oil
1 small red onion, finely chopped
2 garlic cloves, chopped
1kg/2¼lb Swiss chard, thickly sliced
2.5ml/½ tsp grated nutmeg
4 eggs, and
3 hard-boiled eggs
pinch of salt and ground black pepper

For the pastry

500g/18oz/4½ cups gluten-free self-raising/self-rising flour blend, plus extra for dusting
5ml/1 tsp xanthan gum
5ml/1 tsp salt
130g/4½oz/generous ½ cup hard baking margarine
75ml/5 tbsp water
1 egg yolk, lightly beaten

1 Heat the oil in a large pan or wok over medium heat and fry the onion for 5 minutes, until softened and starting to brown.

2 Stir in the garlic and Swiss chard and cook, stirring occasionally, for 5 minutes until the chard has wilted. Turn up the heat a little and stir until the liquid has evaporated and the mixture is fairly dry.

3 Stir in the nutmeg, salt and pepper to taste, then remove from the heat and leave to cool.

4 To make the pastry, sift the flour, xanthan gum and salt into a mixing bowl, then rub in the margarine using your fingers or two forks. Add the water and draw the pastry together with your fingers. Knead to form a smooth dough and leave to rest in a cool place for 10 minutes.

5 Preheat the oven to 180°C/350°F/Gas 4 and oil a rectangular baking dish or tray measuring about 25 x 15cm/10 x 6in. Divide the dough into two pieces, one larger than the other.

6 On a floured surface, thinly roll out the larger piece of pastry and use it to line the dish or tray, leaving the edges of the pastry hanging over the sides.

7 Beat the 4 eggs lightly together and stir them into the cooled chard filling. Pour the mixture into the pastry-lined tray.

8 Cut the hard-boiled eggs in half and press them into the filling, distributing them evenly. Dampen the edges of the pastry.

9 Roll out the remaining dough and cover the pie, sealing the edges by pressing them together with your fingers. Trim the edges and cut out decorations for the top of the pie from the pastry trimmings, if you wish.

10 Brush the surface of the pie with the egg yolk to glaze and bake for about 45 minutes until the pastry is crisp and golden brown.

11 Remove from the oven and leave to cool for about 5 minutes before serving. This pie is good served warm or at room temperature.

Energy 610kcal/2536kJ; Protein 12.8g; Carbohydrate 72.4g, of which sugars 2g; Fat 30g, of which saturates 2.4g; Cholesterol 188mg; Calcium 115mg; Fibre 1.1g; Sodium 581mg.

Salmon puff pastry pie

This majestic pie, also known as coulibiac, consists of a crisp gluten-free puff pastry case filled with cured salmon, hard-boiled eggs and rice. It makes a superb gluten-free dinner party centrepiece and can be prepared up to 12 hours ahead and baked when your guests arrive.

SERVES 4

4 eggs
50g/2oz/¼ cup long grain rice
300g/11oz gravlax or smoked salmon
15g/½oz/¼ cup chopped fresh dill
45ml/3 tbsp crème fraîche or double/heavy cream
a little gluten-free plain/all-purpose flour blend, for dusting
450g/1lb gluten-free puff pastry (see page 102), chilled, or ready-made, thawed if frozen
1 egg yolk and 5ml/1 tsp water
15ml/1 tbsp fresh gluten-free breadcrumbs (see page 18)
pinch of salt and ground black pepper

1 Put the eggs in a pan, cover with cold water and bring to the boil. Reduce the heat to low and simmer for 10 minutes. When the eggs are cooked, immediately drain and put them under cold running water. Remove the shells, then chop the eggs into small pieces.

2 Meanwhile, bring a pan of salted water to the boil, add the rice and stir to loosen the grains at the bottom of the pan. Simmer for about 20 minutes, until tender. Drain and rinse under cold water.

3 Cut the gravlax or smoked salmon into strips and put in a large mixing bowl. Add the chopped eggs, rice, dill and crème fraîche or cream, and mix together. Season with salt and ground black pepper.

4 Preheat the oven to 220°C/425°F/Gas 7. Dampen a baking tray.

5 On a floured surface, roll out the pastry to a 40 x 20cm/16 x 8in rectangle. Spread the filling lengthways on one half of the pastry. Brush the edges with water and fold the other side over to enclose the filling. Seal by pressing with a fork along the join. Transfer to the baking sheet, cover with clear film or plastic wrap and chill until ready to bake.

6 Whisk together the egg yolk and water. Brush the pastry with the glaze and make some small holes in the top with a fork. Sprinkle the breadcrumbs over the top.

7 Bake for 12–15 minutes, until golden brown. Leave to rest for 10 minutes, then cut into slices and serve hot.

Energy 982kcal/4071kJ; Protein 31.9g; Carbohydrate 58.3g, of which sugars 0.6g; Fat 68.9g, of which saturates 32.7g; Cholesterol 408mg; Calcium 74mg; Fibre 0.7g; Sodium 1702mg.

Chicken & mushroom pie

This is a gluten-free version of a classic pie that goes down well with diners of all ages. Tender chicken cooked with fresh and dried porcini mushrooms, celery and carrots in a well-flavoured sauce and a splash of cream makes a great pie filling, topped with crisp shortcrust pastry.

SERVES 6

15g/½oz/¼ cup dried porcini mushrooms, soaked in hot water for 30 minutes
30ml/2 tbsp cornflour/starch
60ml/4 tbsp single/light cream
250ml/8fl oz/1 cup hot chicken stock
25g/1oz/2 tbsp butter
1 onion, coarsely chopped
2 carrots, sliced
2 celery sticks, coarsely chopped
50g/2oz/¾ cup mushrooms, quartered
450g/1lb cooked chicken, cubed
50g/2oz/½ cup peas
375g/13oz gluten-free shortcrust pastry (see page 100), or ready-made, thawed if frozen
a little gluten-free plain/all-purpose flour blend, for dusting
beaten egg, to glaze
salt and ground black pepper, to taste

1 Drain the porcini mushrooms and pat dry. Preheat the oven to 190°C/375°F/Gas 5.

2 Blend the cornflour with the cream in a pan, then gradually add the hot stock. Bring the mixture to the boil over a medium heat, stirring frequently. Season to taste and set aside.

3 Heat the butter in a large frying pan and cook the onion and carrots over a low heat for about 5 minutes. Add the celery and fresh mushrooms and cook for about 5 minutes more. Stir in the cooked chicken, peas and drained porcini mushrooms.

4 Add the chicken mixture to the cream sauce. Adjust the seasoning if necessary. Spoon the mixture into a 2.5-litre/4-pint oval baking dish.

5 On a floured surface, roll out the pastry to a thickness of about 3mm/⅛in. Cut out an oval 2.5cm/1in larger all around than the pie dish.

6 Lay the pastry over the filling, seal and trim the edges. Crimp all round the pastry edge. Cut out decorations for the top of the pie from the pastry trimmings, if you wish. Glaze with beaten egg and cut slits in the top.

7 Put the pie dish on a baking sheet to catch any drips. Bake for 30 minutes, or until the pastry is golden-brown. Leave to stand for 5 minutes after removing from the oven, and serve hot.

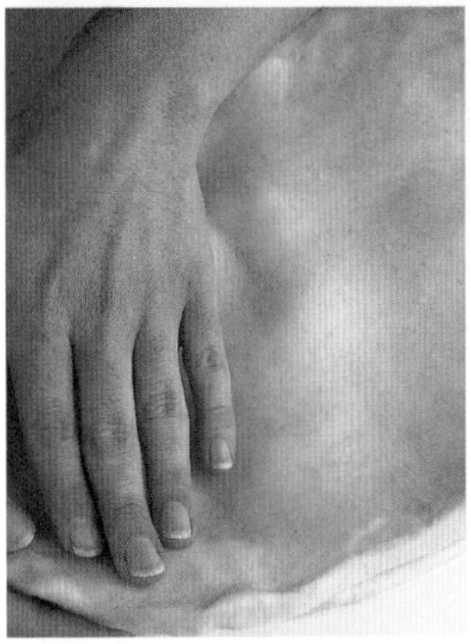

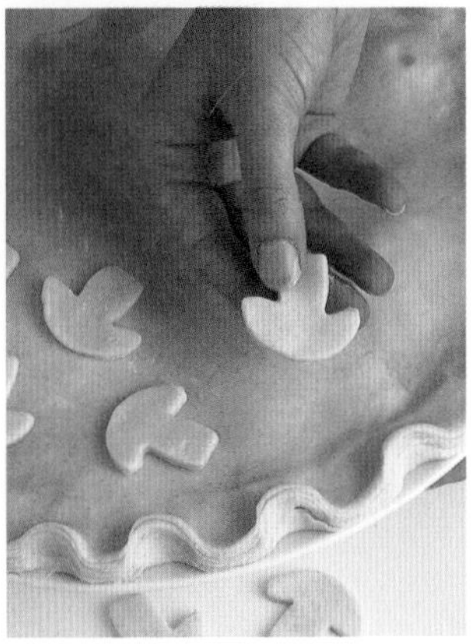

Energy 484kcal/2017kJ; Protein 26.3g; Carbohydrate 40g, of which sugars 4g; Fat 24.6g, of which saturates 14.3g; Cholesterol 117mg; Calcium 38mg; Fibre 2.5g; Sodium 206mg.

Vegan 'sausage' rolls in coconut pastry

Made with crisp coconut pastry, these rolls are filled with 'sausages' made of red lentils and roasted pepper. Smaller ones make great party food, or make bigger ones for packed lunches. You can swap the filling for gluten-free sausagemeat, if you prefer.

MAKES 20 SMALL OR 10 MEDIUM ROLLS

150g/5oz/¾ cup red lentils
300ml/½ pint/1¼ cups vegan stock
1 red bell pepper
50g/2oz/½ cup dried gluten-free white breadcrumbs (see page 18)
5ml/1 tsp smoked paprika
15ml/1 tbsp chopped fresh parsley
275g/10oz or 1 quantity coconut pastry (see page 104)
soya or rice milk, to glaze
30ml/2 tbsp sesame seeds (optional)
salt and ground black pepper, to taste

1 Put the lentils in a bowl, cover with plenty of cold water and rinse well. Tip into a strainer and drain, then transfer to a large pan. Pour in the stock.

2 Bring to the boil, cover with a tight-fitting lid and simmer for 15 minutes, until all the stock has been absorbed. Remove the lid and cook over a low heat for 2–3 minutes, stirring occasionally to prevent sticking.

3 At the end of the cooking time the lentil mixture should be fairly dry, with no excess liquid. Tip the mixture into a large mixing bowl and spread it out as much as possible to allow the steam to evaporate. Stir occasionally as the mixture cools.

4 While the lentils are cooking, preheat a grill or broiler to high. Halve the pepper, then remove the seeds and core. Place the halves skin side up on a baking sheet and grill for about 10 minutes, moving occasionally, until the skin is blackened all over. Put the pepper in a plastic bag, seal the top and leave to steam for 5 minutes – this will help to loosen the skin.

5 Peel away the skin from the pepper halves and chop the flesh finely. Add to the lentils with the breadcrumbs, smoked paprika, parsley, and salt and pepper to taste. Stir well. Cover and chill in the fridge for 20 minutes.

6 Preheat the oven to 200°C/400°F/Gas 6 and line a baking sheet with baking parchment.

7 Roll out the pastry between two pieces of baking parchment to a rectangle slightly larger than 30 x 25cm/12 x 10in. Trim the edges straight, then cut the pastry lengthwise into two strips.

8 Divide the cooled lentil mixture in half. Shape one half into a long sausage shape along the middle of one of the pastry strips. Brush the long edges of the pastry with soya or rice milk. With the help of the baking parchment, roll up the pastry and gently press along the seam with your fingers or a fork to seal. Repeat with the remaining pastry strip and lentil mixture.

9 Brush the outside of the rolls with a little soya or rice milk, to glaze. Using a sharp knife, cut each long roll into five 6cm/2½in rolls or ten 2.5cm/1in rolls. Make two or three small slits in the top of each one, sprinkle with sesame seeds, if liked, then gently transfer the rolls to the baking sheet.

10 Bake for 15–20 minutes or until the pastry is lightly coloured and cooked though. Serve hot or cold.

Energy 88kcal/371kJ; Protein 3.4g; Carbohydrate 14g, of which sugars 0.9g; Fat 2.4g, of which saturates 1.7g; Cholesterol 10mg; Calcium 22mg; Fibre 1.1g; Sodium 34mg.

Beef & mushroom suet pudding

Based on a great British classic, this steamed pudding has a light, herby gluten-free pastry crust made with a mixture of butter and vegetable suet, which provides the desired short, crumbly texture while being robust enough to encase the very savoury filling.

SERVES 6

60ml/4 tbsp gluten-free plain/all-purpose flour blend
675g/1½lb braising steak, diced
45ml/3 tbsp sunflower oil
1 large onion, finely chopped
225g/8oz mushrooms, sliced
1 bay leaf
15ml/1 tbsp Worcestershire sauce
75ml/2½fl oz/⅓ cup red wine
475ml/16fl oz/2 cups beef stock
butter, for greasing
salt and ground black pepper, to taste

For the pastry

275g/10oz/2½ cups gluten-free self-raising/self-rising flour blend
2.5ml/½ tsp gluten-free baking powder
2.5ml/½ tsp salt
15ml/1 tbsp chopped parsley
75g/3oz/1½ cups gluten-free shredded vegetable suet
50g/2oz/¼ cup butter, frozen and grated
1 egg, lightly beaten
150ml/¼ pint/⅔ cup cold water

1 Put the flour in a mixing bowl, season, then add the meat and toss to coat. Heat the oil in a frying pan and fry the meat in batches until browned all over. Transfer to a large casserole. Preheat the oven to 160°C/325°F/Gas 3.

2 Add the onion to the pan and sauté for 10 minutes, until soft. Transfer to the casserole with the mushrooms, bay leaf, Worcestershire sauce, wine and stock. Cook for 2 hours, until the meat is very tender. Leave to cool. Butter a deep 1.75-litre/3-pint heatproof bowl.

3 For the pastry, sift the flour, baking powder and salt into a mixing bowl and stir in the parsley followed by the suet and butter.

4 Make a well in the middle, add the egg and enough cold water to mix, and gather into a soft dough.

5 Use three-quarters of the pastry to line the heatproof bowl, allowing the excess to fall over the sides, and then spoon in the filling, reserving the juices to serve as gravy.

6 Roll out the reserved pastry to make a round large enough to use as a lid for the pudding. Place this on top of the pudding, pressing the edges together to seal.

7 Cover with a pleated, double-thickness layer of baking parchment, and then foil, tied with string. Steam for 3 hours. Invert on to a plate and serve with the gravy.

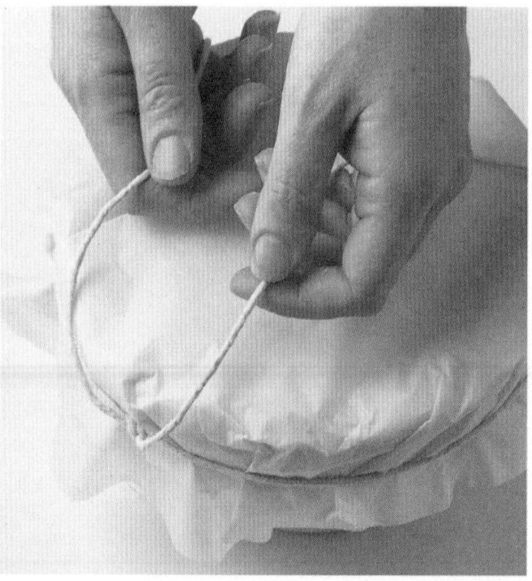

Energy 603kcal/2512kJ; Protein 30.8g; Carbohydrate 49.8g, of which sugars 3g; Fat 30.3g, of which saturates 13.1g; Cholesterol 122mg; Calcium 31mg; Fibre 1.9g; Sodium 171mg.

Batters

Some of the best foods are the simplest, and most batters are basically a combination of flour, eggs and milk, lightly beaten together to make a mixture that can be used to create all sorts of dishes. As well as pouring batter into a pan to make traditional flat pancakes or using it to coat ingredients before shallow- or deep-frying them, such as when making onion bhajis or cheesy fish gougons, you can also make batters that are thick enough to pipe directly into very hot oil, for instance churros to serve with the thickest, richest hot chocolate. And then there are fluffy Yorkshire puddings, Belgian waffles topped with fresh summer berries and whipped cream, and moreish Asian-inspired spring rolls made with rice wrappers ... the list goes on.

Fortunately, all the batters for these delights work well with a whole range of gluten-free flours: while basic ones can be made with ready-blended gluten-free plain/all-purpose flours, either store-bought or made yourself (see page 21), you can also use single-grain or seed gluten-free products such as buckwheat, tapioca flour and quinoa flours to give very different results that bring new flavours and textures as well as added nutritional benefits to the table.

All sorts of extras can then be added to the core batter mixture to further alter the thickness and taste. Finely chopped, grated or mashed vegetables such as potatoes bring flavour and nutrition. Whisked egg whites are used to lighten, as in Potato & Dill Pancakes. Raising agents turn batter into spongy, plump drop scones, and yeast works in much the same way to create little Buckwheat Blinis. The batter liquid can be also be varied with fruit juice, non-dairy milks such as coconut milk, beer, or even just plain water – all of which are suitable for those avoiding dairy. Quick to make and cook, mostly easy, mostly cheap – what's not to love about batters!

Pancake batter

Pancakes and crêpes are popular all around the world, and can be used in many different ways: topped with lemon and sugar, drizzled with syrup or piled with fresh fruit for a sweet snack, or wrapped around all manner of tasty savoury fillings. Buckwheat flour lends them a lovely nutty flavour, but coconut, rice and quinoa flours all also work well.

MAKES 6

40g/1½oz/⅓ cup white rice flour
40g/1½oz/⅓ cup brown rice flour
25g/1oz/¼ cup tapioca starch
25g/1oz/¼ cup potato starch
15ml/1 tbsp buckwheat flour
1.5ml/¼ tsp xanthan gum
pinch of salt
1 egg
15g/½oz/1 tbsp unsalted butter, melted
225ml/8fl oz/1 cup milk
vegetable oil, for frying

1 Put all the dry ingredients in a bowl and stir to combine. Make a small well in the middle.

2 Add the egg, melted butter and half of the milk and gradually whisk into the flour. Add the rest of the milk and whisk to make a smooth batter.

3 Heat a pan over a medium-high heat, until very hot. Pour in a little vegetable oil, tilting the pan to ensure the surface is coated.

4 Pour in a ladleful of batter. Tilt the pan to spread the batter thinly and cook for 30 seconds, until set and browned underneath.

5 Turn the pancake with a flat implement and cook on the second side, until browned.

6 Remove from the pan and place on a plate. Cover loosely with foil and keep hot in a warm oven. Cook the remaining batter to make additional pancakes.

RICE WRAPPERS

Gluten free • Dairy free • Vegan

Paper-thin rice wrappers can be eaten fresh, steamed, or deep-fried until crisp and golden.

MAKES 12

60ml/4 tbsp white rice flour
60ml/4 tbsp potato starch
pinch of salt
90ml/6 tbsp water

1 Put the rice flour, potato starch and salt in a bowl and stir in the water to make a thick gluey paste.

2 Cover a 20cm/8in microwaveable plate with clear film or plastic wrap, stretching it smooth. Spoon some rice paper paste on to the clear film, spreading it thinly and evenly with the back of a spoon into a circle about 18cm/7in in diameter. Microwave for 40–50 seconds until dry (the time will depend on the power of your microwave).

3 Turn the plate upside down on to a circle of baking parchment, peeling the clear film off the plate, so that the rice wrapper is between the parchment and clear film. Allow it to cool, then peel off the clear film. Repeat with the remaining mixture. Use straight away.

Pancakes: Energy 138kcal/580kJ; Protein 3.6g; Carbohydrate 22.5g, of which sugars 1.8g; Fat 3.9g, of which saturates 2g; Cholesterol 46mg; Calcium 55mg; Fibre 0.5g; Sodium 31mg.
Wrappers: Energy 35kcal/146kJ; Protein 0.8g; Carbohydrate 7.8g, of which sugars 0.1g; Fat 0.1g, of which saturates 0g; Cholesterol 0mg; Calcium 2mg; Fibre 0.5g; Sodium 2mg.

Drop scone batter

These little pancakes are made with buttermilk, which adds a lovely tangy taste as well as helping them to rise, since the acid in the buttermilk reacts with the bicarbonate of soda. Ready-mixed gluten-free flour works well, as do quinoa and sorghum flours.

MAKES 12

225g/8oz/2 cups gluten-free plain/all-purpose flour blend
5ml/1 tsp bicarbonate of soda/baking soda
25–50g/1–2oz/2–4 tbsp sugar
1 egg
about 300ml/½ pint/1¼ cups buttermilk
butter and oil, mixed, or white vegetable fat, for frying

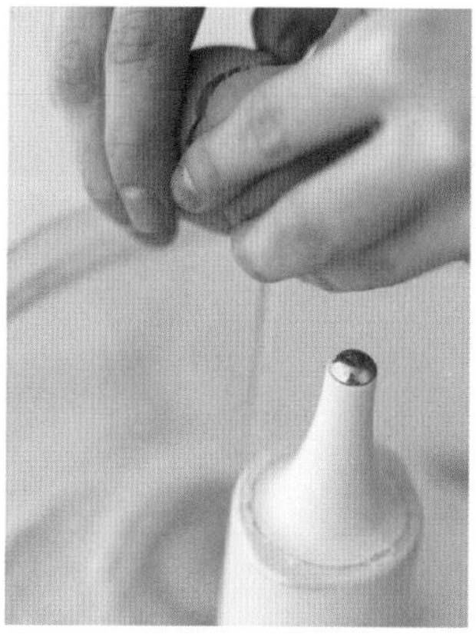

1 In a food processor or a large mixing bowl, mix together the flour and bicarbonate of soda, and enough sugar to taste if you are making sweet drop scones.

2 Add the egg, mix everything together, then gradually pour in enough of the buttermilk to make a thick, smooth batter.

3 Heat a heavy pan and add the butter and oil, or white fat. Heat until it sizzles.

4 Place spoonfuls of the batter on to the hot pan and cook for 2–3 minutes, until bubbles rise to the surface.

5 Flip the pancakes over with a spatula or turner, and cook for a further 2–3 minutes. Remove from the pan and serve warm – they are delicious spread with butter and honey.

DAIRY-FREE DROP SCONES

Gluten free • Dairy free • Vegetarian

Making the batter with pineapple juice instead of milk cuts down on fat and adds to the taste and sweetness, without adding refined sugar, as well as making these light little drop scones dairy free.

MAKES 12

115g/4oz/1 cup gluten-free self-raising/self-rising flour blend
115g/4oz/1 cup sorghum flour
2.5ml/½ tsp gluten-free baking powder
5ml/1 tsp ground cinnamon
2 eggs
300ml/½ pint/1¼ cups pineapple juice

1 Preheat a griddle or heavy-based frying pan.

2 Put the flours in a mixing bowl, add the baking powder and cinnamon, and make a well in the centre.

3 Add the eggs with half the juice to the well, and incorporate the surrounding flour to make a smooth batter. Beat in the remaining pineapple juice.

4 Lightly grease the griddle or pan. Drop tablespoons of the batter on to the surface, leaving them until they bubble and the bubbles begin to burst.

5 Flip the drop scones and cook until the underside is golden brown. Wrap cooked ones in a clean napkin while continuing to cook successive batches.

Plain: Energy 91kcal/380kJ; Protein 2.4g; Carbohydrate 18.3g, of which sugars 3.4g; Fat 0.9g, of which saturates 0.3g; Cholesterol 20mg; Calcium 34mg; Fibre 0.2g; Sodium 22mg.
Dairy-free: Energy 93kcal/390kJ; Protein 2.3g; Carbohydrate 17.9g, of which sugars 2.7g; Fat 1.4g, of which saturates 0.4g; Cholesterol 39mg; Calcium 8mg; Fibre 0.2g; Sodium 16mg.

Yorkshire pudding batter

This popover batter puffs up as it cooks to make light and fluffy puddings. Make sure that the tray and oil are really hot, and give the batter a good stir just before your pour it into the tins, as it will separate during standing due to the lack of gluten.

MAKES 8

75g/3oz/¾ cup gluten-free plain/all-purpose flour blend
50g/2oz/½ cup cornflour/starch
1.5ml/¼ tsp salt
3 eggs
120ml/4fl oz/½ cup milk
oil or white vegetable fat, for greasing

1 Preheat the oven to 220°C/425°F/Gas 7.

2 Sift the flour, cornflour/starch and salt into a bowl, make a well in the middle and break the eggs into it.

3 Make up the milk to 150ml/¼ pint/⅔ cup with cold water. Add half of the milk and water and gradually whisk into the flour. Add the rest and whisk to make a smooth batter. Leave to stand for 5 minutes.

4 Meanwhile, grease eight 10cm/4in Yorkshire pudding tins or muffin pans and put on the top shelf of the preheated oven for 5 minutes, until very hot.

5 Give the batter a good stir, then immediately pour it into the hot tins, making sure that the holes are no more than half full. Cook for 15 minutes, then reduce the heat to 200°C/400°F/Gas 6 and cook for a further 5 minutes, or until crisp and dark golden brown.

TOAD-IN-THE-HOLE

Gluten free

The mixture for this British classic is slightly thinner than the one used for Yorkshire puddings, creating a rich, pillowy batter that puffs up round the sausages.

SERVES 6

190g/6½oz/1⅔ cups gluten-free plain/all-purpose flour blend
1.5ml/¼ tsp salt
3 eggs, beaten
150ml/¼ pint/⅔ cup milk
30ml/2 tbsp oil
500g/18oz gluten-free sausages

1 Preheat the oven to 220°C/425°F/Gas 7. Put the flour and salt in a bowl, make a well and add the eggs.

2 Mix the milk with 150ml/¼ pint/⅔ cup cold water. Using a whisk, gradually stir the liquid into the flour mixture, until smooth. Leave to stand.

3 Pour the oil into a sturdy roasting pan and add the sausages (cut in half crosswise if they're large). Put into the hot oven and cook for 10 minutes, until the oil is very hot and the sausages begin to brown.

4 Stir the batter and quickly pour it around the sausages, and return to the oven.

5 Cook for about 45 minutes, or until the batter is puffed up, set and golden brown. Serve immediately.

Pudding: Energy 96kcal/403kJ; Protein 3.8g; Carbohydrate 14g, of which sugars 0.7g; Fat 2.9g, of which saturates 0.9g; Cholesterol 88mg; Calcium 32mg; Fibre 0.1g; Sodium 41mg.
Toad: Energy 459kcal/1909kJ; Protein 16.1g; Carbohydrate 34.5g, of which sugars 3.6g; Fat 28.7g, of which saturates 9.4g; Cholesterol 167mg; Calcium 133mg; Fibre 0.3g; Sodium 868mg.

Batter for deep-frying

From fritters and fried fish to tempura and dumplings, batters crop up in many guises. The main differences between them are the type and quantity of liquid used, whether milk or water, and the inclusion, or not, of eggs. This recipe is for fish, but the batter can be used with many other foods, too. Ready-mixed gluten-free flour is best here.

SERVES 4

115g/4oz/1 cup gluten-free self-raising/self-rising flour blend
150ml/¼ pint/⅔ cup water
vegetable oil, for deep-frying
675g/1½lb skinned fish fillet, cut into four pieces
salt and ground black pepper, to taste

1 Stir the flour and a pinch of salt together in a bowl, then make a well in the middle.

2 Gradually whisk in the water to make a smooth batter. Leave for 30 minutes.

3 Heat the oil in a deep-fat fryer or large heavy pan to 190°C/375°F (do not over-fill). A piece of gluten-free bread will sizzle and turn golden when hot enough.

4 Season the pieces of fish with salt and pepper. Stir the batter, then dip the fish into it, one piece at a time, allowing the excess to drain off.

5 Working in two batches if necessary, carefully lower the fish into the hot oil using a long-handled spatula or tongs, and fry for 6–8 minutes, until crisp and brown. Drain the fish on kitchen paper and keep warm.

Variation

For a richer batter, reduce the volume of water to 120ml/4fl oz/½ cup and whisk 1 egg into the flour before you add the water.

TEMPURA BATTER

Gluten free • Dairy free

This enriched batter is ideal for coating vegetable strips, as here, or prawns, shrimp and small fish.

SERVES 4

250g/9oz/2¼ cups gluten-free plain/all-purpose flour blend
2 egg yolks
500ml/17fl oz/2¼ cups iced water
5ml/1 tsp salt
2 aubergines/eggplants, cut into batons
2 red bell peppers, seeded and cut into batons
vegetable oil, for deep-frying

1 Preheat the oil in a wok or deep-fryer to 190°C/375°F.

2 Set aside 30ml/2 tbsp of the flour. Put the egg yolks in a large bowl and beat in the water. Tip in the remaining flour with the salt and stir briefly together – the mixture should resemble thick pancake batter but be lumpy and not properly mixed. If it is too thick, add a little more water. Do not leave to stand.

3 Dust the vegetable batons with the reserved flour, then dip a few into the batter. Carefully lower into the hot oil. Cook for 3–4 minutes, until golden and crisp, then drain. Repeat with the remaining batons.

Plain: Energy 553kcal/2297kJ; Protein 27.6g; Carbohydrate 19.3g, of which sugars 0g; Fat 41.1g, of which saturates 5.5g; Cholesterol 0mg; Calcium 83mg; Fibre 1g; Sodium 300mg.
Tempura: Energy 410kcal/1706kJ; Protein 6g; Carbohydrate 56.4g, of which sugars 6.2g; Fat 17.9g, of which saturates 2.7g; Cholesterol 101mg; Calcium 25mg; Fibre 4.3g; Sodium 9mg.

Buckwheat blinis with mushroom caviar

Buckwheat flour is traditionally used to make these tasty little blinis, used here in combination with gluten-free bread flour for lightness both in terms of flavour and texture.

SERVES 4

For the blinis

115g/4oz/1 cup bought gluten-free white bread flour blend or home-made white bread flour blend (see page 42)
50g/2oz/½ cup buckwheat flour
5ml/1 tsp easy-blend/rapid rise dried yeast
300ml/½ pint/1¼ cups milk
2 eggs, separated
oil, for greasing

For the 'caviar'

350g/12oz mixed wild mushrooms, such as chanterelle and porcini, trimmed and chopped
5ml/1 tsp celery salt
30ml/2 tbsp walnut oil
15ml/1 tbsp lemon juice
45ml/3 tbsp chopped fresh parsley
200ml/7fl oz gluten-free sour cream
freshly ground black pepper

1 To make the 'caviar', place the mushrooms in a glass bowl, toss with the celery salt and cover with a weighted plate. Leave for 2 hours until the juices have run out. Rinse the mushrooms, then drain and press out as much liquid as you can. Return to the bowl and toss with the oil, lemon juice, parsley and pepper. Chill.

2 Sift the flours into a large mixing bowl. Sprinkle over the yeast and stir in, then make a well in the middle. Heat the milk until lukewarm, pour into the flour, add the egg yolks and stir to make a smooth batter.

3 Cover with a clean damp dish towel and leave in a warm place for 1 hour.

4 Whisk the egg whites in a clean grease-free bowl until stiff, then fold into the risen batter.

5 Heat an iron pan or heavy griddle to a moderate temperature. Lightly grease with vegetable oil, then drop spoonfuls of the batter on to the surface. When bubbles rise to the top of each pancake, turn them over and cook briefly on the other side.

6 Spoon the mushroom caviar on top of the blinis, top with sour cream and a grind of pepper, and serve.

Energy 390kcal/1623kJ; Protein 11.8g; Carbohydrate 39.4g, of which sugars 5.7g; Fat 21.1g, of which saturates 8.7g; Cholesterol 150mg; Calcium 160mg; Fibre 2g; Sodium 99mg.

Potato & dill pancakes

Made with mashed potato and just a little gluten-free flour to bind, these pancakes are lifted by the addition of whipped egg whites, and flavoured with aromatic dill.

SERVES 6

275g/10oz peeled potatoes
2 eggs, separated
150ml/¼ pint/⅔ cup milk
40g/1½oz/⅓ cup gluten-free plain/all-purpose flour blend
30ml/2 tbsp chopped fresh dill
oil or butter, for greasing
salt and ground black pepper, to taste
gluten-free sour cream mixed with wholegrain mustard, to serve

1 Cut the potatoes into chunks and cook them in boiling salted water for about 15 minutes, or until tender, then drain and mash to form a smooth purée.

2 Put the potato purée in a bowl and beat in the egg yolks, milk and flour with a wooden spoon to make a batter. Season to taste with salt and pepper and whisk in the chopped dill, reserving a little for a garnish.

3 Whisk the egg whites in a clean bowl to stiff peaks, then gently fold into the potato mixture.

4 Heat a non-stick frying pan over a medium heat and grease it with a little oil or butter.

5 Spoon about 30ml/2 tbsp of batter into the pan to make a pancake, measuring about 7.5cm/3in across. Cook for 3–4 minutes, until the underside is set and golden brown.

6 Turn the pancake over and cook the other side for 3–4 minutes, until golden brown. Transfer to a plate and keep warm while you make the remaining pancakes in batches. Serve with a mustard sour cream, and dill.

Energy 66kcal/282kJ; Protein 2.3g; Carbohydrate 13.7g, of which sugars 1.9g; Fat 0.7g, of which saturates 0.3g; Cholesterol 17mg; Calcium 42mg; Fibre 0.9g; Sodium 16mg.

Gluten free

Tapioca pancakes

Tapioca flour can be used to make a thin, chewy pancake, delicious served with a butter or dairy-free spread, and salt.

SERVES 6
450g/1lb/4 cups tapioca flour
285ml/9fl oz/1 cup plus 2 tbsp water
butter or spread and salt, to serve

Cook's tip
These are delicate, and can become brittle as they cool, so are not suitable for wrapping round fillings.

1 Put the tapoica flour in a bowl and drizzle half the water over it. Use your hands to mix, breaking up any large clumps. Gradually add the rest of the water, mixing in the same way.

2 Push the mixture, a little at a time, through a strainer. The result should look like grated Parmesan cheese.

3 Heat a small heavy non-stick frying pan over a low heat. Sprinkle a thin, even layer of the batter over the base of the pan, leaving no gaps or holes.

4 Cook for 1 minute, then lift the edges of the pancake with a spatula and shake the pan to loosen it from the bottom. Turn over or flip the pancake and cook the other side for 1 minute.

5 Slide the pancake on to a plate, spread generously with butter or other spread if you like, and sprinkle with salt. Roll up and serve straight away; they are a good accompaniment to a stew or other moist dish.

Gluten free • Dairy free • Vegan

Teff pancakes

These Ethiopian fermented pancakes are made from teff flour with the addition of sorghum flour to soften and lighten the flavour.

SERVES 4
175g/6oz/1½ cups teff flour
50g/2oz/½ cup sorghum flour
5ml/1 tsp easy-blend/rapid-rise dried yeast
2.5ml/½ tsp salt
600ml/1 pint/2½ cups cold water
75ml/5 tbsp near-boiling water

1 Sift the flours into a large mixing bowl. Stir in the yeast and salt, then make a hollow in the middle.

2 Pour half of the cold water into the hollow, then whisk in the flour to make a smooth batter. Gradually whisk in the rest of the cold water. Cover and leave at room temperature for 48 hours, until it smells sour.

3 Carefully tip away the watery liquid that has formed on top of the thicker batter. Stir the batter: it should be bubbly and slightly puffy. Transfer 75ml/5 tbsp to a bowl, add the near-boiling water and whisk well. Pour this warm mixture back into the rest of the batter, mix well, then leave to stand for a further 20 minutes.

4 Heat a large non-stick frying pan over a medium heat. Ladle in enough batter to cover the surface with a thin layer. Cover with a lid and steam for about 3 minutes, until the surface is covered with tiny bubbles and is just dry. Remove to a plate and keep warm while you make the remaining pancakes, then serve immediately.

Tapioca Energy 269kcal/1148kJ; Protein 0.3g; Carbohydrate 71.3g, of which sugars 0g; Fat 0.1g, of which saturates 0g; Cholesterol 0mg; Calcium 6mg; Fibre 0.4g; Sodium 3mg.
Teff Energy 207kcal/865kJ; Protein 5g; Carbohydrate 47.8g, of which sugars 0.2g; Fat 0.9g, of which saturates 0g; Cholesterol 0mg; Calcium 8mg; Fibre 1.6g; Sodium 247mg.

Pancake roll with spinach

This stuffed pancake is made from a basic batter of gluten-free flour, milk, egg and butter, which is then baked in a thin layer in the oven rather than in a pan, before being filled with wilted spinach and rolled up like a roulade. Grated cheese works well as a garnish.

SERVES 4

For the batter

2 eggs
100ml/3½fl oz/scant ½ cup milk
50g/2oz/½ cup gluten-free plain/all-purpose flour blend
5ml/1 tsp gluten-free baking powder

For the filling

50g/2oz/¼ cup butter
500g/18oz fresh or frozen spinach
1.5ml/¼ tsp grated nutmeg
salt and ground black pepper
freshly grated Parmesan cheese, to garnish

1 Preheat the oven to 180°C/350°F/Gas 4. Beat the eggs and milk together in a mixing bowl.

2 Sift the flour, 5ml/1 tsp salt and the baking powder into a large mixing bowl, then add the egg and milk mixture and whisk together until smooth. Leave to stand for a few minutes.

3 Cut a piece of baking parchment so that it is slightly bigger than a 25cm x 35cm/10in x 14in shallow baking tin/pan, and position in the tin. Melt a tablespoon of the butter and brush all over the baking parchment.

4 Stir the batter as it will have settled during standing, then pour it into the tin and spread evenly. Bake in the preheated oven for about 20 minutes, until set.

5 Meanwhile, cook the spinach in only the water clinging to its leaves after washing, for 5 minutes until wilted, or until thawed if using frozen spinach. Drain well and squeeze out as much water as possible with your hands. Chop the spinach slightly.

6 Melt the remaining butter in a pan, then add to the chopped spinach. Mix together and season with the nutmeg, salt and pepper.

7 Spread the spinach across the baked pancake. Roll the pancake up like a roulade and cut into thick slices before serving. Garnish with cheese.

Variation

For a dairy-free version, use rice or almond milk instead of dairy milk, dairy-free margarine instead of butter, and vegan ready-grated cheese.

Energy 225kcal/933kJ; Protein 8.8g; Carbohydrate 13.3g, of which sugars 3.2g; Fat 15.2g, of which saturates 7.9g; Cholesterol 144mg; Calcium 262mg; Fibre 3.6g; Sodium 304mg.

Rice-wrapper summer rolls

These delightful rolls are made with naturally gluten-free rice wrappers, which are filled with crunchy raw summer vegetables and fresh herbs to create a light and refreshing snack or appetizer. Serve with a gluten-free dipping sauce of your choice.

SERVES 4

12 home-made (see page 128) or store-bought rice wrappers
1 lettuce, leaves separated
2–3 carrots, cut into julienne strips
1 small cucumber, peeled, seeded, and cut into julienne strips
3 spring onions/scallions, trimmed and cut into julienne strips
225g/8oz mung beansprouts
1 bunch of fresh mint leaves, roughly chopped
1 bunch of fresh coriander/cilantro leaves, roughly chopped
dipping sauce, to serve (see Cook's Tips)

1 If using bought rice wrappers (home-made ones don't need dampening), pour some lukewarm water into a shallow dish and soak the wrappers, two or three at a time, for about 5 minutes, until pliable. Place on a clean dish towel and cover with a second dish towel to keep them moist.

2 Work with one wrapper at a time. Place a lettuce leaf towards the edge nearest to you, leaving about 2.5cm/1in to fold over. Place a mixture of the vegetables on top, followed by some fresh mint and coriander.

3 Fold the edge nearest to you over the filling, tuck in the sides, and roll tightly to the edge on the far side. Place the filled roll on a plate and cover with clear film or plastic wrap, so it doesn't dry out. Repeat with the remaining rice wrappers and vegetables.

4 Serve with a dipping sauce of your choice. If you are making these rolls ahead of time, keep them in the fridge under a damp dish towel, so they stay moist.

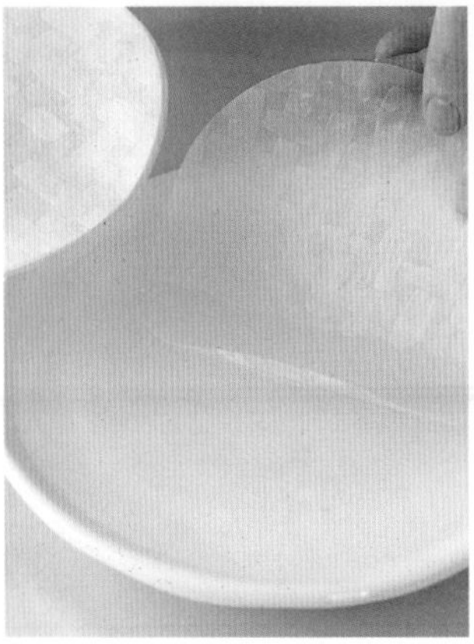

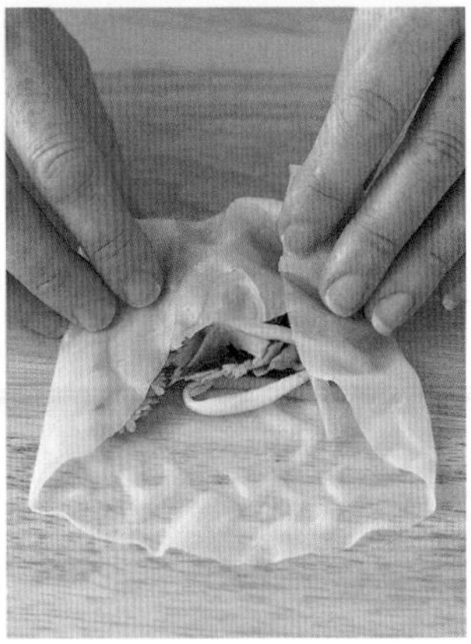

Cook's tips

- In Vietnam, these crunchy filled rolls are often served with a light peanut dipping sauce, whereas in Cambodia, they are accompanied by a dipping sauce called tuk trey (also the name of the national fish sauce), which is similar to the Vietnamese dipping sauce called nuoc cham, except that it has chopped peanuts in it. Check the bottles to ensure they are gluten free. The rolls are also delicious with any dipping sauce.
- Rice wrappers can be bought in Chinese and South-east Asian markets, but do check that they are not made in a factory that handles gluten products.

Energy 159kcal/668kJ; Protein 6g; Carbohydrate 31.9g, of which sugars 6.3g; Fat 1.1g, of which saturates 0.1g; Cholesterol 0mg; Calcium 102mg; Fibre 5g; Sodium 25mg.

Vietnamese spring rolls

Immensely popular, freshly fried spring rolls are very moreish, especially when dipped in a piquant sauce. The rice wrappers are gluten free, and you can tweak the filling to suit your palate, adding more or less seasoning and varying the vegetables.

SERVES 4

12 home-made (see page 128) or store-bought rice wrappers
25g/1oz dried bean thread/ cellophane noodles, soaked in warm water
15g/½oz dried cloud ear/ wood ear mushrooms, soaked in warm water for 15 minutes
1 egg
15ml/1 tbsp gluten-free nuoc cham (a Vietnamese dipping sauce)
1 garlic clove, crushed
5ml/1 tsp palm or soft light brown sugar
2 spring onions/scallions, finely sliced
150g/5oz/1½ cups minced/ ground pork
75g/3oz/¾ cup cooked crab meat or raw prawns/shrimp
salt and ground black pepper
vegetable oil, for deep-frying
sliced fresh chilli and gluten-free Thai fish sauce, to serve

1 If using bought wrappers (home-made don't need dampening), pour some lukewarm water into a dish and soak the wrappers, two or three at a time, for about 5 minutes, until pliable. Place on a clean dish towel and cover with a second towel to keep them moist.

2 To make the filling, drain and squeeze dry the soaked noodles and mushrooms and chop into small pieces.

3 Beat the egg in a bowl. Stir in the nuoc cham, garlic and sugar. Add the spring onions, noodles, mushrooms, pork, and crab meat or prawns. Season well with salt and ground black pepper.

4 Take one wrapper and spoon about 15ml/1 tbsp of the filling on one side, just in from the edge. Fold the nearest edge over the filling, fold over the sides, tucking them in, then roll the whole wrapper into a tight cylinder. Place on a plate and cover with clear film or plastic wrap to keep it moist. Continue making rolls in the same way, using the remaining wrappers and filling.

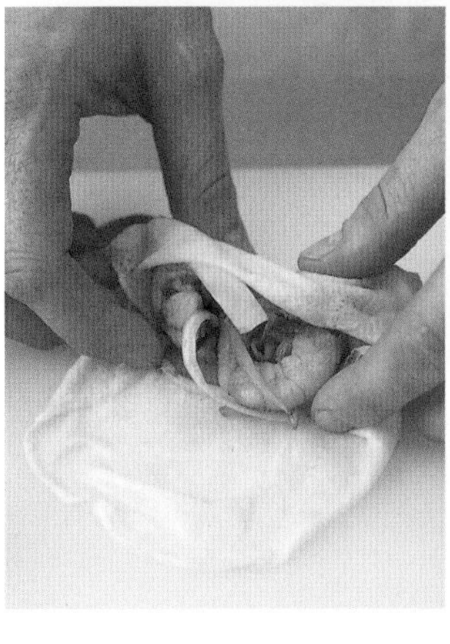

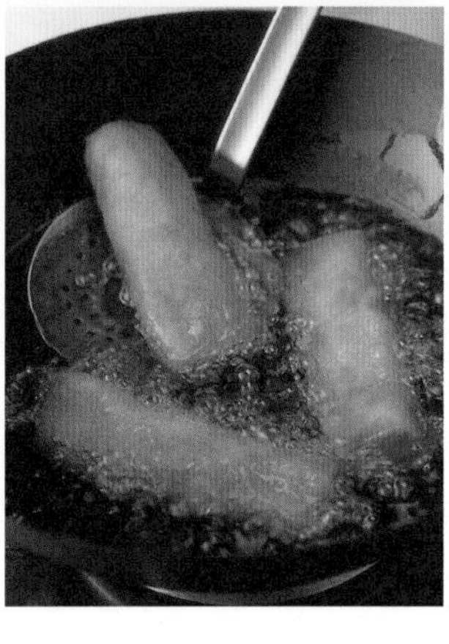

5 Heat oil for deep-frying in a wok or heavy pan (do not over-fill). Make sure it is hot enough by dropping in a piece of (gluten-free) bread; it should sizzle. Cook the rolls in batches, turning so that they are golden all over.

6 Drain them on kitchen paper and serve immediately with sliced fresh chilli and fish sauce for dipping.

Energy 389kcal/1621kJ; Protein 15.5g; Carbohydrate 29.9g, of which sugars 1.8g; Fat 23.1g, of which saturates 3.9g; Cholesterol 96mg; Calcium 21mg; Fibre 1.7g; Sodium 131mg.

Filled rice flour pancakes

These pancakes are made with a combination of three gluten-free flours to achieve the correct structure, texture and taste. Don't be daunted by the long list of spices for the filling; it is quick and easy to make and you can use leftover cooked potatoes to save time.

MAKES 8

600g/1½lb floury potatoes, such as Maris Piper or King Edward
60ml/4 tbsp sunflower oil or light olive oil
2.5ml/½ tsp black mustard seeds
2.5ml/½ tsp cumin seeds
1.25ml/¼ tsp fenugreek seeds
1 large onion, finely sliced
1–3 fresh green or red chillies, finely chopped (seeded if liked)
2.5ml/½ tsp ground turmeric
5ml/1 tsp ground coriander
5ml/1 tsp ground cumin
5ml/1 tsp salt, or to taste
30ml/2 tbsp fresh coriander/cilantro or parsley leaves, finely chopped

For the batter

115g/4oz/1 cup fine polenta/cornmeal
115g/4oz/⅔ cup rice flour
75g/3oz/⅔ cup gluten-free plain/all-purpose flour blend
2.5ml/½ tsp salt, or to taste
150g/5oz/⅔ cup natural/plain yogurt
450ml/16fl oz/2 cups water
10ml/2 tsp oil, for frying

Variation

You could substitute the potato with sweet potato or parsnip for a sweet and spicy alternative.

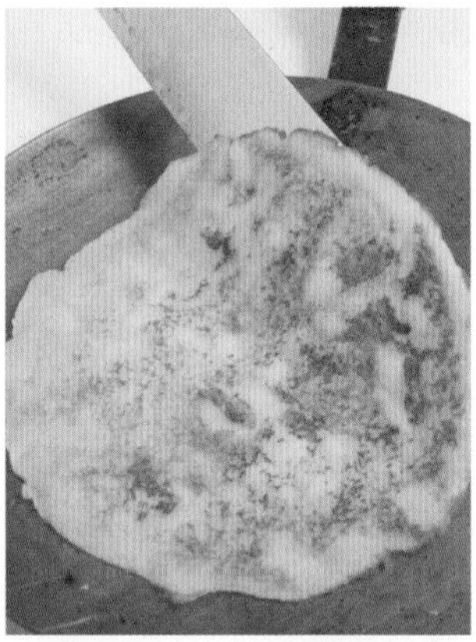

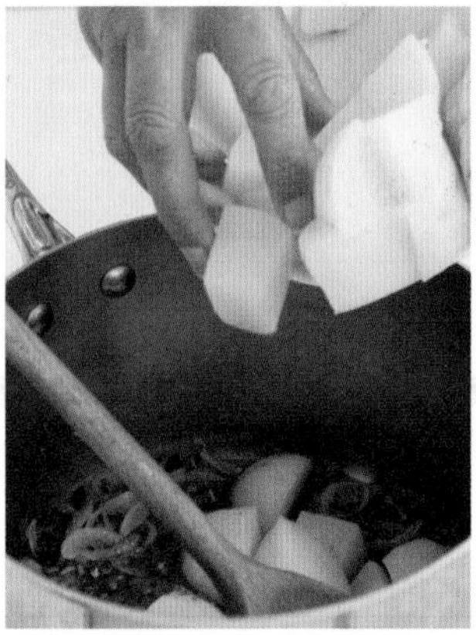

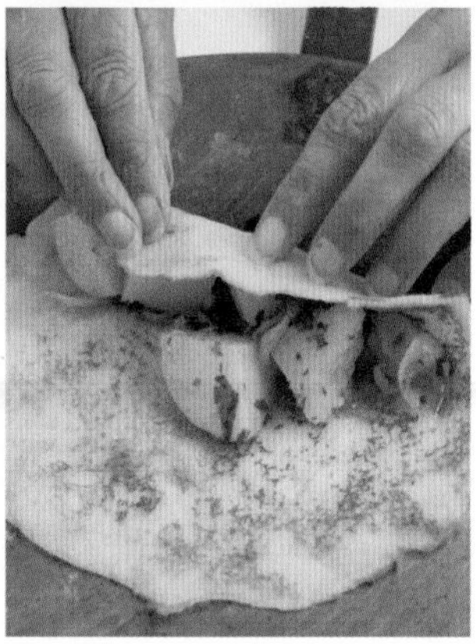

1 For the filling, boil the potatoes (in their skins to stop them going mushy), until just soft. Cool, peel and cut them into 2.5cm/1in cubes.

2 Meanwhile, to make the pancakes, combine all the dry batter ingredients thoroughly in a large mixing bowl. Make a well in the middle.

3 Beat the yogurt in a bowl until smooth, then blend with the water. Gradually add the blended yogurt to the dry ingredients, beating well.

4 Place a heavy non-stick griddle (23cm/9in wide) or frying pan over a medium heat and add 10ml/2 tsp oil. Brush the oil quickly all over the surface and allow to heat up for a few minutes.

5 Using a measuring cup, pour about 125ml/4fl oz/½ cup of the pancake batter on to the griddle, spread it quickly and evenly and let the mixture set for 2 minutes.

6 Sprinkle 15ml/1 tbsp water around the edges, wait for 15–20 seconds, then turn the pancake over with a metal spatula or a fish slice. Cook for a further 2–3 minutes or until brown patches appear underneath. Cook the remaining pancakes in the same way and place on a wire rack in a single layer.

7 Return to the filling. Heat the 60ml/4 tbsp oil in a saucepan over a medium heat. When hot, but not smoking, add the mustard, cumin and fenugreek seeds. Add the onion and chillies and stir-fry for 8–9 minutes or until the onion is a light golden colour. Add the turmeric, coriander and cumin. Cook for 1 minute.

8 Add the potatoes and salt and stir until the potatoes are heated through. Stir in the fresh coriander. Remove from the heat and divide into eight equal portions.

9 Place the griddle used to cook the pancakes over a low heat. Lay a pancake on it, put a portion of the filling on one side, roll it up and heat for 1 minute. Place the pancake in a very low oven while you finish making the rest; do not leave them too long or they will dry out.

Energy 245kcal/1025kJ; Protein 4.2g; Carbohydrate 41.1g, of which sugars 1g; Fat 7.4g, of which saturates 0.9g; Cholesterol 25mg; Calcium 20mg; Fibre 1.9g; Sodium 11mg.

Vegetable fritters

These light and crunchy vegetable fritters are made with a gluten-free batter to which cornflour has been added to ensure a crisp result. Simple to prepare and easy to cook, serve them with sweet chilli sauce if you don't have the soy sauce dip ingredients to hand.

SERVES 4–6

1 potato, thinly sliced
1 small carrot, thinly sliced
½ small white onion, sliced
½ courgette/zucchini, sliced
1 fresh chilli, seeded and sliced
salt and ground black pepper, to taste
vegetable oil, for frying

For the batter

115g/4oz/1 cup gluten-free plain/all-purpose flour blend
45ml/3 tbsp cornflour/starch
1 egg, beaten
250ml/8fl oz/1 cup water
5ml/1 tsp salt

For the dip

30ml/2 tbsp gluten-free soy sauce
15ml/1 tbsp water
15ml/1 tbsp Chinese white radish (daikon), grated
5ml/1 tsp vinegar
5ml/1 tsp sesame seeds

1 To make the batter, sift the flour and cornflour into a bowl. Make a well in the middle.

2 Blend the egg, water and salt with a wire whisk until smooth, then pour into the well and gradually work in the flour mixture until it combines to form a smooth batter. The batter should be thick enough to hold the vegetables together but to still pour slowly from a ladle.

3 Place the potato, carrot, onion, courgette and chilli in a bowl. Mix together, then pour in the batter and mix it into the vegetables, adding a small amount of seasoning.

4 For the dip, combine the soy sauce, water, grated radish, vinegar and sesame seeds in a bowl. Set aside.

5 Heat a little vegetable oil in a frying pan or wok over a medium heat. Ladle three or four small portions of the fritter mixture into the pan (depending on the size of pan) and cook until they are set and golden brown underneath. Turn and cook the fritters on the second side until they are golden.

6 Drain the fritters on kitchen paper and keep hot in a warm oven. Cook the remaining fritter mixture in the same way.

7 Divide the dipping sauce among small individual dishes. Serve the hot fritters on platters with the dishes of dipping sauce alongside.

Energy 217kcal/908kJ; Protein 3.3g; Carbohydrate 30.6g, of which sugars 3.3g; Fat 9.4g, of which saturates 1.4g; Cholesterol 50mg; Calcium 24mg; Fibre 1.8g; Sodium 386mg.

Onion bhajis

Bhajis are extremely popular all over the world, and are quick to rustle up. These classic onion ones are coated in a gram and rice flour batter, seasoned with all sorts of aromatic spices and pepped up with fresh chilli, but you can play with the spices to suit your palate.

SERVES 4–6

2 fresh green chillies, chopped (seeded if preferred)
450g/1lb onions, sliced into half rings and separated
15ml/1 tbsp fresh coriander/cilantro leaves and stalks, finely chopped
sunflower oil or light olive oil, for deep-frying
gluten-free chutney of your choice, to serve (optional)

For the batter

150g/5oz/1¼ cups gram flour
25g/1oz rice flour
5ml/1 tsp salt, or to taste
a pinch of bicarbonate of soda/baking soda
2.5ml/½ tsp ground turmeric
5ml/1 tsp ground cumin
5ml/1 tsp cumin seeds
2.5ml/½ tsp asafoetida
200ml/7fl oz/¾ cup water

1 For the batter, sift the gram flour into a large mixing bowl and add the rice flour, salt, bicarbonate of soda, turmeric, ground cumin, cumin seeds and asafoetida.

2 Mix these dry ingredients together thoroughly. Gradually pour in the water and mix until a thick batter is formed.

3 Add the chillies, onion rings and coriander, and stir until all the ingredients are well coated with the batter.

4 Heat the oil in a pan suitable for deep-frying (don't over-fill) over a medium heat until it reaches 180°C/350°F on a thermometer, or drop about ¼ teaspoon of the batter into the hot oil and if it floats up to the surface immediately without turning brown, then the oil is at the right temperature for deep-frying.

5 Carefully lower about a tablespoon of the onion batter mixture at a time into the hot oil. Keep to a single layer and avoid overcrowding the pan as this will lower the temperature of the oil and the bhajis will not crisp up.

6 Reduce the heat slightly and continue to cook until the bhajis are golden brown and crisp. This should take 8–10 minutes. Remove to kitchen paper to drain and repeat the process with the remaining batter until it is all used up.

7 Serve the onion bhajis on their own or with a chutney of your choice.

Energy 338kcal/1413kJ; Protein 12.3g; Carbohydrate 30.8g, of which sugars 4.3g; Fat 18.4g, of which saturates 2.1g; Cholesterol 0mg; Calcium 124mg; Fibre 9.3g; Sodium 284mg.

Cheesy fish goujons in beer batter

This gluten-free batter incorporates beer, which creates a light and crisp coating for fried fish, with or without the cheese. It is important to check the lager brand is gluten free but these are readily available, or you can also use sparkling water.

SERVES 4

375g/13oz white fish, such as plaice or sole fillets, cod or haddock
a little cornflour/starch
salt and ground black pepper
vegetable oil, for deep-frying
dill and lemon wedges, to garnish

For the batter

75g/3oz/¾ cup gluten-free plain/ all-purpose flour blend
25g/1oz/¼ cup freshly grated Parmesan cheese
5ml/1 tsp bicarbonate of soda/ baking soda
pinch of salt
1 egg, separated
150ml/¼ pint/⅔ cup ice-cold gluten-free lager or sparkling water
90ml/6 tbsp ice-cold water

For the sour cream dip

60ml/4 tbsp gluten-free sour cream
60ml/4 tbsp gluten-free mayonnaise
2.5ml/½ tsp grated lemon rind
30ml/2 tbsp chopped gherkins and/or capers
15ml/1 tbsp chopped fresh dill
salt and ground black pepper

1 To make the dip, mix everything together, then chill in the fridge until required.

2 To make the batter, sift the flour into a bowl. Mix in the other dry ingredients, make a well in the middle, then whisk in the egg yolk and the lager or sparkling water to give a thick, smooth batter. Slowly whisk in the 90ml/6 tbsp iced water. Chill for a few minutes.

3 Meanwhile, skin the fish and cut into thin strips of similar length. Dip the fish lightly in seasoned cornflour.

4 Heat about 7.5cm/3in oil in a large, heavy pan. Whisk the egg white for the batter until stiff and gently fold into the batter, until just blended.

5 Stir the batter, then dip in the floured fish, drain off any excess and drop the fish gently into the hot fat.

6 Cook the fish in batches, so that the goujons don't stick to one another, for 3–4 minutes, turning once. When the batter is golden and crisp, remove the fish with a slotted spoon. Place the goujons on kitchen paper on a plate and keep warm while cooking the rest.

7 Serve hot, garnished with sprigs of dill and accompanied by the sour cream dip and lemon wedges.

Energy 338kcal/1406kJ; Protein 21.5g; Carbohydrate 15.6g, of which sugars 0.7g; Fat 21g, of which saturates 5.7g; Cholesterol 133mg; Calcium 132mg; Fibre 0.2g; Sodium 239mg.

Tempura butterflied prawns

Japanese tempura batter is gluten free, light and crisp, and thin enough to allow you to see the pink prawns. It can also be used to coat baby vegetables, but you should lightly cook them first. Make sure the water you use is well chilled, as this stops foods from absorbing too much oil.

SERVES 4

16 large prawns/shrimp
vegetable oil, for deep-frying
gluten-free dipping sauce, to serve

For the batter

40g/1½oz/⅓ cup rice flour
40g/1½oz/⅓ cup cornflour/starch
2.5ml/½ tsp gluten-free baking powder
75ml/2½fl oz/⅓ cup ice-cold water, preferably sparkling, or soda water

1 Clean the prawns and shell them, removing the heads but leaving the tails intact. Using a sharp knife, slit each prawn lengthways halfway through the back, then spread them flat so that they resemble butterflies. Remove the black intestinal tract.

2 Mix the flour, cornflour and baking powder in a bowl. Make a small hollow in the middle, pour in the water and stir to make a smooth batter.

3 Heat the oil in a wok or deep-fryer to 190°C/375°F. Dip each prawn in turn in the batter, gently shaking off the excess, and add to the hot oil. Repeat with more prawns, but do not overcrowd the wok or fryer.

4 After 2–3 minutes, when the prawns are golden brown, lift them out and drain on kitchen paper. Keep them warm while you cook successive batches. Serve hot, with the dipping sauce.

Energy 184kcal/769kJ; Protein 9.5g; Carbohydrate 17.2g, of which sugars 0g; Fat 8.7g, of which saturates 1g; Cholesterol 98mg; Calcium 44mg; Fibre 0.3g; Sodium 101mg.

Veggie toad-in-the-hole

A gluten-free batter is used to create this family favourite, presented here as a vegetarian version though the batter works for any toad-in-the-hole. You could of course buy ready-made sausages but making them yourself ensures they are gluten free.

SERVES 4

For the sausages

250g/9oz firm tofu, drained
150g/5oz/2½ cups gluten-free fresh breadcrumbs (see page 18)
½ small onion, coarsely chopped
small bunch of fresh parsley, thyme, sage or rosemary, finely chopped, or 10ml/2 tsp dried herbs
5ml/1 tsp gluten-free Dijon mustard
5ml/1 tsp gluten-free soy sauce
1 egg
salt and ground black pepper, to taste

For the gravy

30ml/2 tbsp vegetable oil
1kg/2¼lb onions, thinly sliced
105ml/7 tbsp red or dry white wine or water
300ml/½ pint/1¼ cups vegetable stock
small bunch fresh thyme, woody stems removed, chopped (optional)

For the batter

115g/4oz/1 cup gluten-free plain/all-purpose flour blend
75g/3oz/⅔ cup cornflour/starch
3 eggs, beaten
175ml/6fl oz/¾ cup milk
salt and ground black pepper, to taste

1 For the vegetarian sausages, put all the ingredients in a food processor and process to a thick paste. Scrape out the mixture and divide it into eight portions. Roll them into sausage shapes with your hands. The mixture will be slightly wet, but will form the shape quite easily.

2 Put the sausages on a large plate in a single layer, cover with clear film or plastic wrap and chill in the fridge until required.

3 To make the onion gravy, heat the oil in a large non-stick frying pan. Add the onions and cook over a medium heat for 5 minutes, until beginning to turn golden. Reduce the heat to its lowest setting, cover the pan, then cook for 10 minutes, stirring occasionally, until softened and coloured.

4 Add the wine or water and stock and bring to the boil. Add the herbs, if using. Simmer, uncovered, for 10 minutes, until the gravy is reduced and thickened.

5 Meanwhile, preheat the oven to 220°C/425°F/Gas 7. Generously oil a small roasting pan and put in the oven to heat.

6 To make the batter, sift the flour and cornflour into a large mixing bowl and season with salt and pepper. Make a well in the middle, then add the eggs and half of the milk.

7 Gradually stir in the flour until fully incorporated, then beat until smooth. Stir in the remaining milk to make a smooth thick batter.

8 Carefully remove the hot roasting pan from the oven and arrange the sausages in the base in a single layer with a little space between each. Pour in the batter, return the roasting pan to the oven and bake for 40–45 minutes, or until the batter is well risen and a rich golden brown.

9 Serve cut into portions with two sausages each, and accompanied by the onion gravy, and cooked vegetables as you like.

Energy 519kcal/2179kJ; Protein 24.1g; Carbohydrate 71.6g, of which sugars 17.8g; Fat 17.2g, of which saturates 3.4g; Cholesterol 1mg; Calcium 312mg; Fibre 5.9g; Sodium 1044mg.

Apple batter pudding

Also known as clafoutis, this dessert uses a sweet version of a gluten-free Yorkshire pudding or popover batter, and is very quick and simple to put together, as well as being extremely adaptable. Serve with cream whipped with a dash of fruit liqueur, or scoops of vanilla ice cream.

SERVES 4

30ml/2 tbsp sunflower oil
450g/1lb eating apples, peeled, cored and thickly sliced
15ml/1 tbsp gluten-free icing/confectioners' sugar

For the batter

115g/4oz/1 cup gluten-free plain/all-purpose flour blend
2.5ml/½ tsp gluten-free baking powder
pinch of salt
5ml/1 tsp ground cinnamon
50g/2oz/¼ cup caster/superfine sugar
1 egg, beaten
300ml/½ pint/1¼ cups milk

1 Preheat the oven to 220°C/425°F/Gas 7. Pour the oil in a roasting pan, about 25 x 30cm/10 x 12in, and swirl around the base and up the sides to coat evenly.

2 Add the apple slices, spreading them out evenly. Put the pan in the oven for 10 minutes.

3 Meanwhile, make the batter. Sift the flour, baking powder, salt and cinnamon into a large mixing bowl. Stir in the sugar, then make a well in the middle. Add the egg and gradually whisk in the milk to make a smooth batter.

4 Carefully remove the hot pan from the oven and pour the batter over the apples. Return to the pan to the oven and bake for 25–30 minutes, until well risen and dark golden brown.

5 Dust the top of the pudding with icing sugar and serve immediately, while the pudding is still puffy.

Variation

You can use different fruit in place of the apple in this dish, depending on personal preference and availability. Rhubarb (drain off the juice after roasting), pears, plums and cherries are all good choices and should be cooked in the oven as in step 2. You could also use fresh raspberries, blackberries or blueberries (simply add these to the hot pan just before pouring in the batter; don't cook them first). Adjust the sugar in the batter depending on the sweetness of the fruit you use. You will need a little more with fruit such as rhubarb and less with fruits such as raspberries and blueberries. Use soft light brown or coconut sugar if you prefer.

Energy 325kcal/1366kJ; Protein 6.4g; Carbohydrate 56.8g, of which sugars 33.9g; Fat 8.9g, of which saturates 2g; Cholesterol 62mg; Calcium 108mg; Fibre 3g; Sodium 58mg.

Puffed fritters in syrup

These delicious fritters are made with a leavened gluten-free batter that is then fried in a pan, like pancakes, which puff up considerably to make tender little cakes. These are then bathed in an aromatic syrup, but you could just serve them straight from the pan, too.

SERVES 6

For the batter

175g/6oz/1½ cups gluten-free plain/all-purpose flour blend
50g/2oz/½ cup rice flour
pinch of salt
2.5ml/½ tsp easy-blend/rapid rise dried yeast
50ml/¼ pint/⅔ cup warm water
sunflower oil, for frying

For the syrup

225g/8oz/1 cup sugar
150ml/¼ pint/⅔ cup water
30ml/2 tbsp orange blossom water

1 Sift the flour and rice flour into a large mixing bowl. Stir in the salt, sprinkle over the yeast and stir again. Make a well in the middle.

2 Slowly pour the warm water into the well, gradually mixing in the flour as you do so, to make a soft, sticky dough. You may need to add a little more water, depending on your flour, since these vary.

3 Cover the bowl with a damp dish towel or some clear film or plastic wrap, and leave in a warm place for 2 hours or until the dough is bubbly and has risen to twice its original size.

4 Meanwhile, prepare the syrup. Place the sugar and water in a heavy pan over a low heat and slowly bring to the boil, stirring until the sugar has dissolved. Do not stir after this point. Turn up to a medium heat and simmer for about 10 minutes or until the syrup is thick enough to coat the back of a spoon.

5 Remove the pan from the heat and let the syrup cool, leaving the pan uncovered so that any steam can evaporate. When it is nearly cool, stir in the orange blossom water.

6 Heat 15ml/1 tbsp sunflower oil in a non-stick frying pan or skillet. Using two teaspoons, place small blobs of the batter mixture on the surface of the hot pan, spacing them slightly apart to allow room for spreading.

7 Fry the fritters in batches for a few minutes on each side, until golden brown all over, then place on a plate lined with kitchen paper while you cook the remaining batter in the same way.

8 Once they are all cooked, transfer the warm fritters to the pan of syrup to soak for 10–15 minutes.

9 Scoop out the fritters and serve at room temperature with a little of the syrup drizzled over them.

Energy 269kcal/1138kJ; Protein 2g; Carbohydrate 68g, of which sugars 38.1g; Fat 0.5g, of which saturates 0.1g; Cholesterol 0mg; Calcium 23mg; Fibre 0.5g; Sodium 12mg.

Lemon & raisin sorghum pancakes

Making pancakes is a lovely way to start the weekend. Nobody will notice any difference between these and regular pancakes, but there is a nutritional boost from the sorghum flour, with its slow-release energy and micronutrients.

MAKES 16

1 egg
120ml/4fl oz/½ cup plain/natural yogurt
120ml/4fl oz/½ cup milk
115g/4oz/1 cup sorghum flour
15ml/1 tbsp gluten-free baking powder
50g/2oz/¼ cup sugar
grated rind of 1 lemon
25g/1oz raisins
vegetable oil, for frying
butter and maple syrup, to serve

1 Whisk the egg, yogurt and milk in a jug or bowl until combined. Put the flour and baking powder into a large mixing bowl and make a well in the middle.

2 Add the egg mixture to the well and use a whisk to incorporate the flour mixture, a little at a time, to make a smooth batter. Add the sugar and lemon rind. Allow to stand for 20 minutes.

3 When you are ready to cook, pour a little oil into a frying pan or pancake pan and use kitchen paper to spread it evenly over the base.

4 Place the pan over a medium heat, and when hot spoon in enough batter to form two or three pancakes, about 6–7.5cm/2½–3in in diameter.

5 Sprinkle a few raisins on each pancake and cook for 1–2 minutes on each side.

6 When the pancakes are puffed and golden on both sides, remove from the pan, top with a little butter, and keep warm while you cook the remaining batter.

7 Serve the pancakes warm with extra butter, if you wish, and maple syrup poured over.

Energy 71kcal/297kJ; Protein 2.1g; Carbohydrate 9.3g, of which sugars 5.7g; Fat 3.1g, of which saturates 0.5g; Cholesterol 15mg; Calcium 31mg; Fibre 0g; Sodium 19mg.

Quinoa crêpes

Quinoa flour is a lovely pale cream colour with a slightly coarser texture than traditional flour and with a higher protein content. Here, the crêpes are filled with fresh fruit and yogurt, but you could serve them with lemon and sugar or a spoonful of honey or chocolate spread.

MAKES 4

115g/4oz/1 cup quinoa flour
1 large egg
350ml/12fl oz/1½ cups milk or soya milk
30ml/2 tbsp vegetable oil, for frying
strawberries, sliced, and gluten-free thick yogurt, to serve

1 Sift the flour into a large mixing bowl and make a well in the middle. Beat the egg and milk together, then pour the egg mixture into the well and use a whisk to slowly incorporate the flour mixture, a little at a time, to make a smooth batter.

2 Alternatively place all of the ingredients into a bowl or liquidizer and briefly blend with a hand blender or food processor just until smooth.

3 Heat a little of the oil in a frying pan until it is hot but not smoking. Add enough batter to cover the base of the pan, tipping it quickly to ensure that it spreads evenly.

4 Cook over medium heat until the pancake is set and golden underneath, then flip it using a spatula. Cook the other side for a couple of minutes, until golden brown.

5 Add a little more oil to the pan and repeat until all the batter has been used, keeping the cooked pancakes warm in a low oven until ready for serving. Make sure your pan is well oiled before you cook each pancake.

6 Serve the pancakes warm, filled with strawberries and yogurt, or whichever fillings you prefer.

Energy 201kcal/845kJ; Protein 8.8g; Carbohydrate 20.1g, of which sugars 5.9g; Fat 10.1g, of which saturates 2.2g; Cholesterol 63mg; Calcium 136mg; Fibre 0g; Sodium 76mg.

Buckwheat & apple pancakes

These substantial yeasted buckwheat pancakes are lightened with some gluten-free plain flour – in the same way as blinis – and feature a distinctive apple ring that is cooked into the batter. Make sure you use a firm eating variety of apple, so it holds its shape.

SERVES 4

125g/4½oz/1¼ cups buckwheat flour
125g/4½oz/1¼ cups gluten-free plain/all-purpose flour blend
7g/½ tbsp easy-blend/rapid-rise dried yeast
pinch of salt
30ml/2 tbsp sugar
2 eggs, at room temperature
500ml/17fl oz/generous 2 cups milk, buttermilk or an equal mixture of milk and water
oil or butter, for greasing
1 eating apple, cored and cut into 4 thick slices
honey, to serve

1 In a blender, a food processor or by hand, whisk both types of flour with the yeast, a pinch of salt, the sugar, eggs and chosen liquid to make a smooth batter. Pour the batter into a jug or bowl, cover and leave to stand for at least 1 hour.

2 Just before cooking, stir to incorporate any flour that has settled. The batter should be thick but pourable. Set a 24cm/9½in non-stick frying pan over a medium-high heat. When it is hot, grease it with butter or oil.

3 Off the heat, place an apple ring in the middle of the pan, then pour in enough batter to coat the pan. Immediately tilt the pan and swirl the batter to coat the base. Tiny bubbles will form on the surface.

4 Return to the heat and cook for 1–3 minutes, until the surface looks dry and the edges are lightly browned. Run a wide spatula under the pancake to loosen it. Flip it and cook for 30 seconds more, until cooked through. Keep warm while cooking the rest. Serve with honey.

Energy 368kcal/1545kJ; Protein 12.2g; Carbohydrate 68.2g, of which sugars 16.9g; Fat 6.4g, of which saturates 2.4g; Cholesterol 123mg; Calcium 174mg; Fibre 1.8g; Sodium 97mg.

Ricotta-filled crêpes

The basic gluten-free batter for these delicious crêpes is enriched with butter, which adds flavour and depth and makes them beautifully tender. After cooking, they are filled with a creamy ricotta mixture, then returned to the pan to heat through and lightly set the filling.

SERVES 4

For the batter

50g/2oz/¼ cup butter
3 eggs
2.5ml/½ tsp salt
pinch of caster/superfine sugar
200ml/7fl oz/scant 1 cup warm water
185g/6½oz/1⅔ cups gluten-free plain/all-purpose flour blend
350ml/12fl oz/1½ cups milk
vegetable oil, for frying

For the filling

500g/18oz/2½ cups ricotta cheese
2 egg yolks
30ml/2 tbsp caster/superfine sugar, plus extra for dusting
gluten-free sour cream or crème fraîche, to serve

1 Melt the butter in a small pan or in the microwave. Whisk the eggs, salt and sugar together in a large mixing bowl. Add the water, then gradually whisk in the flour.

2 Stir the milk into the egg and flour mixture, a little at a time, and then add the melted butter.

3 Heat a non-stick frying pan over a medium heat. Brush it with a little oil and pour in a thin layer of batter. As soon as the surface has set, turn the crêpe over with a wide spatula and cook the other side.

4 Fry the remaining crêpes in the same way, brushing the pan with oil each time and stacking when cooked.

5 To make the filling, put the ricotta cheese and egg yolks in a bowl and blend together. Sprinkle over the sugar and stir until everything is well mixed.

6 Place 45ml/3 tbsp of the filling in the middle of each crêpe and fold over to create an envelope.

7 Heat the oil in a frying pan. Gently add the crêpe envelopes, join-side down, and fry over a medium heat, for 1–2 minutes. Carefully turn the pancakes over using the wide spatula and fry the other sides for 1–2 minutes, until golden brown all over and the filling is cooked and lightly set.

8 Serve the pancakes hot with sour cream or crème fraîche and a sprinkling of sugar.

Energy 649kcal/2710kJ; Protein 26.3g; Carbohydrate 50.5g, of which sugars 15.2g; Fat 39.4g, of which saturates 19g; Cholesterol 368mg; Calcium 512mg; Fibre 1.9g; Sodium 308mg.

Belgian waffles with fruit

These waffles are famous throughout the world, and make a wonderful breakfast. Recipes vary, but the essential ingredients remain simple: white (gluten-free) flour, yeast and eggs mixed with milk, beer or sparkling water. You will need a special waffle iron to make these.

MAKES 8–10

500g/18oz/5 cups gluten-free plain/all-purpose flour blend
pinch of salt
15ml/1 tbsp easy-blend/rapid-rise dried yeast
30ml/2 tbsp soft light brown sugar or coconut crystals/sugar
8g/⅓oz sachet vanilla sugar or 5ml/1 tsp pure vanilla extract
4 egg yolks and 6 egg whites
500ml/17fl oz/generous 2 cups sparkling water or milk, at room temperature
200g/7oz/scant 1 cup butter, melted and cooled, plus extra for greasing (if required)
gluten-free icing/confectioners' sugar, for dusting
whipped cream and prepared fruit, to serve

1 Sift the flour and salt into a large mixing bowl. Stir in the yeast and sugar, with the vanilla sugar, if using.

2 In a jug or bowl, beat the egg yolks with the sparkling water or milk. Stir in the vanilla extract, if using.

3 Make a well in the middle of the dry ingredients and add the egg yolk mixture. Beat, gradually incorporating the dry ingredients to make a smooth batter. Stir in the melted butter.

4 Whisk the egg whites until stiff peaks form, then carefully fold them into the batter.

5 Cover the bowl with clear film or plastic wrap and leave the mixture in a warm place for 45–60 minutes or until it has doubled in bulk.

6 Preheat a 17 x 9cm/6½ x 3½in waffle iron and grease it if the instruction book says to do so.

7 Pour in batter to the level recommended in your instruction book (generally about three-quarters full) and bake for 4–5 minutes, until golden brown. The cooked waffle should be crisp on the outside and soft and airy inside.

8 When the first batch of waffles is done, place them on a baking tray and keep in a warm oven until you have made the rest.

9 Transfer the warm waffles to plates and dust with icing sugar. Serve with whipped cream and assorted berries and chopped seasonal fruits so everyone can add their own topping.

Energy 368kcal/1531kJ; Protein 5.5g; Carbohydrate 43.2g, of which sugars 3.4g; Fat 19.3g, of which saturates 11.2g; Cholesterol 123mg; Calcium 15mg; Fibre 0.5g; Sodium 161mg.

Sesame & banana fritters

The batter for these vegan fritters is made from rice flour blended with coconut milk and thickened with desiccated coconut and sesame seeds to make a crunchy coating. 'Apple bananas' are used here, but you can also use ordinary small bananas, or other fruits, such as wedges of apple or peach.

SERVES 3–4

50g/2oz/¼ cup desiccated/dry unsweetened shredded coconut
50g/2oz/¼ cup caster/ superfine sugar
5ml/1 tsp ground cinnamon
2.5ml/½ tsp gluten-free baking powder
115g/4oz/1 cup rice flour
30ml/2 tbsp sesame seeds
600ml/1 pint/2½ cups coconut milk
6 small or apple bananas
sunflower oil, for deep-frying
gluten-free icing/confectioners' sugar, to dust
ice cream (dairy free if preferred), to serve, optional

1 Place the desiccated coconut, sugar, cinnamon, baking powder, rice flour, sesame seeds and coconut milk in a large mixing bowl and whisk thoroughly to form a smooth batter.

2 Cover the bowl with clear film or plastic wrap and place in the fridge to rest for 30 minutes to 1 hour.

3 When ready to cook, peel the bananas and carefully slice the flesh in half lengthways. If you are using ordinary large bananas, cut them in half widthways, before halving them lengthways.

4 Fill a wok or deep heavy pan one-third full of sunflower oil and heat to 180°C/350°F (or until a piece of batter, dropped into the oil, browns in 15 seconds).

5 Working in batches, dip the halved bananas into the batter, drain off any excess and gently lower them into the oil. Deep-fry for 3–4 minutes, or until golden.

6 Remove the bananas from the wok using a slotted spoon and drain well on kitchen paper. Repeat until you have deep-fried all of the bananas.

7 Serve hot or warm, dusted with icing sugar, with scoops of vanilla ice cream if you like.

Cook's tip

Apple bananas are exceptionally sweet, which is why they are sometimes known as 'candy apple bananas'. Grown in tropical countries, they have a firm flesh with a pinkish tinge.

Energy 429kcal/1795kJ; Protein 4.8g; Carbohydrate 56.2g, of which sugars 33.1g; Fat 21.1g, of which saturates 8.7g; Cholesterol 0mg; Calcium 111mg; Fibre 6.3g; Sodium 175mg.

Churros with hot chocolate

Churros are long, golden doughnuts made with a stiff batter, piped into lengths which are deep-fried and rolled in sugar while still hot. They are especially delicious served with real hot chocolate, or a chocolate or caramel dipping sauce.

SERVES 4

200g/7oz/1¾ cups gluten-free plain/all-purpose flour blend
150ml/¼ pint/⅔ cup milk
150ml/¼ pint/⅔ cup water
2 eggs, beaten
vegetable oil, for deep-frying
gluten-free icing/confectioners' sugar or regular sugar, for dusting

For the hot chocolate

115g/4oz plain/semisweet chocolate
400ml/14fl oz/1⅔ cups milk

1 To make the churros, sift the flour on to a small sheet of baking parchment. Bring the milk and water to the boil in a pan. Tip in the flour and beat vigorously with a wooden spoon, stirring until the dough forms a ball and no longer sticks to the sides of the pan.

2 Remove the pan from the heat and let the dough cool a little. Gradually beat in the eggs, adding just enough to give a piping consistency. Spoon the mixture into a piping bag fitted with a large fluted nozzle.

3 Preheat the oven to 150°C/300°F/Gas 2. To cook the churros, heat the oil in a deep pan or wok (don't over-fill) until a piece of dough sizzles as soon as it hits the oil. Squeeze the piping bag over the pan, snipping off 10cm/4in lengths of dough with kitchen scissors.

4 Fry the churros in batches of four or so, until golden, then remove them with a slotted spoon, and drain on kitchen paper. Place on a baking tray and keep warm in the oven while you cook the rest in the same way.

5 Once you have finished frying the churros, make the hot chocolate. Melt the chocolate in a heatproof bowl set over a pan of barely simmering water.

6 Bring the milk to the boil in a small pan. When the chocolate has melted, remove it from the heat and stir in a little milk. Now whisk in the remaining milk – a hand-held blender is good for this – until frothy. Pour into mugs.

7 Remove the churros from the oven, roll in sugar, pile into a dish and serve them with the hot chocolate.

Energy 506kcal/2114kJ; Protein 12.4g; Carbohydrate 64.7g, of which sugars 24.6g; Fat 22.7g, of which saturates 8.4g; Cholesterol 125mg; Calcium 192mg; Fibre 1.5g; Sodium 103mg.

Baked ring doughnuts

For those intolerant to gluten, this recipe never fails to please, and they have the added benefit of being baked rather than deep-fried,which means they are slightly healthier than regular doughnuts. These have a chocolate topping, but you could just toss them in sugar.

MAKES 12

non-stick baking oil spray (see Cook's tip) or oil or melted butter, for greasing
100g/3¾oz/scant ½ cup butter, softened
150g/5oz/¾ cup caster/superfine sugar
5ml/1 tsp vanilla extract
2 eggs
300g/11oz/2¾ cups gluten-free plain/all-purpose flour blend
5ml/1 tsp xanthan gum
10ml/2 tsp gluten-free baking powder
pinch of salt
150ml/¼ pint/⅔ cup full-fat/whole milk

For the topping

100g/3¾oz dark/bittersweet chocolate, broken into pieces
100ml/3½fl oz/scant ½ cup golden/light corn syrup
50g/2oz/¼ cup butter

1 Preheat the oven to 180°C/350°F/Gas 4. Spray a 12-cup or two 6-cup doughnut baking pans with non-stick baking oil, or brush with oil.

2 Place the softened butter, sugar and vanilla in a large mixing bowl and beat together with a wooden spoon. Alternatively, you can use a hand-held electric mixer. Whisk in the eggs one at a time, making sure the first is fully incorporated before adding the next.

3 Put the flour, xanthan gum, baking powder and salt in a bowl and stir together to mix well. Sift these dry ingredients into the butter and sugar mixture, then gently fold in. Gradually add the milk and mix just until it all comes together.

4 Transfer the mixture to a piping bag fitted with a round nozzle, then pipe the mixture into the prepared baking pan, dividing it evenly between the cups. Piping the mixture makes it easier to create neat circles, but you can spoon the mixture into the tin, if you prefer.

5 Place the baking pan in the middle of the oven and bake for 15 minutes, or until golden brown.

6 Remove from the oven and leave to stand for about 5 minutes before removing the doughnuts from the tin and placing them on a wire rack.

7 Meanwhile, for the topping, place the chocolate, syrup and butter in a non-stick pan and melt over a low heat, stirring until smooth and glossy.

8 Spoon the glaze over the doughnuts, while they are warm, allowing it to drizzle down the sides. Leave to set.

Cook's tip

Some baking oil sprays contain flour, so check that you have a gluten-free brand before using.

Variation

For cinnamon doughnuts, lightly brush the doughnuts with melted butter. Mix 30ml/2 tbsp caster/superfine sugar with 5ml/1 tsp ground cinnamon in a bowl and dip in the doughnuts to lightly coat them.

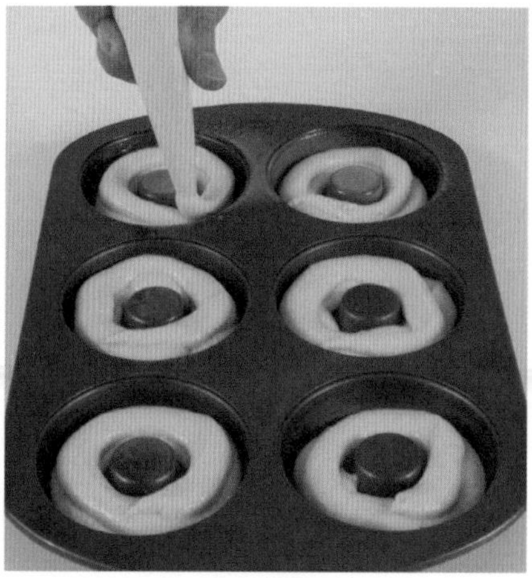

Energy 346kcal/1456kJ; Protein 5.4g; Carbohydrate 51.4g, of which sugars 26g; Fat 14.6g, of which saturates 8.6g; Cholesterol 67mg; Calcium 90mg; Fibre 1.6g; Sodium 267mg.

Crumpets

Crumpets are a traditional English tea-time treat with an unusual dense and spongy texture from the combination of the yeast and the bicarbonate of soda. Made here with a gluten-free yeast batter, and cooked quickly in metal rings on a griddle, they are best served hot.

MAKES 10

200g/7oz/1¾ cups gluten-free self-raising/self-rising flour blend
pinch of salt
2.5ml/½ tsp bicarbonate of soda/baking soda
5ml/1 tsp easy-blend/rapid-rise dried yeast
150ml/¼ pint/⅔ cup milk
200ml/7fl oz/scant 1 cup water
oil, for greasing

1 Sift the flour, salt and bicarbonate of soda into a mixing bowl and stir in the yeast. Make a well in the middle.

2 Heat the milk with the water in a small pan or in the microwave, until lukewarm.

3 Pour the milk into the well and beat or whisk together vigorously to make a thick, smooth batter.

4 Cover the bowl with a clean dish towel and leave in a warm place for about 1 hour, until the mixture has a spongy texture.

5 Heat a griddle or heavy frying pan. Lightly oil the hot pan surface and the inside of metal crumpet rings, each measuring about 8cm/3½in in diameter. Place the rings on the hot griddle or frying pan and leave for 1–2 minutes, until hot.

6 Spoon the batter into the rings to a depth of about 1cm/½in. Cook over medium-high heat for 6 minutes, until the surface is set and holes have appeared.

7 When set, carefully lift off the metal rings and flip the crumpets over, cooking the second side for 1 minute, until lightly browned.

8 Lift off the griddle and leave to cool on a wire rack. Repeat with the remaining crumpet mixture.

9 Just before serving, toast the crumpets on both sides so that the surface is quite hard. Serve hot, with butter and jam or a spread of your choice.

Cook's tip

Crumpets freeze beautifully, and if you aren't going to eat them on the day of making it is a good idea to do this as soon as they are cool and then toast them straight from the freezer on a defrost setting. Alternatively, if you are cooking a lot of crumpets from frozen, it's easier and quicker to put them under the grill or broiler than in the toaster. Start the grill on low so that the crumpets have time to defrost thoroughly, then turn it up to medium to finish toasting them. Check they are cooked through, as they will look cooked even when still frozen inside.

Energy 78kcal/325kJ; Protein 1.5g; Carbohydrate 16.7g, of which sugars 0.8g; Fat 0.5g, of which saturates 0.2g; Cholesterol 1mg; Calcium 18mg; Fibre 0.2g; Sodium 6mg.

Scones & savoury crackers

A freshly baked, slightly warm scone, generously buttered or topped with cream and fruity jam is a special pleasure – one that with a few simple ingredient swaps you can still indulge in. In this chapter, as well as gluten-free traditional English scones, you'll find versions dotted with aromatic caraway seeds, and savoury ones made with caramelized onions and walnuts – delicious with a bowl of chunky vegetable soup.

To make sure the scones aren't dry and crumbly as a result of the gluten-free flour, you'll need to add either extra xanthan gum or beaten egg, or moist ingredients such as ground almonds or mashed sweet potatoes. Once it has come together, you can roll out the dough and cut it into rounds or, if you prefer a more rustic look – and quicker and easier preparation – pat or roll the dough into a large round, transfer it to the baking sheet, then cut almost right the way through into portion-sized wedges. Then, after baking and when barely cool, cut or split the round into individual portions. This technique has the added advantage of ensuring a more moist scone, since there are fewer outside edges exposed to the drying heat of the oven.

The same applies to crackers, which are made in a similar way: rubbing fat into flour to make a stiff dough before shaping and baking. Gluten-free oats, seeds and stronger-tasting flours such as quinoa and sorghum come into their own for these bakes, and hard baking margarine makes an excellent substitute for butter if you prefer to make them dairy free. Multiseed Crackers, Herby Seeded Oatcakes, Quinoa & Poppy Seed Twists – there's something here for everyone.

Classic scones

A traditional scone is always popular, but making a good gluten-free version can be difficult, as those based on bought gluten-free flour alone can be crumbly and a little dry. Here, ground almonds keep them moist and the addition of xanthan gum makes the dough easy to roll.

MAKES 12

about 150ml/1¼ pint/⅔ cup milk plus 15ml/1 tbsp lemon juice, or 150ml/1¼ pints/⅔ cup buttermilk
300g/11oz/2¾ cups gluten-free self-raising/self-rising flour blend, plus extra for dusting
3.75ml/¾ tsp gluten-free baking powder
2.5ml/½ tsp xanthan gum
pinch of salt
115g/4oz/1 cup ground almonds
115g/4oz/½ cup butter or hard baking margarine
1 egg, lightly beaten
jam and thick whipped cream, to serve

1 Preheat the oven to 200°C/400°F/Gas 6. Put the milk in a jug or bowl and stir in the lemon juice, unless you are using buttermilk.

2 Sift the flour, baking powder, xanthan gum and salt into a large mixing bowl. Stir in the almonds. Rub in the butter or margarine with your fingertips until the mixture resembles fine breadcrumbs. Make a small well.

3 Mix the egg and soured milk together, reserve 15ml/1 tbsp, then pour the rest into the flour and mix quickly to form a soft dough, adding a little more milk, if needed.

4 Knead the dough very lightly until it just comes together as a ball, then roll it out on a floured surface until it is slightly thicker than 2.5cm/1in.

5 Using a 5cm/2in cutter, stamp out 12 scones and place them on a well-floured baking sheet. Re-roll any trimmings and cut out more if you can.

6 Brush the tops of the scones lightly with the reserved egg-and-milk mixture, then bake for about 20 minutes, or until risen and golden brown.

7 Wrap the scones in a clean dish towel to keep them warm and soft until ready to serve with jam and a generous dollop of cream.

Energy 232kcal/961kJ; Protein 4.4g; Carbohydrate 21.3g, of which sugars 1.1g; Fat 14.3g, of which saturates 5.8g; Cholesterol 40mg; Calcium 43mg; Fibre 0.3g; Sodium 72mg.

Caraway scones

These gluten-free scones are flavoured with caraway seeds, which give a warm, old-fashioned aroma as they bake, but you can leave them out if you prefer. Light and slightly sweetened, buttermilk works together with the baking powder to make the scones extra light.

MAKES 12

350g/12oz/2½ cups gluten-free self-raising/self-rising flour blend, plus extra for dusting
5ml/1 tsp gluten-free baking powder
5ml/1 tsp xanthan gum
115g/4oz/1 cup ground almonds
115g/4oz/½ cup butter or hard baking margarine
50g/2oz/½ cup caster/superfine sugar, plus extra for dusting
30ml/2 tbsp caraway seeds (optional)
1 egg, beaten
200ml/7fl oz/scant1 cup buttermilk
butter, to serve

1 Preheat the oven to 200°C/400°F/Gas 6. Line a baking sheet with baking parchment.

2 Sift the flour, baking powder and xanthan gum into a large mixing bowl, then add the ground almonds and mix to combine.

3 Add the butter or hard baking margarine to the dry ingredients and, with your fingertips, rub it in until the mixture resembles fine breadcrumbs. Stir in the sugar and caraway seeds, if using. Make a small well in in the middle of the mixture.

4 Mix the egg with the buttermilk in a jug or pitcher. Pour most of the liquid into the dry ingredients (you won't need it all) and mix quickly to make a soft dough. Transfer the dough to a lightly floured surface.

5 Roll out until the dough is slightly thicker than 2.5cm/1in. Using a 5cm/2in cutter, cut into rounds, gathering up the offcuts and re-rolling to make more.

6 Arrange the rounds on the lined baking sheet, setting them quite close together so they support each other as they rise. Brush the tops of the scones with the remaining buttermilk mixture.

7 Put into the hot oven and bake for about 20 minutes until risen and golden brown.

8 Transfer the scones to a wire rack and dust the tops with sugar, then wrap them in a clean dish towel to keep them warm and soft until you are ready to serve them, preferably warm, spread with butter.

Energy 285kcal/1184kJ; Protein 4.8g; Carbohydrate 29.2g, of which sugars 5.7g; Fat 16.6g, of which saturates 7.2g; Cholesterol 46mg; Calcium 49mg; Fibre 0.3g; Sodium 94mg.

Caramelized onion & walnut scones

Oatmeal adds texture and helps bring the dough together as it absorbs liquid. These are excellent with soup or a robust vegetable stew. Alternatively, roll them thinner and make small scones to use as gluten-free bases for cocktail savouries, served topped with soft goat's cheese.

MAKES 12

90g/3½oz/7 tbsp butter
15ml/1 tbsp olive oil
1 Spanish/Bermuda onion, chopped
2.5ml/½ tsp cumin seeds, lightly crushed, plus a few extra
200g/7oz/scant 1⅔ cups gluten-free self-raising/self-rising flour blend, plus extra for dusting
5ml/1 tsp gluten-free baking powder
5ml/1 tsp xanthan gum
salt and ground black pepper
25g/1oz/¼ cup gluten-free oatmeal
5ml/1 tsp light muscovado/brown sugar
90g/3½oz/scant 1 cup chopped walnuts
5ml/1 tsp chopped fresh thyme
about 150ml/¼ pint/⅔ cup buttermilk or soured milk
coarse sea salt, for sprinkling

1 Melt 15g/½oz/1 tbsp of the butter with the oil in a small pan and cook the onion gently, covered, for about 10 minutes, until soft but not browned. Uncover, then continue to cook gently until it begins to brown.

2 Add the crushed cumin seeds and increase the temperature slightly. Cook, stirring occasionally, until the onion browns and begins to caramelize around the edges. Cool. Preheat the oven to 200°C/400°F/Gas 6.

3 Sift the flour, baking powder and xanthan gum into a large mixing bowl, then add 2.5ml/½ tsp salt, a generous grinding of black pepper, the oatmeal and the sugar. Add the remaining butter and rub it in with your fingertips until the mixture resembles breadcrumbs.

4 Add the cooled cooked onion, walnuts and fresh thyme, then bind to make a soft, but not sticky, dough using just enough buttermilk or soured milk (you may not need it all).

5 Roll or pat out the mixture to just over 1cm/½in thick. Stamp out scones using a floured 5–6cm/2–2½in cutter. Re-roll any trimmings and cut out more if you can.

6 Place the scones quite close together on a floured baking tray, glaze with the leftover milk and scatter with a little sea salt and a few whole cumin seeds.

7 Bake for 12–15 minutes, until risen and golden. Cool for a few minutes on a wire rack and serve warm.

Energy 195kcal/809kJ; Protein 2.9g; Carbohydrate 17.4g, of which sugars 2.1g; Fat 12.7g, of which saturates 4.7g; Cholesterol 16mg; Calcium 30mg; Fibre 1.1g; Sodium 54mg.

Sweet potato scones

These are gluten-free scones with a difference. A sweet potato gives them a pale orange colour and sweet flavour, and replaces some of the flour, as well as making them meltingly soft in the middle, just waiting to be spread with butter and served with jam or some salty cheese.

MAKES 24

150g/5oz/1¼ cups gluten-free plain/all-purpose flour blend, plus extra for dusting
20ml/4 tsp baking powder
5ml/1 tsp xanthan gum
5ml/1 tsp salt
15g/½oz/1 tbsp soft light brown sugar
150g/5oz cooked sweet potatoes
150ml/¼ pint/⅔ cup milk
50g/2oz/¼ cup butter, melted, plus extra for greasing

1 Preheat the oven to 230°C/450°F/Gas 8. Grease a baking sheet with a little butter. Sift the flour, baking powder, xanthan gum and salt into a large mixing bowl, then add the sugar.

2 In a separate large bowl, mash the sweet potatoes with the milk and melted butter. Beat well.

3 Add the flour mixture to the sweet potato and stir to make a dough. Turn out on to a lightly floured surface and knead until soft and pliable. Roll or pat out the dough to a 1cm/½in thickness. Cut into rounds using a floured 4cm/1½in cutter, then arrange the rounds quite close together on the baking sheet.

4 Bake for about 15 minutes, until risen and golden. Cool for a few minutes on a wire rack and serve warm.

Energy 50kcal/208kJ; Protein 0.7g; Carbohydrate 7.6g, of which sugars 1.3g; Fat 1.9g, of which saturates 1.2g; Cholesterol 5mg; Calcium 19mg; Fibre 0.3g; Sodium 116mg.

Berry & yogurt scones

These fruity scones are made with a mixture of gluten-free flours including sorghum. They can either be baked as individual scones or you can shape the dough into a thick round on the baking sheet, mark it into triangles and break it into wedges after baking.

MAKES 8

175g/6oz/1½ cups dried mulberries (see Variations)
120ml/4fl oz/½ cup hot tea
150g/5oz/1¼ cups potato flour/starch, plus extra for dusting
150g/5oz/1¼ cups tapioca flour/starch
50g/2oz/½ cup sorghum flour
50g/2oz/½ cup rice flour
5ml/1 tsp xanthan gum
10ml/2 tsp gluten-free baking powder
10ml/2 tsp soft light brown sugar
pinch of salt
115g/4oz/¼ cup ground almonds
115g/4oz/½ cup butter or hard baking margarine, plus extra for greasing
5ml/1 tsp lemon juice
150ml/¼ pint/⅔ cup full-fat/whole natural/plain yogurt
2 eggs, lightly beaten
milk, for brushing

1 Put the dried mulberries into a small mixing bowl and pour over the hot tea. Set aside for about 20 minutes.

2 Preheat the oven to 220°C/425°F/Gas 7. Grease a large baking sheet with butter or margarine.

3 Sift the potato, tapioca, sorghum and rice flours, xanthan gum, baking powder, sugar and salt into a large mixing bowl. Stir in the ground almonds.

4 Rub in the butter or margarine with your fingertips, until it is the consistency of breadcrumbs.

5 Drain the dried fruit and discard the liquid. Mix in the mulberries using your fingers.

6 Stir the lemon juice into the yogurt in a jug or bowl, then stir in the eggs.

7 Make a small well in the middle of the dry ingredients, then quickly stir in enough of the yogurt mixture to make a soft dough.

8 Dust the counter with potato flour, put the dough on it and use your hands to form a flat long rectangle that is about 2.5cm/1in thick and 6cm/2½in wide.

9 Cut the dough into diagonal quarters, and then cut these wedges in half again to make eight even-sized triangular pieces.

10 Put the scones on the prepared baking sheet, spaced about 2.5cm/1in apart. Brush the tops with a little milk, to glaze.

11 Bake for 15–20 minutes in the preheated oven, until well risen and golden brown. Cool for a few minutes on a wire rack and serve warm.

Variations

- If you can't track down dried mulberries, this recipe works wonderfully with dried cherries, cranberries or blueberries, or chopped dates.
- You can use ordinary tea for soaking the dried fruit, or a fruit tea, such as apple or cranberry, if you prefer.

Energy 466kcal/1955kJ; Protein 8.6g; Carbohydrate 61.6g, of which sugars 18.8g; Fat 22g, of which saturates 8.8g; Cholesterol 89mg; Calcium 100mg; Fibre 2.4g; Sodium 140mg.

Quinoa & poppy seed twists

These crisp twists are delicious served fresh and still warm from the oven. Enriched with olive oil and flavoured with poppy seeds and herbs, they are made with a combination of quinoa and gluten-free plain flours so that they are substantial yet light at the same time.

MAKES 12

175g/6oz/1½ cups quinoa flour
50g/2oz/½ cup gluten-free plain/all-purpose flour blend, plus extra for dusting
2.5ml/½ tsp xanthan gum
60ml/4 tbsp poppy seeds
10ml/2 tsp mixed dried herbs
2.5ml/½ tsp salt
2.5ml/½ ground black pepper
75ml/5 tbsp olive oil
150ml/¼ pint/⅔ cup cold water
non-dairy milk, to glaze

1 Sift the flours and xanthan gum together into a large mixing bowl. Mix in the poppy seeds, dried herbs, salt and pepper.

2 Stir in the oil and then the cold water little by little to form a soft, pliable pastry. Knead on a lightly floured surface for just a few seconds, until smooth.

3 Shape into a disc, wrap in clear film or plastic wrap and chill for 30 minutes in the fridge.

4 Preheat the oven to 190°C/375°F/Gas 5. Line a medium baking sheet with baking parchment.

5 On a floured surface, roll the pastry into a rough rectangle about 6 x 12cm/2½ x 4½in and 1cm/½in thick. Trim the edges to make them straight.

6 Cut the pastry into 12 even strips, then twist each one a couple of times as you transfer them to the prepared baking sheet. Lightly press the ends of the sticks down so that they do not untwist during baking.

7 Brush with milk and bake for 15–18 minutes, until golden brown and crisp. Transfer to a wire rack to cool.

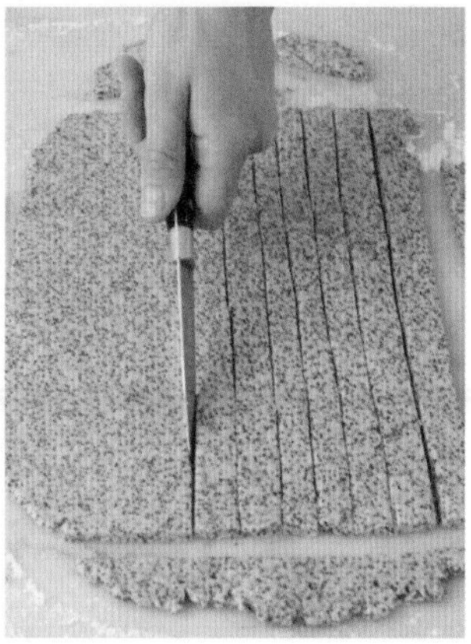

Variations

- Use sesame seeds instead of some or all of the poppy seeds for a nutty flavour.
- If you wish, you could add 30ml/2 tbsp finely chopped olives to the pastry mix.
- For a light smoked paprika coating, sprinkle 5ml/1 tsp smoked paprika over the floured surface before rolling out the pastry.
- For Parmesan straws, sprinkle the pastry twists with freshly grated Parmesan cheese before baking.

Energy 303kcal/1267kJ; Protein 9.8g; Carbohydrate 34.4g, of which sugars 2.7g; Fat 23.2g, of which saturates 3.3g; Cholesterol 0mg; Calcium 272mg; Fibre 0.1g; Sodium 30mg.

Herby seeded oatcakes

Using a combination of sorghum flour and oatmeal creates just the right blend of texture and taste in these crisp oatcakes. The addition of sunflower seeds boosts their nutrients and adds to the crunch, while the thyme lends a distinctive savoury flavour.

MAKES 32

175g/6oz/1½ cups sorghum flour, plus extra for dusting
175g/6oz/1½ cups gluten-free fine oatmeal
2.5ml/½ tsp xanthan gum
1.5ml/¼ tsp bicarbonate of soda/baking soda
5ml/1 tsp salt
75g/3oz/6 tbsp white vegetable fat
15ml/1 tbsp fresh thyme leaves, chopped
90–105ml/6–7 tbsp water
30ml/2 tbsp sunflower seeds

1 Preheat the oven to 150°C/300°F/Gas 2. Sprinkle two non-stick baking sheets with sorghum flour.

2 Put the flour, oatmeal, xanthan gum, bicarbonate of soda and salt into a large mixing bowl and stir together to mix.

3 Rub in the fat until the mixture resembles fine breadcrumbs. Stir in the thyme. Add enough water to the dry ingredients to mix to a stiff but not sticky dough.

4 Gently knead the dough on a lightly floured surface until smooth, then cut in half and roll out one piece to make a 23–25cm/9–10in round.

5 Sprinkle half the seeds over the dough and press them in with the rolling pin. Cut into triangles and arrange on one of the baking sheets, spacing them apart to allow for spreading. Repeat with the remaining dough.

6 Bake for 45–60 minutes until crisp but not brown. Cool on wire racks.

Energy 68kcal/282kJ; Protein 1.1g; Carbohydrate 8.5g, of which sugars 0g; Fat 3.3g, of which saturates 1g; Cholesterol 2mg; Calcium 4mg; Fibre 0.6g; Sodium 2mg.

Multiseed crackers

These chunky crackers have plenty of flavour and texture provided by the different gluten-free flours and the seeds used. You could also add a teaspoon or two of ground flaxseed to the mixture if you like. They taste fabulous with robust farmhouse and blue cheeses.

MAKES 14

175g/6oz/1½ cups gluten-free plain/all-purpose flour blend, plus extra for dusting
50g/2oz/½ cup millet flour
25g/1oz/¼ cup buckwheat flour
2.5ml/½ tsp xanthan gum
2.5ml/½ tsp gluten-free baking powder
2.5ml/½ tsp celery salt
115g/4oz/½ cup butter, chilled and diced
1 egg, beaten
45ml/3 tbsp milk, plus extra for brushing
15ml/1 tbsp pumpkin seeds
15ml/1 tbsp sunflower seeds
15ml/1 tbsp sesame seeds

1 Preheat the oven to 180°C/350°F/Gas 4. Put the flours, xantham gum, baking powder and celery salt in a large mixing bowl and stir together. Rub in the butter until the mixture resembles fine breadcrumbs.

2 Add the egg and milk and mix to a stiff dough. Roll out on a floured surface to about 5mm/¼in thick.

3 Using a pastry brush, brush a little milk over the rolled dough. Sprinkle all the pumpkin, sunflower and sesame seeds over the top in an even layer.

4 Very gently, roll the rolling pin back and forth over the seeds to press them into the dough.

5 Stamp out rounds using a floured 10cm/4in cutter, then place on a non-stick baking sheet, spacing them slightly apart to allow for spreading. Alternatively, use a sharp knife to trim off the rough edges of the rolled-out dough, then cut the dough into equal-size squares, rectangles or triangles.

6 Bake the crackers for about 15 minutes, or until they are just beginning to brown. Carefully transfer the crackers to a wire rack to cool completely.

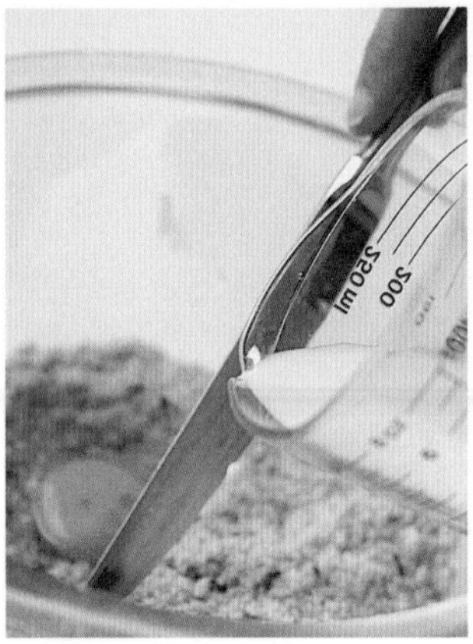

Cook's tips

• To make your own celery salt, grind five parts lightly toasted celery seeds with one part sea salt. Transfer to an airtight container and store in a cool, dark place.

• You can also use other seeds if you prefer. Try using poppy seeds or whole flaxseeds/linseeds in place of the sesame seeds.

Energy 151kcal/626kJ; Protein 2.3g; Carbohydrate 14.8g, of which sugars 0.3g; Fat 9.1g, of which saturates 4.7g; Cholesterol 34mg; Calcium 13mg; Fibre 0.4g; Sodium 58mg.

Sun-dried tomato crackers

These buttery gluten-free treats have all the flavours of a classic pizza – cheese, tomato, oregano and olives – in a short, melt-in-the-mouth cracker format. They are great as a snack or addition to lunchboxes and are also wonderful as a tasty nibble to pass round with drinks.

MAKES 25

175g/6oz/1½ cups gluten-free plain/all-purpose flour blend
2.5ml/½ tsp xanthan gum
150g/5oz/½ cup butter, chilled and diced
150g/5oz/1¼ cups grated mature/sharp Cheddar cheese
15ml/1 tbsp sun-dried tomato paste
25g/1oz semi-dried tomatoes, coarsely chopped
15ml/1 tbsp dried oregano
30ml/2 tbsp pitted black olives, drained
30–45ml/2–3 tbsp water
60ml/4 tbsp sesame seeds

1 Put all the ingredients, except the water and sesame seeds, into a food processor. Process in bursts, using the pulse button, until the mixture resembles fine breadcrumbs. Don't overprocess the ingredients.

2 Add enough water to mix to a soft dough, then turn out the mixture and shape it into a neat log about 25cm/10in long.

3 Spread out the sesame seeds over a sheet of baking parchment or on a large plate. Roll the dough log in the seeds until the sides are thoroughly coated. Wrap in clear film or plastic wrap and chill for about 2 hours.

4 Preheat the oven to 180°C/350°F/Gas 4. Remove the clear film. Cut into 1cm/½in slices and place on baking parchment on baking sheets, spaced slightly apart. Bake for 15–20 minutes, or until golden brown. Transfer to a wire rack to cool.

Energy 115kcal/475kJ; Protein 2.4g; Carbohydrate 5.7g, of which sugars 0.1g; Fat 9.2g, of which saturates 4.8g; Cholesterol 19mg; Calcium 63mg; Fibre 0.4g; Sodium 117mg.

Cookies & slices

There's no need to miss out on sweet treats just because you can't eat gluten, and cookies are probably the easiest of all bakes to make: most have just a few ingredients, are simple to assemble, and quick to cook. What's more, unlike breads, cakes and pastries, cookies don't always need gluten substitutions such as xanthan gum to make them work. In fact, the lack of gluten in alternative flours is a definite plus when it comes to making melt-in-the-mouth crumbly biscuits.

Whatever type they are, once baked, allow the gluten-free cookies to at least partially cool on the baking tray to allow them to set and stop them breaking before you then remove them carefully with a flat, wide spatula and transfer them to a wire rack to cool completely. Store in an airtight container, and if the cookies are the soft or slightly sticky type, place a sheet of baking parchment between each layer.

The simplest cookies are 'drop cookies', so called because the dough is soft enough to drop off the spoon and on to the baking sheet. These include Fruit & Millet Cookies and Almond Florentines. Other cookies, such as Carob Chip Shortcake Cookies, are rolled out and stamped with a cutter into simple rounds, or into fun shapes as you prefer. Like gluten-free pastry, it is easier to roll these doughs out between two sheets of baking parchment. There are also mixtures that you simply roll into balls and that spread out during baking, such as Ginger Cookies. And, for the more experienced cook, Cappuccino Swirls are piped directly on to the baking sheet.

Slices, by contrast, are cooked in a large tin or pan, then cut into pieces after baking. Some are thin and crunchy, others thick and chewy. These often have more than one layer, so you can combine taste and textures. Coconut Mint Slice and Apple Shortcake Slice are examples of these, and both are ideal for bake sales or for feeding a crowd, being easy to make, impressive to look at, and delicious to eat.

Fruit & millet cookies

Molasses has a rich, dark colour and adds a malty flavour. It's combined here with millet, which is highly nutritious and contains more iron than other grains. Quick to make, these chunky gluten-free cookies are packed with fruit and nuts and make a satisfying treat.

MAKES 25–30

90g/3½oz/7 tbsp soft baking margarine
150g/5oz/⅔ cup light muscovado/brown sugar
30ml/2 tbsp black treacle/molasses
1 large egg
115g/4oz/1 cup gluten-free plain/all-purpose flour
5ml/1 tsp ground psyllium husk
50g/2oz/½ cup millet flakes
50g/2oz/½ cup almonds, roughly chopped
175g/6oz/1 cup dried fruit

1 Preheat the oven to 190°C/375°F/Gas 5. Line two large baking sheets with baking parchment.

2 Put the margarine, muscovado sugar, treacle and egg in a large mixing bowl and beat together with an electric whisk or wooden spoon, until well combined.

3 Stir in the flour, ground psyllium husk, millet flakes, almonds and dried fruit. Put tablespoonfuls of the mixture on to the prepared baking sheets. Bake for about 15 minutes, until brown.

4 Leave on the baking sheets for a few minutes, then transfer to a wire rack to cool completely.

Energy 93kcal/390kJ; Protein 1.1g; Carbohydrate 14.3g, of which sugars 10g; Fat 3.7g, of which saturates 0.7g; Cholesterol 8mg; Calcium 17mg; Fibre 0.2g; Sodium 29mg.

Carob chip shortcake cookies

Perfect for anyone on a gluten- or dairy-free diet, these lovely cookies are best eaten freshly made, preferably while still slightly warm from the oven. You could also use milk or white chocolate chips if you are able to eat dairy.

MAKES 12

75g/3oz/⅔ cup brown rice flour
75g/3oz/⅔ cup white rice flour
25g/1oz/¼ cup tapioca flour
1.5ml/¼ tsp xanthan gum
25g/1oz/2 tbsp soft light brown sugar
75g/3oz/6 tbsp baking margarine
50g/3oz/⅓ cup carob or dark chocolate chips, or cacao nibs
1 egg
15ml/1 tbsp clear honey
demerara/raw sugar, for sprinkling

1 Preheat the oven to 160°C/325°F/Gas 3. Line two baking sheets with baking parchment.

2 Put the flours, xanthan gum and sugar in a large mixing bowl and rub in the margarine. Stir in the carob.

3 Beat the egg and honey together, add to the dry ingredients and mix to a dough.

4 Roll the dough out between two sheets of baking parchment to a thickness of about 8mm/⅓in.

5 Stamp out the dough into rounds using a plain 5cm/2in round cutter. Place the rounds on the prepared baking sheets. Prick each cookie once with a fork and sprinkle with sugar.

6 Bake for about 15–20 minutes, or until firm. Cool on a wire rack.

Energy 139kcal/579kJ; Protein 1.6g; Carbohydrate 17.8g, of which sugars 5.7g; Fat 6.9g, of which saturates 3.3g; Cholesterol 17mg; Calcium 8mg; Fibre 0.5g; Sodium 44mg.

Date & walnut cookies

Dates and walnuts are perfect partners and here they flavour little gluten-free shortbread-type cookies. These are sliced from a roll of dough that you can make ahead and keep in the fridge for a few days or freeze, ready for the next time you get cravings for freshly baked cookies.

MAKES 24

115g/4oz/½ cup butter, softened
115g/4oz/½ cup light muscovado sugar
5ml/1 tsp vanilla extract
1 large egg, beaten
75g/3oz/¾ cup ground almonds
50g/2oz/⅓ cup dried chopped dates
25g/1oz/¼ cup buckwheat flour
75g/3oz/¾ cup rice flour
40g/1½oz/⅓ cup tapioca flour/starch
10g/¼oz ground linseed
pinch of salt
50g/2oz/⅓ cup chopped walnuts

1 Cream the butter, sugar and vanilla until pale and smooth. Gradually add the egg and ground almonds alternately, beating well after each addition.

2 Put the dates, flours, ground linseed and salt into a food processor and blend for a few seconds until the dates are coarsely ground. Add to the bowl with the walnuts and mix to form a dough.

3 Roll the dough into a 5cm/2in-diameter log. Wrap in clear film or plastic wrap and chill for at least 1 hour.

4 Preheat the oven to 180°C/350°F/Gas 4 and line two baking sheets with baking parchment.

5 Remove the dough from the fridge and slice it into 5mm/¼in-thick cookies. Arrange on the baking sheets about 5cm/2in apart.

6 Bake for 14–16 minutes, until golden brown at the edges. Leave on the sheets for 5 minutes to firm up, then transfer to a wire rack to cool. The cookies will become crisp and crumbly as they cool.

Energy 119kcal/494kJ; Protein 1.7g; Carbohydrate 11.7g, of which sugars 6.6g; Fat 7.4g, of which saturates 2.9g; Cholesterol 20mg; Calcium 15mg; Fibre 0.3g; Sodium 34mg.

Almond Florentines

Flour-free, sugar-free and vegan, these Florentines are thin and crisp with a gorgeous colour. By grinding your own almonds, the brown skin of the nut is included. Not only does this mean the cookies have more fibre, but also that the mixture is less absorbent, resulting in a crisper cookie.

MAKES 12

200g/7oz/1½ cups raw whole almonds
1.5ml/¼ tsp bicarbonate of soda/ baking soda
30ml/2 tbsp coconut oil
50ml/2fl oz/¼ cup maple syrup
1.5ml/¼ tsp almond extract

1 Preheat the oven to 160°C/325°F/Gas 3. Line a baking sheet with baking parchment.

2 Put the almonds in a food processor and blitz them for about 30 seconds, until ground into tiny crumbs.

3 Pour them into a mixing bowl, add the bicarbonate of soda and mix with a fork.

4 Melt the coconut oil then pour the oil, maple syrup and almond extract into the dry ingredients and stir to combine.

5 Spoon the sticky mixture on to the baking sheet using a teaspoon, leaving plenty of space in between them to allow for spreading, and flatten each spoonful into a cookie shape.

6 Bake for 15–16 minutes, until golden brown. Leave the Florentines to cool until hardened on the baking sheet, then transfer to a wire rack to cool completely.

Variations

- If you want to buy ready-ground almonds, use 175g/6oz/1½ cups.
- You could use other nuts, such as hazelnuts or walnuts.

Energy 135kcal/560kJ; Protein 3.5g; Carbohydrate 4g, of which sugars 3.2g; Fat 11.8g, of which saturates 2.9g; Cholesterol 0mg; Calcium 43mg; Fibre 0g; Sodium 3mg.

Peanut butter cookies

Speedy, delicious and flourless, this recipe will make you wonder why you ever made peanut butter cookies any other way. If you are quick, it will take you only 20 minutes from getting out the mixing bowl to having hot baked cookies.

MAKES 12

250g/9oz/1 cup peanut butter
100g/3¾oz/¾ cup coconut crystals/sugar or soft light brown sugar
1 egg, beaten
2.5ml/½ tsp bicarbonate of soda/baking soda
2.5ml/½ tsp ground cinnamon (optional)

Variations

You can use smooth or crunchy peanut butter, or another type of nut butter, for these cookies. Adding a pinch of sea salt and dark chocolate chips (about 50g/2oz) takes them to another dimension!

1 Preheat the oven to 180°C/350°F/Gas 4. Line a baking sheet (with sides) with baking parchment.

2 Put all the ingredients in a mixing bowl and mix well to form a dough, using a wooden spoon.

3 Roll the dough into small balls and flatten each one, working quickly. Put the cookies on the baking sheet, spaced about 5cm/2in apart.

4 Bake for 10–12 minutes, until the edges are browned.

5 Leave to cool on the baking sheet for 5 minutes before transferring to a wire rack to cool completely. The cookies will be still soft to the touch after baking, becoming crisper as they cool.

Energy 167kcal/695kJ; Protein 5.4g; Carbohydrate 11.4g, of which sugars 10.1g; Fat 11.4g, of which saturates 2.8g; Cholesterol 19mg; Calcium 13mg; Fibre 0g; Sodium 80mg.

Orange quinoa cookies

These satisfying, intensely orangey cookies are made with a combination of quinoa flour and flakes for bulk and texture, held together with a mixture of butter, sugar and syrup. Baking time is important, so watch them carefully; they should be dark golden and crisp but don't let them scorch.

MAKES 18–20

250g/9oz/1 1/8 cups butter, softened, or soft baking margarine
175g/6oz/generous 1 3/4 cups soft light brown sugar
115g/4oz/1 cup quinoa flour
115g/4oz/1 cup quinoa flakes
finely grated rind of 3 oranges
45ml/3 tbsp golden/light corn syrup
10ml/2 tsp vanilla extract
gluten-free icing/confectioners' sugar, for dusting

1 Preheat the oven to 190°C/375°F/Gas 5. Line two large baking sheets with baking parchment.

2 With an electric mixer or a wooden spoon, beat the butter or margarine and sugar until light and fluffy.

3 Stir in the quinoa flour and flakes with the orange rind, golden syrup and vanilla extract, and combine.

4 Place large teaspoonfuls of the mixture on the baking sheets, slightly flattening each one with the back of a damp spoon and leaving a little space for them to spread. Bake for 12–15 minutes, until golden.

5 Remove from the oven and leave on the baking sheets for a few minutes before transferring to a wire rack to cool. Dust with icing sugar and serve.

Variation

Add 25g/1oz chocolate chips with the dry ingredients.

Energy 176kcal/734kJ; Protein 2g; Carbohydrate 19g, of which sugars 11g; Fat 11g, of which saturates 7g; Cholesterol 27mg; Calcium 16mg; Fibre 10.5g; Sodium 84mg.

Ginger cookies

These intensely flavoured cookies are crisp on the outside and slightly soft in the middle thanks to a combination of gluten-free flours and the raising agent. They are a real treat for ginger lovers, as they contain both dried ginger and pieces of succulent preserved stem ginger.

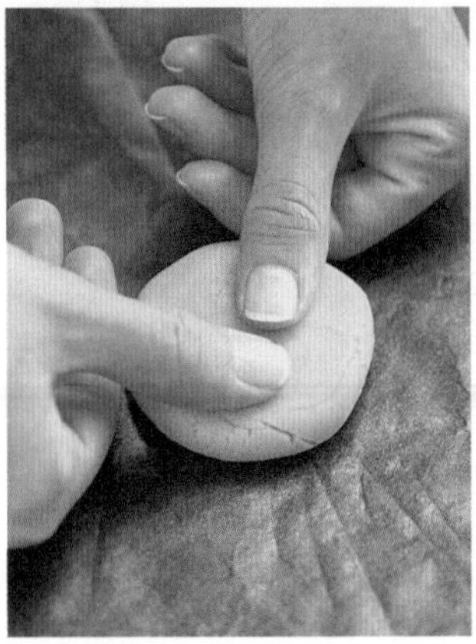

MAKES 25 SMALL OR 15 LARGE

50g/2oz/½ cup sorghum flour
50g/2oz/½ cup potato flour
40g/1½oz/⅓ cup tapioca flour
1.5ml/¼ tsp xanthan gum
5ml/1 tsp bicarbonate of soda/baking soda
10ml/2 tsp ground ginger
50g/2oz/¼ cup soft light brown sugar
115g/4oz preserved stem ginger, patted dry and chopped
50g/2oz/¼ cup hard baking margarine
75ml/5 tbsp maple syrup
5ml/1 tsp black treacle

1 Preheat the oven to 180°C/350°F/Gas 4. Line two baking sheets with baking parchment or lightly greased greaseproof or waxed paper.

2 Sift the flours, xanthan gum, bicarbonate of soda and ground ginger into a large mixing bowl and stir to combine. Stir in the sugar, followed by half the chopped stem ginger.

3 Put the margarine in a small, heavy pan with the maple syrup and black treacle. Heat gently, stirring, until all has melted. Remove from the heat and set aside to cool until just warm.

4 Pour the melted mixture over the dry ingredients and stir until evenly mixed.

5 Shape the dough into 25 small or 15 large balls, depending on the cookie size you require. Place the balls, spaced well apart to allow for spread, on the prepared baking sheets.

6 Gently flatten the balls, then press a few pieces of the remaining preserved stem ginger into the top of each of the cookies.

7 Bake for about 12–15 minutes, depending on the size of the cookies, until light golden in colour. Remove from the oven.

8 Leave to cool for 1 minute on the baking sheets to firm up. Using a palette knife or metal spatula, transfer to a wire rack to cool completely.

Energy 52kcal/218kJ; Protein 0.6g; Carbohydrate 8.9g, of which sugars 4.3g; Fat 1.7g, of which saturates 0.4g; Cholesterol 0mg; Calcium 5mg; Fibre 0.4g; Sodium 16mg.

Cappuccino swirls

These luxurious piped mocha-flavoured cookies have a melt-in-the-mouth texture. Drizzled with white and dark chocolate after baking, they are perfect when you want a special cookie to serve with a mid-morning latte or for afternoon tea.

MAKES 18

10ml/2 tsp instant coffee powder
15ml/1 tbsp near-boiling water
150g/5oz/1¼ cups gluten-free plain/all-purpose flour blend
2.5ml/½ tsp xanthan gum
115g/4oz/½ cup cornflour/starch
15ml/1 tbsp unsweetened cocoa powder
225g/8oz/1 cup butter, softened
50g/2oz/¼ cup caster/superfine sugar

For the decoration

50g/2oz white chocolate
25g/1oz dark/bittersweet chocolate

1 Preheat the oven to 190°C/375°F/Gas 5. Line two baking sheets with baking parchment.

2 Put the coffee powder in a cup, add the water and stir until dissolved. Set aside to cool. Sift together the flour, xanthan gum, cornflour and cocoa powder into a large mixing bowl.

3 Put the butter and sugar in another mixing bowl and beat until creamy. Add the coffee and the sifted flour and mix well.

4 Spoon the dough into a piping or pastry bag fitted with a plain nozzle. Pipe 18 spirals, slightly apart, on to the prepared baking sheets.

5 Bake for 10–15 minutes, or until the cookies are firm but not browned. Remove from the oven and leave on the baking sheets for 1 minute, then transfer to a wire rack to cool.

6 Meanwhile, melt the white and dark chocolate separately in small heatproof bowls set over a pan of hot water.

7 Place the cooled cookies close together on kitchen paper. Using a teaspoon, take some white chocolate and flick it over the cookies from left to right to create small lines of chocolate drizzle over them.

8 When all the white chocolate has been used, repeat with the dark chocolate, flicking it over the cookies so the dark chocolate is at an angle to the white chocolate. Leave to set, then serve.

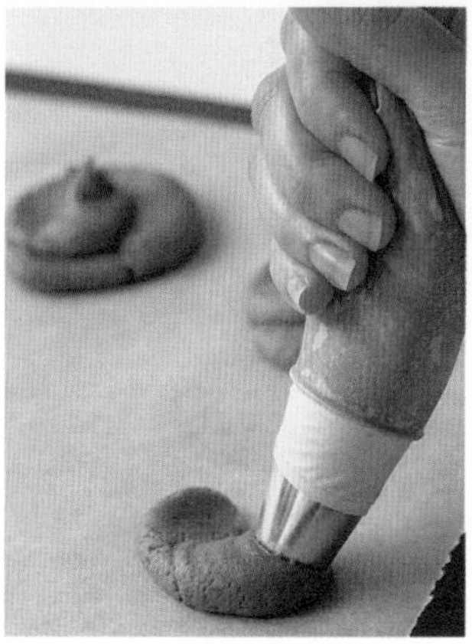

Energy 177kcal/738kJ; Protein 0.8g; Carbohydrate 18.2g, of which sugars 5.6g; Fat 11.6g, of which saturates 7.2g; Cholesterol 27mg; Calcium 5mg; Fibre 0.2g; Sodium 79mg.

Chocolate macaroons

These easy-to-make macaroons mostly consist of moist desiccated coconut in place of flour, held together with a syrup made from egg whites and sugar. This mixture is then allowed to cool before being shaped, baked and filled with a luscious puddle of dark chocolate.

MAKES 18

100g/3¾oz/2 cups desiccated/dry unsweetened shredded coconut
125g/4¼oz caster/superfine sugar
2 egg whites
10ml/2 tsp honey
2.5ml/½ tsp vanilla extract
small pinch of salt
100g/3¾oz dark/bittersweet chocolate, broken into pieces

1 Combine all of the ingredients except for the chocolate in a heavy pan and cook over a medium heat for about 7 minutes, stirring constantly, until the mixture is opaque and sticky. The coconut should just begin to scorch on the bottom of the pan.

2 Transfer the coconut mixture to a large mixing bowl and allow it to cool completely.

3 Preheat the oven to 160°C/325°F/Gas 3. Line a baking sheet with baking parchment.

4 Drop tablespoonfuls of the mixture on to the baking sheet. Using the end of a wooden spoon, make small depressions in the middle of each macaroon.

5 Place in the oven and bake for about 12 minutes, until the macaroons are just golden around the edges.

6 Remove from the oven and leave on the baking sheet to firm up for 2 minutes before transferring the macaroons to a wire rack to cool completely.

7 Meanwhile, melt the chocolate in a heatproof bowl placed over a pan of barely simmering water, making sure the water does not touch the bowl. Leave until the chocolate is melted.

8 Transfer the melted chocolate to a piping or pastry bag with a fine nozzle and use it to fill the indented middle of each macaroon. Alternatively, you can use a teaspoon, but it is easier and less messy to use a piping bag.

9 Leave to cool, until the chocolate is almost set. These macaroons are best eaten on the day they are made, although they can be stored in an airtight container for up to one week.

Energy 258kcal/1088kJ; Protein 6g; Carbohydrate 42g, of which sugars 20g; Fat 9g, of which saturates 3g; Cholesterol 34mg; Calcium 99mg; Fibre 2g; Sodium 45mg.

Nut butter cookies

If you enjoy a spoonful of nut butter from the jar, you will love these crumbly cookies, which are quick and easy to make and contain just a few gluten-free ingredients. Half are plain and half are chocolate-flavoured but you can make a batch of just one or other if you prefer.

MAKES 12

225g/8oz/1 cup smooth cashew nut butter
30ml/2 tbsp maple syrup
10ml/2 tsp raw cacao powder or unsweetened cocoa powder
30ml/2 tbsp finely chopped cashew nuts, for sprinkling (optional)
2.5ml/½ tsp gluten-free icing/confectioners' sugar, for dusting

1 Preheat the oven to 180°C/350°F/Gas 4. Line a baking sheet with baking parchment.

2 Put half of the cashew nut butter and half of the maple syrup into a mixing bowl and mix together with a spoon.

3 Put the remaining cashew nut butter and maple syrup in another mixing bowl. Sift over 7.5ml/1½ tsp of the raw cacao or cocoa powder. Mix it all together until blended.

4 Shape each batch of mixture into 6 walnut-sized balls, to make 12 mixed plain and chocolate cookies. Arrange the balls on the prepared baking sheet, spacing them slightly apart to allow room for the cookies to spread out when cooking. Sprinkle the balls with chopped cashew nuts, if using.

5 Bake the cookies for 5–7 minutes, or until beginning to brown around the edges.

6 Remove from the oven and dust the plain ones with icing sugar and the chocolate ones with the remaining 2.5ml/½ tsp cacao or cocoa powder.

7 Leave to cool on the baking sheet. Store in an airtight container where they will keep for up to 4 days.

Variation

For an extra-special effect you can make chocolate- or jam-filled thumbprint cookies. Use your thumb or the end of a wooden spoon dipped in gluten-free icing sugar to make a dip in the middle of each cookie before baking. After baking, and while the cookies are still hot, spoon or pipe a little smooth jam or some chocolate hazelnut spread into the dips and leave to cool.

Energy 119kcal/499kJ; Protein 3.7g; Carbohydrate 6.8g, of which sugars 1.5g; Fat 9.6g, of which saturates 2.5g; Cholesterol 0mg; Calcium 3mg; Fibre 0.1g; Sodium 8mg.

Chocolate cherry cookies

These indulgent cookies are just as chocolatey as chocolate chip cookies. They are rich in raw cacao powder, with the added depth of flavour and sweetness of the cherries. You could replace the cherries with another dried fruit, like dried figs.

MAKES 30

115g/4oz/½ cup mesquite powder
80g/3¼oz/1 cup raw cacao powder or unsweetened cocoa powder
225g/8oz/2 cups brown rice flour
115g/4oz/1 cup gluten-free oat flour
165g/5½oz/1 cup potato starch
10ml/2 tsp cream of tartar
2.5ml/½ tsp gluten-free baking powder
225g/8oz/1 cup unsalted butter, softened, plus extra for greasing
275g/10oz/2 cups coconut crystals/sugar or soft light brown sugar
3 large eggs
50g/2oz/½ cup dried unsweetened cherries

1 Preheat the oven to 180°C/350°F/Gas 4. Lightly grease two baking sheets.

2 Sift the mesquite, cacao or cocoa powder, rice flour, oat flour, potato starch, cream of tartar and baking powder into a mixing bowl.

3 In a separate mixing bowl, beat the butter with the coconut crystals or sugar using an electric whisk on high for about 3 minutes, until fluffy.

4 Beat the eggs into the butter mixture one by one, then beat the flour mixture into the butter mixture. Stir in the dried cherries with a spoon.

5 Roll the cookie dough into small balls, flatten them, then place them on the baking sheets, spaced about 2.5cm/1in apart.

6 Bake for about 15 minutes until set, then leave to cool on a wire rack before serving.

Energy 127kcal/532kJ; Protein 2.5g; Carbohydrate 20.8g, of which sugars 6.9g; Fat 6.1g, of which saturates 3.5g; Cholesterol 36mg; Calcium 10mg; Fibre 2.9g; Sodium 39mg.

Flapjack cookies with ginger & turmeric

Flapjacks are universally popular and very useful if you can't tolerate wheat, but they can be high in fat and refined sugar. These are made with a small amount of vegetable margarine and maple syrup for natural sweetness, so are a healthier option.

MAKES 16

75g/3oz/½ cup hard baking margarine
60ml/4 tbsp/¼ cup maple syrup
30ml/2 tbsp crunchy hazelnut or almond butter or unsweetened peanut butter
110g/4oz/1 cup gluten-free jumbo rolled oats
40g/1½oz/¼ cup quinoa flakes
7.5ml/1½ tsp ground ginger
2.5ml/½ tsp ground turmeric
1 dessert apple, cored and coarsely grated
20ml/4 tsp sesame seeds

1 Preheat the oven to 180°C/350°F/Gas 4. Line two baking sheets with baking parchment.

2 Put the margarine, maple syrup and nut butter in a large pan and heat gently, stirring until the margarine has melted.

3 Stir in the oats, quinoa flakes, spices and grated apple and mix well. Scoop out 16 heaped tablespoons on to the lined sheets. Flatten slightly with a fork then sprinkle with the sesame seeds.

4 Bake for 10–12 minutes, until browned, then remove from the oven and leave to cool on the parchment. Store in a plastic container in the fridge for up to 2 days.

Variation
Turmeric gives these a golden colour and subtle flavour, but you can use a different spice; ground cinnamon or mixed/apple pie spice would work well here.

Energy 104kcal/434kJ; Protein 1.9g; Carbohydrate 10.3g, of which sugars 3.1g; Fat 6.4g, of which saturates 2.2g; Cholesterol 1mg; Calcium 17mg; Fibre 1.1g; Sodium 38mg.

Chocolate popcorn slice

Packed with concentrated energy and flavour, these gluten-free treats are a no-bake twist on muesli bars. You can vary the topping and use different dried fruits or toasted nuts if you prefer.

MAKES 10

15ml/1 tbsp vegetable oil
50g/2oz/¼ cup popping corn
115g/4oz/scant ½ cup smooth peanut butter or other nut butter
45ml/3 tbsp coconut oil
100g/3¾oz dark/bittersweet chocolate, broken into pieces
30ml/2 tbsp maple syrup

For the topping

30ml/2 tbsp dried cranberries
30ml/2 tbsp dried goji berries
15ml/1 tbsp pumpkin seeds
15ml/1 tbsp sunflower seeds

1 Line a shallow 20cm/8in square cake tin/pan with baking parchment.

2 Heat the oil in a medium-sized pan with a lid, add the popping corn, cover and cook over a medium heat for 3–4 minutes, shaking the pan from time to time until all the corn has popped. Remove the lid and take the pan off the heat.

3 Put the peanut or other nut butter, coconut oil, chocolate and maple syrup in a second large pan and heat gently over a low heat, stirring from time to time, until the chocolate has melted and the mixture is smooth and glossy.

4 Take the pan off the heat then stir in the popped corn, discarding any kernels that haven't popped.

5 Coat the popcorn well in the chocolate, then tip the mixture into the lined tin, roughly spread it with the back of a spoon to level, then sprinkle with the cranberries, goji berries and seeds.

6 Chill for about an hour, until set, then lift out of the tin, peel away the paper and cut into 10 bars. These can be stored in the fridge for up to 2 days.

Variations

- Replace the popcorn with some gluten-free cornflakes or puffed rice cereal.
- Children may prefer a slightly less intense chocolate flavour, so you could use half dark chocolate and half milk chocolate.
- These bars are dairy-free and vegan if you ensure that you are using milk-free dark chocolate.

Energy 27kcal/90kJ; Protein 0.5g; Carbohydrate 1.7g, of which sugars 1.1g; Fat 1.6g, of which saturates 0.7g; Cholesterol 0.1mg; Calcium 1.4mg; Fibre 0.1g; Sodium 4mg.

Hazelnut praline slice

For those who love naturally gluten-free puffed rice refrigerator cake and chocolate hazelnut spread, this is a double delight. To make it even more tempting, it's covered with a hazelnut praline.

MAKES 16

15ml/1 tbsp golden/light corn syrup or brown rice syrup
15ml/1 tbsp liquid glucose
100g/3¾oz gluten-free marshmallows
75g/3oz/6 tbsp butter or hard baking margarine
120g/4oz/4 cups gluten-free puffed rice cereal
50g/2oz/½ cup chopped roasted hazelnuts

For the praline

50g/2oz/¼ cup caster/superfine sugar
50g/2oz/½ cup roasted hazelnuts

For the topping

100g/3¾oz plain/semisweet chocolate, broken into pieces
15ml/1 tbsp butter
30ml/2 tbsp chocolate hazelnut spread
60ml/4 tbsp chopped roasted hazelnuts

1 Grease a 20cm/8in square cake tin/pan, then line it with baking parchment.

2 To prepare the praline, heat the sugar in a pan until it has melted. Do not stir; swirl it to ensure that the sugar does not burn. Cook until the caramel is golden brown.

3 Spread the hazelnuts out on a silicone mat or greased baking sheet and pour over the caramel. Leave to cool completely, then blitz the praline in a food processor or blender to very fine crumbs.

4 Place the golden syrup, glucose, marshmallows and butter or margarine in a pan and heat gently until melted. Stir in the hazelnut praline powder, then add the puffed rice and chopped hazelnuts and combine.

5 Spoon the mixture into the tin and press out with the back of a spoon into an even layer. Leave to cool.

6 For the topping, place a heatproof bowl over a pan of simmering water, then add the chocolate and the butter. Stir until melted and combined. Stir in the chocolate hazelnut spread. The mixture will thicken.

7 Spread the chocolate mixture over the top of the crispy cake and sprinkle with the chopped hazelnuts.

8 Leave in the fridge to set for 3 hours, then cut into 16 bars or squares, and serve.

Energy 262kcal/1093kJ; Protein 2.6g; Carbohydrate 22.7g, of which sugars 15.1g; Fat 18.5g, of which saturates 5.4g; Cholesterol 16mg; Calcium 55mg; Fibre 1.2g; Sodium 139mg.

Coconut mint slice

Coconut and mint are perhaps not a combination that you would often put together but they marry really well in this indulgent slice, made with a combination of gluten-free flour, desiccated coconut and cocoa powder. The pretty brown and white layers look elegant displayed on a tea table.

MAKES 20

For the coconut base

225g/8oz/generous 1 cup butter, plus extra for greasing
170g/6oz/¾ cup caster/superfine sugar
200g/7oz/generous 1⅔ cups gluten-free plain/all-purpose flour blend
2.5ml/½ tsp xanthan gum
60g/2oz/½ cup raw cacao powder or unsweetened cocoa powder
100g/3½oz desiccated/dry unsweetened shredded coconut

For the peppermint layer

350g/11½oz/3 cups gluten-free icing/confectioners' sugar, sifted
50g/1¾oz/3 tbsp butter, softened
5ml/1 tsp peppermint extract
15ml/1 tbsp cream cheese
15–30ml/1–2 tbsp milk

For the ganache

200g/7oz plain/semisweet chocolate
30ml/2 tbsp butter
30ml/2 tbsp milk

1 Preheat the oven to 180°C/350°F/Gas 4. Grease a 35 x 25cm/14 x 10in deep baking tin/pan, then line it with baking parchment.

2 For the coconut base, cream together the butter and sugar until light and creamy.

3 Sift in the flour, xanthan gum and cacao or cocoa. Add the coconut and stir together to make a soft dough.

4 Spoon the dough into the tin and press it out flat using your fingertips, which you may need to lightly dust with flour, or a sheet of baking parchment.

5 Bake the coconut base in the preheated oven for 15–20 minutes, until firm. Remove from the oven and leave to cool completely.

6 For the peppermint layer, whisk together the icing sugar, butter, peppermint extract, cream cheese and milk until very light and creamy. It is best to do this with an electric mixer.

7 Spread the peppermint icing over the coconut base and chill in the fridge for about an hour.

8 For the ganache, break the chocolate into pieces and place with the butter and milk in a heatproof bowl over a pan of simmering water. Stir until the butter and chocolate have melted and combined and you have a smooth, glossy mixture.

9 Leave the ganache until it is just cool and then spread it over the peppermint icing. Return to the fridge and leave to set for at least 3 hours or overnight.

10 Lift out the slice, remove the lining paper, cut into about 20 bars and serve. This slice will store in an airtight container in the fridge for up to 3 days.

Variation

If you aren't keen on coconut, you could replace it with an equal quantity of ground almonds or other nuts.

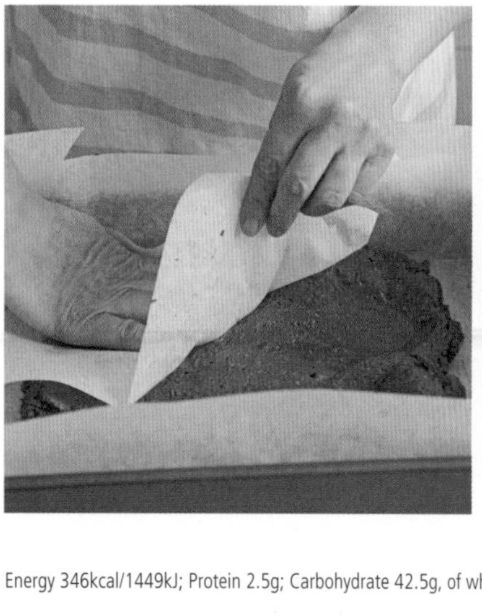

Energy 346kcal/1449kJ; Protein 2.5g; Carbohydrate 42.5g, of which sugars 34.3g; Fat 19.6g, of which saturates 13g; Cholesterol 34mg; Calcium 32mg; Fibre 2.1g; Sodium 129mg.

Apple shortcake slice

This traybake has a buttery gluten-free shortbread-style base, a thick fruity apple filling, and crumble topping. It will be popular at any tea-time table and can also be served as a cold dessert with gluten-free crème fraîche or whipped cream.

MAKES 24

1kg/2¼lb cooking apples
90g/3½oz/½ cup caster/superfine sugar
5ml/1 tsp ground cinnamon
250g/9oz/generous 1 cup butter, softened, or soft baking margarine
90g/3½oz/¾ cup gluten-free icing/confectioners' sugar, sifted
225g/8oz/2 cups gluten-free plain/all-purpose flour blend, plus extra for dusting
2.5ml/½ tsp xanthan gum

For the crumble topping

150g/5oz/1¼ cups gluten-free self-raising/self-rising flour blend
75g/3oz/6 tbsp caster/superfine sugar
90g/3½oz/7 tbsp butter or hard baking margarine, chilled and diced

1 Peel and core the apples, then chop them into small pieces and place in a pan over a gentle heat with the sugar, ground cinnamon and 75ml/5 tbsp water.

2 Simmer until the apple is soft, adding a splash more water if necessary. Remove from the heat and leave to cool completely.

3 Cream together the butter or soft baking margarine and icing sugar until light and creamy. Mix in the flour and xanthan gum to make a soft dough.

4 Lightly dust your hands with flour, then press the dough into the lined tin in an even layer. Chill in the fridge for 30 minutes.

5 Preheat the oven to 180°C/350°F/Gas 4. Line a 35 x 25cm/14 x 10in deep baking tin/pan.

6 For the crumble topping, sift the flour into a mixing bowl and stir in the sugar. Rub the butter or margarine cubes into the flour with your fingertips, until the mixtures resembles large breadcrumbs.

7 Spread the cooled apple over the shortbread base and then sprinkle over the crumble in a thin layer. Bake for 25–30 minutes until the crumble is golden brown.

8 Remove from the oven and leave to cool in the tin, then cut into 24 squares.

Energy 217kcal/906kJ; Protein 1g; Carbohydrate 27.4g, of which sugars 14.9g; Fat 11.9g, of which saturates 7.4g; Cholesterol 30mg; Calcium 6mg; Fibre 1.1g; Sodium 87mg.

Oaty apricot slice

This slice is more delicate than standard flapjack thanks to the inclusion of gluten-free flour and amaranth flour, but still has the same oaty goodness. If you are short of time or they are out of season, replace the fresh apricots with about 30 ready-to-eat dried ones.

MAKES 24

450g/1lb fresh apricots, halved and pitted
200g/7oz/scant 1 cup butter or hard baking margarine
225g/8oz/2 cups gluten-free plain/all-purpose flour blend
75g/3oz/⅔ cup amaranth flour
2.5ml/½ tsp xanthan gum
225g/8oz/generous 2 cups gluten-free rolled oats
175g/6oz/scant 1 cup caster/superfine sugar
30ml/2 tbsp golden/light corn syrup
1 egg, beaten
grated rind of 1 lemon

1 Preheat the oven to 140°C/275°F/Gas 1. Line a 35 x 25cm/14 x 10in deep baking tin/pan with baking parchment, or greaseproof or waxed paper.

2 Lay the apricots in a roasting dish, cut side up, then bake for about an hour until the fruit is soft. Remove from the oven and leave to cool.

3 Turn the oven temperature up to 180°C/350°F/Gas 4. Melt the butter or margarine in a small pan or in a bowl in the microwave, then set aside and set aside to cool.

4 Place the flours, xanthan gum, oats and sugar in a large mixing bowl and stir together to combine.

5 Pour in the cooled melted butter, golden syrup and the beaten egg and mix in. The dough should be loose and crumbly but should hold together when you press it gently with your fingers.

6 Spoon just over half of the mixture into the prepared tin and press down flat with clean fingertips so that the whole base is covered.

7 Roughly chop the cooled apricots into small pieces and mix with the lemon rind. Arrange over the oaty base mixture so that the apricots are evenly distributed.

8 Sprinkle the remaining oat mixture on top of the apricots and press down. Bake for 25–30 minutes, until the top of the slice is golden brown.

9 Remove from the oven and leave to cool in the tin, then cut into 24 bars or squares.

Energy 186kcal/778kJ; Protein 2.4g; Carbohydrate 26.8g, of which sugars 10g; Fat 8.1g, of which saturates 4.5g; Cholesterol 27mg; Calcium 13mg; Fibre 1.4g; Sodium 61mg.

Apricot & pecan flapjack

A tried-and-tested favourite made even more delicious by the addition of maple syrup, fruit and nuts, this gluten-free traybake is a real energy booster at any time of day – great for kids and adults alike. Chop and change the nuts and dried fruit, to suit your taste.

MAKES 10

150g/5oz/10 tbsp unsalted butter or hard baking margarine, diced, plus extra for greasing
150g/5oz/⅔ cup light muscovado/ brown sugar
30ml/2 tbsp maple syrup
200g/7oz/generous 2 cups gluten-free rolled oats
50g/2oz/½ cup pecan nuts, chopped
50g/2oz/¼ cup ready-to-eat dried apricots, chopped

1 Preheat the oven to 160°C/325°F/Gas 3. Lightly grease an 18cm/7in square shallow baking tin/pan.

2 Put the butter or margarine, sugar and maple syrup in a large pan and heat gently until the butter has melted.

3 Remove from the heat and stir in the oats, nuts and apricots until everything is well combined.

4 Spread the mixture evenly in the prepared tin and, using a knife, score the mixture into 10 bars.

5 Bake the flapjacks for about 25–30 minutes, or until golden but still slightly wobbly in the middle if you shake the pan (it will firm up as it cools).

6 Remove from the oven and cut through the scored lines. Leave until just warm before removing from the tin and slicing into individual bars.

Energy 298kcal/1255kJ; Protein 3.3g; Carbohydrate 34.7g, of which sugars 19.9g; Fat 17.1g, of which saturates 7.8g; Cholesterol 32mg; Calcium 25mg; Fibre 2.6g; Sodium 11mg.

Cranberry, chia & apple muesli bars

These tasty energy-packed low-fat muesli bars are sweetened with apples, dried cranberries and just a little sugar, then mixed with the tiniest amount of coconut oil to keep them moist. Egg and chia seeds bind it all together. Make sure you choose a muesli that contains gluten-free oats.

MAKES 12

250g/9oz or 2 small dessert apples, cored and diced
30ml/2 tbsp water
30ml/2 tbsp coconut oil
150g/5oz/1¼ cups gluten-free muesli
10ml/2 tsp chia seeds
30ml/2 tbsp dried cranberries
50g/2oz/4 tbsp light muscovado/brown sugar
1 egg, beaten

1 Preheat the oven to 180°C/350°F/Gas 4. Line a 20cm/8in square cake tin/pan with baking parchment.

2 Put the apples, water and oil in a pan, cover and simmer for 5 minutes, until the apples are soft. Mash the apples.

3 Stir the muesli, chia seeds and cranberries into the apple mixture, then mix in the sugar and beaten egg. Tip the mixture into the lined tin and press into an even layer with the back of a spoon.

4 Bake for 30–35 minutes, until golden brown. Score into bars with a sharp knife and leave to cool in the tin. Once cold, peel off the paper and cut into bars. Store in a plastic container in the fridge for up to 2 days.

Variation

You could use 250g/9oz ready-made apple sauce in place of the apples and water, and omit the coconut oil.

Energy 107kcal/449kJ; Protein 2.3g; Carbohydrate 17g, of which sugars 10.5g; Fat 3.7g, of which saturates 2g; Cholesterol 19mg; Calcium 16mg; Fibre 2.3g; Sodium 24mg.

Sweet pastry & desserts

There are few who can resist a slice of a fruit-laden tart, fluffy citrus pudding or decadent chocolate dessert, and you'll find recipes for all of them in this chapter. You'll also discover how to make gluten-free versions of classic sweet pastry, such as pâte sucrée and almond pastry, using a range of different flours in place of wheat ones. Because of their sugar content, these are a little softer than plainer savoury pastry, so make sure you chill them after making and assembling; don't be tempted to cut down on the times recommended for this. There are also lots of general tips for pastry making on pages 100–105, so do have a read before you try the recipes here. If you follow the simple guidelines, there is no reason why even beginners should not be able to create good gluten-free pastry.

Once you've mastered them, the range of foods on offer is vast. Fruit-laden pies are always welcome, and ones included here are Double-crust Apple Pie with egg-enriched lemon-flavoured pastry, Cherry Pie with a nutty-flavoured sorghum flour pastry, or Pear Tarte Tatin, with buttery puff pastry. Tarts make equally delicious desserts and can have more indulgent fillings, such as the baked chocolate mousse in Dark Chocolate Hazelnut Tart or Summer Bakewell Tart. Of course, such rich pies should not be served every day of the week, but are they are perfect on special occasions or to round off Sunday lunch, since they can be made in advance and have real wow factor. If, however, you are looking for something lighter after a rich meal, try serving Mango & Coconut Filo Baskets.

Not all pies and tarts are made with pastry crusts, either: for instance, Mississippi Mud Pie and Chocolate Avocado Tart use crushed nuts and dried fruits to make cases firm enough to hold generous fillings. Other alternative ingredients appear in these desserts, too, such as mild-tasting rice flour, which is used in a range of different ways, lending shortness to pastries and helping to thicken fillings. The unassuming flavour of this and some other gluten-free flours allows the other other ingredients to shine; you'll find the citrus in Lemon Surprise Pudding is a little more tangy, and the chocolate in Chocolate Mud Pudding has a rounder and richer flavour, than in wheat-flour versions.

A dessert adds a final flourish to any meal, so whether you opt for a perfect pie or a homely pudding, there's something here for everyone to enjoy.

Pâte sucrée

This rich, crisp sweet pastry, also known as biscuit pastry, is used mainly for making flan and tartlet cases. Because it has a high proportion of sugar, it needs to be chilled for an hour before use. This makes enough for a 23cm/9in flan tin/pan or eight 7.5cm/3in tartlet tins/mini quiche pans.

MAKES 275G/10OZ

175g/6oz/1½ cups gluten-free plain/all-purpose flour blend, plus extra for dusting
2.5ml/½ tsp xanthan gum
1.5ml/¼ tsp salt
75g/3oz/6 tbsp chilled butter or hard baking margarine, diced
50g/2oz/¼ cup caster/superfine sugar
1 egg, lightly beaten
30ml/2 tbsp cold water

1 Sift the flour, xanthan gum and salt together to make a mound on a pastry board or cold work surface. Make a well in the middle and put in the butter and sugar, then pour the beaten egg over the top.

2 Using your fingertips only, with a pecking action, work the butter or margarine, eggs and sugar together. As you do this, pull in a little of the surrounding flour to prevent the mixture from becoming too sticky.

3 When the mixture begins to form a smooth paste, gradually pull in the rest of the flour to make a crumbly mixture. Sprinkle over the water and mix to a soft dough.

4 Lightly knead the dough with the heel of your hand for 1 minute, form it into a ball, then wrap it in clear film or plastic wrap and chill it in the fridge for 1 hour.

5 Roll out on a lightly floured surface, working quickly while it is still cool, as it becomes tacky as it warms. Use as directed in your chosen recipe.

TIPS FOR MAKING PÂTE SUCRÉE

• Allow plenty of time for the pastry to chill and relax in the fridge.

• If the pastry has been chilled for 1 hour or more, allow it to soften at room temperature before rolling out, or it may crack.

• Pies made using sweet pastry should be taken out of the oven as soon as the pastry is golden brown and crisp. Once it reaches this stage, the pastry will burn very quickly because of the sugar content.

• If you find sweet pastry difficult to handle, roll it between sheets of clear film or plastic wrap, so you can easily lift it and place it in the tin/pan.

• Alternatively, press small pieces of the pastry into the tin or pan with your fingers to form an even layer, instead of rolling it out. This gives a less finessed finish, but tastes good.

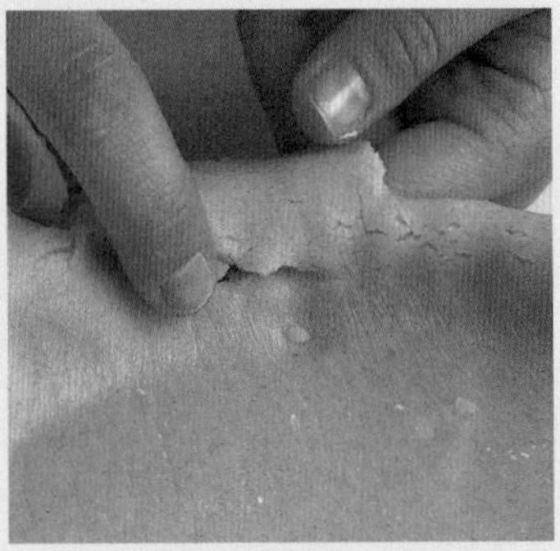

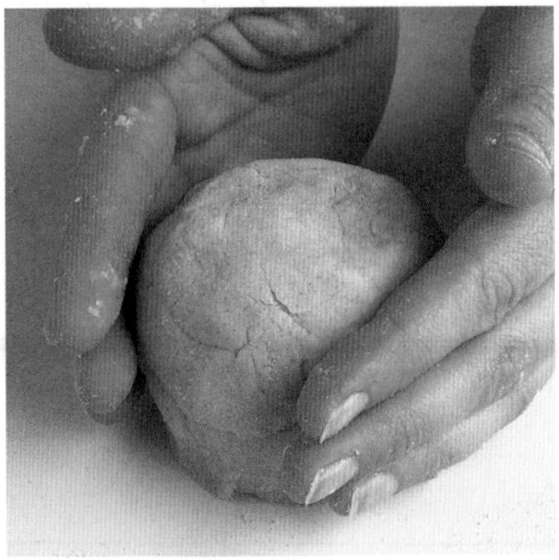

Energy 1463kcal/6097kJ; Protein 16.9g; Carbohydrate 192.5g, of which sugars 53.1g; Fat 70.6g, of which saturates 41.5g; Cholesterol 391mg; Calcium 62mg; Fibre 1.9g; Sodium 541mg.

Almond pastry

This dough resembles pâte sucrée and can be used as an alternative in most gluten-free sweet tart recipes, for extra nutty texture and richness. The addition of ground almonds makes it fairly soft, so it needs chilling for up to an hour before using. This is sufficient for a 23cm/9in flan tin/pan.

MAKES 350G/12OZ

150g/5oz/1¼ cups gluten-free plain/all-purpose flour blend
2.5ml/½ tsp xanthan gum
pinch of salt
30ml/2 tbsp caster/superfine sugar
50g/2oz/½ cup ground almonds
90g/3½oz/7 tbsp chilled butter or hard baking margarine, diced
1 egg
1–2 drops almond extract
15–30ml/1–2 tbsp cold water

1 Sift the flour, xanthan gum and salt into a large mixing bowl. Stir in the sugar and ground almonds.

2 Rub in the butter or margarine with your fingertips until the mixture resembles fine breadcrumbs.

3 Beat the egg, almond extract and 15ml/1 tbsp of the water in a bowl. Stir into the dry ingredients, adding a little more of the water if needed to make a soft dough.

4 Wrap in clear film or plastic wrap and chill for about 40 minutes, until firm, before using in your chosen recipe.

Variations

- Make a slightly spiced almond pastry by adding 5ml/1 tsp cinnamon and some grated nutmeg to the flour.
- To make chocolate pastry, replace 30ml/2 tbsp of the flour with unsweetened cocoa powder. Time the cooking carefully when using chocolate pastry, since the dark colour means it is hard to tell when it is cooked. Be guided by the cooking time and look for a dry texture and crisp bottom in flans and tarts.

ORANGE PASTRY

Gluten free • Vegetarian

MAKES 275G/10OZ

175g/6oz/1½ cups gluten-free plain/all-purpose flour blend
2.5ml/½ tsp xanthan gum
pinch of salt
75g/3oz/6 tbsp chilled butter or hard baking margarine, diced
seeds from 4 green cardamom pods
pinch of ground cloves
finely grated rind of 1 orange
30ml/2 tbsp caster/superfine sugar
2 egg yolks
10ml/2 tsp fresh orange juice

1 Sift the flour, xanthan gum and salt into a mixing bowl. Rub in the fat until the mixture resembles breadcrumbs.

2 Crush the cardamon seeds to a powder in a pestle and mortar. Stir into the flour with the cloves, orange rind and sugar. Make a well in the middle.

3 Mix the egg yolks with the juice in a small bowl. Add to the dry ingredients and mix to a dough. Knead briefly until smooth.

4 Wrap in cling film or plastic wrap and chill for 40 minutes, until firm, then use in your chosen recipe.

Almond: Energy 1714kcal/7117kJ; Protein 26.2g; Carbohydrate 155.2g, of which sugars 34.3g; Fat 110.5g, of which saturates 51.4g; Cholesterol 423mg; Calcium 179mg; Fibre 1.6g; Sodium 638mg.
Orange: Energy 1420kcal/5904kJ; Protein 15.2g; Carbohydrate 172.5g, of which sugars 33g; Fat 74.9g, of which saturates 42.7g; Cholesterol 563mg; Calcium 70mg; Fibre 1.9g; Sodium 475mg.

Fruit turnovers

Here, the gluten-free pastry is made in the traditional way, using half butter for flavour and richness and half white shortening for a crisp texture. The addition of an egg enriches it and ensures that it is flexible to handle and shape.

MAKES 8

450g/1lb plums, stoned and chopped
30–45ml/2–3 tbsp caster/superfine sugar

For the pastry

350g/12oz/3 cups gluten-free plain/all-purpose flour blend, plus extra for dusting
5ml/1 tsp xanthan gum
75g/3oz/6 tbsp white cooking fat or vegetable shortening, diced
75g/3oz/6 tbsp chilled butter or hard baking margarine, diced
1 egg, lightly beaten
75ml/5 tbsp cold water
milk and sugar, for brushing and sprinkling

1 Bring the fruit and the sugar to the boil with 15ml/1 tbsp water, then cover and simmer for 5–10 minutes, stirring frequently, until the fruit is soft. You can reduce the liquid by simmering it, uncovered, and stirring until thick. Leave to cool.

2 Sift the flour and xanthan gum into a large mixing bowl, add the fats and rub them into the flour until the mixture resembles fine crumbs (alternatively, process in a food processor). Mix the egg and water together and add to the dry ingredients. Mix to a soft dough.

3 Shape the dough into a ball, then flatten slightly, wrap in clear film or plastic wrap and chill for 30 minutes.

4 Preheat the oven to 190°C/375°F/Gas 5. Line a baking sheet with baking parchment.

5 On a lightly floured surface, roll out the dough to 3–5mm/⅛–¼in thick. Using a small upturned bowl or plate as a guide, cut out eight 15cm/6in circles, re-rolling the pastry offcuts as necessary.

6 Place a spoonful of the cooled fruit on to each pastry circle and brush the edges with water. Fold the pastry over the fruit, pinching the edges to seal them well.

7 Arrange the pastries on the baking sheet, brush with milk, sprinkle with sugar and make a small slit in each.

8 Bake for 20–30 minutes, until golden brown. Sprinkle with a little extra sugar and transfer to a wire rack to cool, or serve them warm.

Energy 343kcal/1435kJ; Protein 5.4g; Carbohydrate 41.3g, of which sugars 8g; Fat 18.5g, of which saturates 9g; Cholesterol 58mg; Calcium 72mg; Fibre 2.6g; Sodium 70mg.

Christmas stars

These pretty pastries are a delicious twist on the usual mince pies, and have a prune filling that is much less sweet than mincemeat. The pastry is made with a mixture of gluten-free rice and gram flours, softened with ground almonds and a hint of cinnamon.

MAKES 9

200g/7oz/1 cup ready-to-eat prunes, chopped

For the pastry

75g/3oz/½ cup rice flour
75g/3oz/⅔ cup gram flour
2.5ml/½ tsp xanthan gum
5ml/1 tsp ground cinnamon
50g/2oz/½ cup ground almonds
30ml/2 tbsp caster/superfine sugar
90g/3½oz/8 tbsp chilled butter or hard baking margarine, diced
1 large egg, lightly beaten
30–45ml/2–3 tbsp cold water
gluten-free icing/confectioners' sugar, for dusting

1 Sift the rice and gram flours, xanthan gum and cinnamon into a large mixing bowl. Stir in the ground almonds and sugar.

2 Add the butter or margarine to the flour and rub in until the mixture resembles fine breadcrumbs. Alternatively, put the dry ingredients in a food processor, pulse for a few seconds to mix, then add the fat and, using a pulsating action, blend to form fine breadcrumbs.

3 Reserve 15ml/1 tbsp of the beaten egg for glazing. Mix the rest of the egg with 30ml/2 tbsp of the water, add to the dry ingredients and mix to a soft dough, adding the rest of the water if needed.

4 Knead briefly and gently to bring together into a ball. Flatten slightly, then wrap in clear film or plastic wrap and chill for 1 hour.

5 Preheat the oven to 200°C/400°F/Gas 6. Roll out the pastry between two sheets of baking parchment to a square about 3mm/⅛in thick, then cut the square into a further nine equal squares. Make a diagonal cut from each corner of the squares towards the middle.

6 Put a spoonful of the chopped prunes in the middle of each square of pastry, then lift each corner of the pastry and fold it over to the middle to form a star shape.

7 Place the stars on a baking sheet and brush with beaten egg. Bake for about 15 minutes or until golden brown. Dust with sugar and serve warm.

Energy 224kcal/933kJ; Protein 3.7g; Carbohydrate 24.8g, of which sugars 11.3g; Fat 12.3g, of which saturates 5.7g; Cholesterol 47mg; Calcium 31mg; Fibre 2.1g; Sodium 74mg.

Mango & coconut filo baskets

Layered squares of gluten-free filo pastry baked in muffin tins make dainty containers for filling with coconut cream and fruit. Make the baskets ahead and fill them no more an hour before serving.

MAKES 6

250g/9oz or ½ quantity gluten-free filo pastry dough (see page 105)
30ml/2 tbsp coconut oil, melted
a little gluten-free plain/all-purpose flour blend, for dusting

For the filling

1 large mango, peeled and stoned
45ml/3 tbsp coconut cream
30ml/2 tbsp smooth apricot jam
seeds from 1 pomegranate
15ml/1 tbsp gluten-free icing/confectioners' sugar, for dusting

1 For the filling, cut half the mango flesh into attractive slices. Put the rest in a food processor or blender. Add the coconut cream and process to a thick purée. Chill.

2 Preheat the oven to 190°C/375°F/Gas 5. Lightly grease six non-stick muffin tins/pans, measuring 7.5cm/3in across and 3cm/1¼in deep, with a little of the oil.

3 Cut the filo pastry dough into two pieces; wrap one in clear film or plastic wrap. Roll out the other on a lightly floured surface, following the instructions on page 105, to a rectangle about 34 x 23cm/13.5 x 9in. Trim the edges straight, then cut into six 12cm/4½in squares.

4 Brush each filo square lightly with oil, then use one square to line one cup of a muffin pan. Place another oiled square on top, offset to make a star-shaped basket. Make two more baskets in the same way. Repeat with the second piece of pastry dough and the rest of the oil to make six baskets, each consisting of two sheets of filo. Warm the jam in a pan or bowl in the microwave and thickly brush it over the base and partway up the sides of the filo cases. Bake for 10 minutes, until light golden, then leave to cool in the tins before removing.

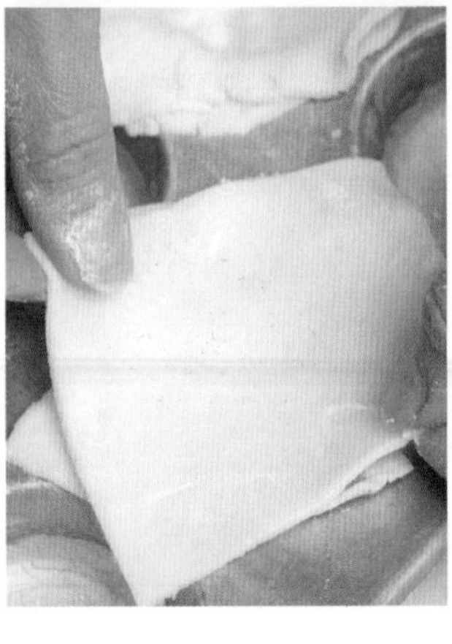

5 Just before serving, spoon the cream filling into the baskets and top each with fresh mango slices, pomegranate seeds and a dusting of icing sugar.

Cook's tip

You can buy coconut cream in small cans (this is not the same as coconut milk). Depending on the brand, it may either be thickened with guar gum or the top section may be thick with a more watery cream underneath. In the case of the latter, use the thicker cream, it needs a similar consistency to thick yogurt.

Energy 199kcal/832kJ; Protein 1.6g; Carbohydrate 28.9g, of which sugars 10g; Fat 8.9g, of which saturates 6.2g; Cholesterol 0mg; Calcium 5mg; Fibre 1.1g; Sodium 5mg.

Lemon & ricotta rolls

These gluten-free filo rolls are packed with a lemon cheesecake mixture that is thickened with sweet rice flour, which has a mild and milky flavour that works well in desserts and bakes.

MAKES 12

250g/9oz or ½ quantity gluten-free filo pastry dough (see page 105)
a little gluten-free plain/all-purpose flour blend, for dusting
40g/1½oz/3 tbsp butter, melted
15ml/1 tbsp poppy seeds
45ml/3 tbsp clear honey or maple syrup
15ml/1 tbsp lemon juice

For the filling

250g/9oz/generous 1 cup ricotta cheese
finely grated rind of 1 lemon
50g/2oz/¼ cup caster/superfine sugar
1 egg
15ml/1 tbsp sweet rice flour

1 To make the filling, put the ricotta and lemon rind in a large mixing bowl and beat for a few seconds to soften.

2 Beat the sugar and egg in a separate mixing bowl with an electric whisk for 1 minute or a balloon whisk for 2–3 minutes, until slightly thickened and foamy.

3 Stir one-third of the egg mixture into the ricotta mixture to loosen, then fold in the rest. Sprinkle over the rice flour and gently fold in.

4 Preheat the oven to 190°C/375°F/Gas 5 and line a baking sheet with baking parchment. Cut the filo pastry dough into two pieces, for ease of handling. Roll out one portion on a lightly floured surface, following the instructions on page 105, to a rectangle about 30 x 20cm/15 x 8in. Trim the edges straight, then cut the sheet in half lengthways, and then into six 15 x 10cm/5 x 4in rectangles. Repeat with the other portion of dough.

5 Brush a pastry strip with some of the melted butter, then place a heaped teaspoon of filling slightly in from one of the long edges and spread it out along the length. Tuck in the two shorter ends by about 1cm/½in, then roll up like a long cigar. Place on the baking sheet.

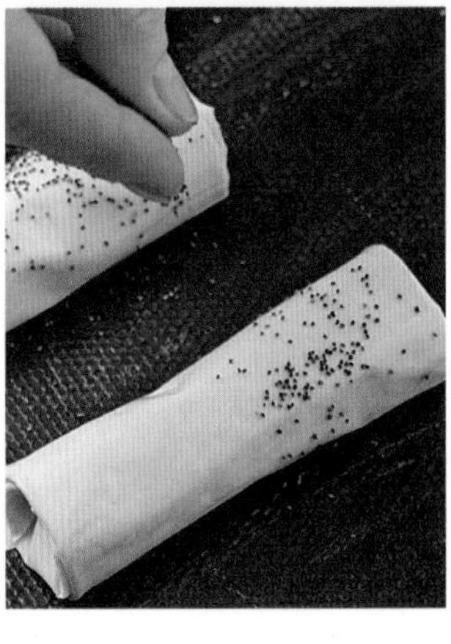

6 Repeat with the remaining pastry and filling to make 12 pastry rolls. Brush the tops of the rolls with the remaining butter and sprinkle with poppy seeds.

7 Bake for 15–20 minutes or until golden brown and crisp. Remove from the oven and transfer to a wire rack to cool. Mix the honey or maple syrup with the lemon juice and drizzle over the pastries just before serving.

Energy 143kcal/599kJ; Protein 3.5g; Carbohydrate 18.1g, of which sugars 7.7g; Fat 7.2g, of which saturates 3.6g; Cholesterol 37mg; Calcium 75mg; Fibre 0.1g; Sodium 50mg.

Chocolate éclairs

A simple white gluten-free flour mix makes excellent choux pastry, but if you have some sweet rice flour, substitute 15ml/1 tbsp for an equal amount of flour. For the crispiest pastries, these are best served within a couple of hours of making, but can be chilled for 24 hours if needed.

MAKES 12

For the pastry

65g/2½oz/9 tbsp gluten-free plain/all-purpose flour blend
pinch of salt
50g/2oz/¼ cup butter, diced
150ml/¼ pint/⅔ cup water
2 eggs, lightly beaten

For the filling & topping

300ml/½ pint/1¼ cups double/heavy cream
10ml/2 tsp gluten-free icing/confectioners' sugar, sifted
1.5ml/¼ tsp vanilla extract
115g/4oz plain/semisweet chocolate
30ml/2 tbsp water
25g/1oz/2 tbsp butter

1 Preheat the oven to 200°C/400°F/Gas 6. Line a large baking sheet with baking parchment.

2 To make the pastry, sift the flour and salt on to a small sheet of baking parchment – this makes it easier to add it all in one go.

3 Heat the butter and water in a pan very gently until the butter melts, then increase the heat and bring to a rolling boil.

4 Remove the pan from the heat and add all the flour in one go. Beat vigorously with a wooden spoon until the flour is incorporated. Return the pan to low heat, then beat until it leaves the sides of the pan and forms a ball.

5 Set the pan aside and allow the choux pastry dough to cool for 2–3 minutes.

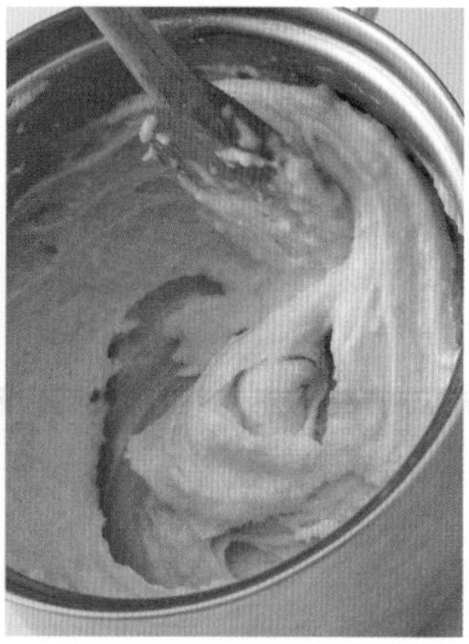

6 Add the beaten eggs a little at a time, beating well after each addition, until you have a smooth, shiny paste, which is thick enough to hold its shape.

7 Spoon the choux pastry into a piping or pastry bag fitted with a 2.5cm/1in plain nozzle. Pipe 10cm/4in lengths on to the prepared baking sheet. Use a wet knife to cut off the pastry at the nozzle.

8 Bake for 25–30 minutes, or until the pastry fingers are well risen and golden brown in colour. Remove from the oven. Make a neat slit along the side of each finger to release the steam.

9 Lower the oven temperature to 180°C/350°F/Gas 4 and bake for a further 5 minutes. Cool on a wire rack.

10 To make the filling, whip the cream with the icing sugar and vanilla extract until it just holds its shape. Spoon into a piping bag fitted with a 1cm/½in plain nozzle and use to fill the éclairs.

11 Place the chocolate and water in a heatproof bowl set over a pan of simmering water, until melted. Remove from the heat and gradually stir in the butter.

12 Dip the top of each éclair in the melted chocolate, then place on a rack. Leave in a cool place until the chocolate is set.

Variation

To make profiteroles instead of chocolate éclairs, simply use the same choux pastry mixture to pipe rounds, instead of fingers, on to baking parchment. Dampen your finger and gently press down any peaks that may form when you lift off the piping bag, or these can burn. Bake the buns for a little less time than the fingers – about 20 minutes – keeping an eye on them towards the end of the cooking time to avoid letting them get too brown; they should be pale golden and risen. Instead of making a slit, poke a hole in the bottom of each bun with a skewer, then return to the oven briefly to dry out. Once cool, fill with cream and top with chocolate as you would éclairs.

Energy 246kcal/1018kJ; Protein 1.8g; Carbohydrate 10.9g, of which sugars 6.5g; Fat 21.9g, of which saturates 13.4g; Cholesterol 67mg; Calcium 19mg; Fibre 0.4g; Sodium 51mg.

Mississippi mud pie

This is an updated and healthier version of the classic Mississippi mud pie, which traditionally used processed ingredients, and is also gluten free, as the pie crust doesn't contain flour, being made from a mixture of nuts, goji berries and maple syrup.

SERVES 8–10

For the pastry

oil, for greasing
225g/8oz/2 cups walnut pieces
115g/4oz/1 cup goji berries
50ml/2fl oz/¼ cup maple syrup
50g/2oz/¼ cup maple sugar or brown sugar and stevia blend

For the filling

60ml/4 tbsp coconut oil
175g/6oz/1¾ cups raw cacao paste
6 eggs, separated
1.5ml/¼ tsp salt
75g/3oz/¾ cup mixed brown sugar and stevia

For the custard

45ml/3 tbsp mixed brown sugar and stevia
50g/2oz/½ cup raw cacao powder or unsweetened cocoa powder
75ml/5 tbsp cornflour/starch
600ml/1 pint/2½ cups almond milk
45ml/3 tbsp coconut oil

For the topping

300ml/½ pint/1¼ cups double/heavy cream
raw cacao powder or unsweetened cocoa powder, for dusting

1 Preheat the oven to 180°C/350°F/Gas 4. Lightly grease a 23cm/9in-diameter springform cake tin/pan with vegetable oil.

2 To make the pastry, put the walnuts, goji berries, maple syrup and sugar in a food processor and process to form a sticky dough.

3 Press the pastry dough into the prepared tin in an even layer, flattening it into the bottom and up the sides with a spoon, leaving a 1cm/½in gap between the top of the crust and the top of the tin.

4 To make the filling, put the coconut oil and cacao paste in a heatproof bowl set over a pan of barely simmering water. Stir until combined.

5 Put the egg yolks, salt and 50g/2oz/½ cup of the brown sugar and stevia blend in a large mixing bowl and beat with an electric whisk on high for 5 minutes, until pale and doubled in volume. Wash and dry the beaters.

6 Put the egg whites in a clean, dry mixing bowl and beat with the electric whisk, starting on low and building up to high over a few minutes. Once stiff, add the remaining 25g/1oz/¼ cup brown sugar and stevia blend and continue whisking until soft peaks form, but no more. Fold the egg white mixture into the egg yolk mixture, then fold in the cacao and coconut oil mixture.

7 Pour the filling into the pastry. Bake for 40 minutes, until the filling has set but is still wobbly when you shake the tin. Leave to cool in the tin on a wire rack, where it will sink in the middle as it cools. Chill in the fridge for at least 3 hours, or overnight.

8 To make the chocolate custard, put the brown sugar and stevia blend in a pan with the cacao or cocoa powder and cornflour and mix to combine. Slowly pour in the almond milk, whisking continuously with an electric whisk on low. Put over a medium heat and continue whisking as the liquid comes to a boil. Boil for just 30 seconds, then pour it into a bowl. Add the coconut oil, and whisk until it has melted and combined into the custard. Leave to cool, then chill in the fridge to set for at least 3 hours, or overnight.

9 Stir the custard with a spatula to break it up, then pour it over the cake and spread evenly, keeping it within the outer crust. Put the cake in the fridge for 30 minutes. Remove from the tin and place on a serving plate or dish.

10 To make the cream topping, whisk the cream in a mixing bowl until it forms stiff peaks. Spread the cream over the top of the pie, sprinkle with cacao or cocoa powder and serve.

Energy 631kcal/2105kJ; Protein 9.4g; Carbohydrate 39.2g, of which sugars 29.8g; Fat 38.4g, of which saturates 16.9g; Cholesterol 150mg; Calcium 62mg; Fibre 1.8g; Sodium 126mg.

Dark chocolate hazelnut tart

Buttery shortcrust enriched with ground hazelnuts makes the perfect case for this luxuriously rich chocolate filling. Use the pastry trimmings to decorate the top of the tart.

SERVES 8

300ml/½ pint/1¼ cups double/heavy cream
150ml/¼ pint/⅔ cup milk
150g/5oz dark/bittersweet chocolate, chopped
4 eggs
45ml/3 tbsp caster/superfine sugar
5ml/1 tsp vanilla extract
15ml/1 tbsp gluten-free plain/all-purpose flour blend
115g/4oz/1 cup hazelnuts, toasted
10ml/2 tsp gluten-free icing/confectioners' sugar, for dusting

For the pastry

150g/5oz/1¼ cups gluten-free plain/all-purpose flour, plus extra for dusting
2.5ml/½ tsp xanthan gum
45ml/3 tbsp caster/superfine sugar
50g/2oz/½ cup ground hazelnuts
90g/3½oz/scant ½ cup chilled butter or hard baking margarine, diced
1 egg, lightly beaten
30ml/2 tbsp cold water

1 Make the pastry. Sift the flour, xanthan gum and sugar into a mixing bowl, then add the hazelnuts. Rub in the fat until the mixture resembles breadcrumbs. Mix the egg and water and stir into the flour to make a dough.

2 Wrap the pastry in clear film or plastic wrap and chill for 30 minutes, then roll out on a floured surface and line a 23cm/9in loose-based flan tin/pan. Trim the edges. Cover and chill. Re-roll the trimmings into a 30cm/12in strip. Cut into six strips, and make two braids. Join these into a circle of a size to fit the pie case. Place on a baking sheet lined with baking parchment, then chill.

3 Preheat the oven to 200°C/400°F/Gas 6. Blind bake the case for 10 minutes. Remove the paper and beans and bake for 5 minutes. Bake the braid for 10 minutes.

4 Bring the cream and milk to the boil in a pan. Add the chocolate and melt. Whisk the eggs, sugar, vanilla and flour in a bowl, then stir in the chocolate mixture and hazelnuts. Pour into the pastry case and bake for 25 minutes.

5 Cool, remove from the tin, transfer to a plate and place the pastry rope on top. Dust with icing sugar.

Energy 538kcal/2230kJ; Protein 8.7g; Carbohydrate 32.3g, of which sugars 18.7g; Fat 42g, of which saturates 19.1g; Cholesterol 178mg; Calcium 82mg; Fibre 2.1g; Sodium 112mg.

Chocolate avocado tart

A chocolate tart crust with a creamy chocolate filling… and all without any sugar, dairy or gluten! This raw vegan paleo recipe is every bit as good as a baked chocolate tart, but healthier.

SERVES 8

2 ripe avocados
60ml/4 tbsp raw cacao powder or unsweetened cocoa powder
30ml/2 tbsp maple syrup
mixed fresh berries, to decorate

For the pastry

115g/4oz/1 cup cashew nuts, soaked in water for at least 4 hours or overnight
40g/1½oz/½ cup gluten-free rolled oats
75g/3oz/½ cup macadamia nuts
60g/2¼oz/¾ cup raw cacao powder or unsweetened cocoa powder
5ml/1 tsp vanilla extract
75g/3oz/about 14 dried stoned/pitted dates

1 For the pastry, drain the cashews and put them in a food processor with the oats, macadamias, cacao or cocoa powder, and vanilla extract. Pulse until broken down and combined, add the dates and process to make a dough.

2 Press the dough into a 25cm/10in-diameter round flan tin/pan, flattening it into the bottom and up the sides of the tin using the back of a spoon. Put it in the freezer for 20 minutes to set.

3 When the pastry case or pie shell is ready, make the creamy filling. Halve the avocados, remove the stones and scoop the flesh into a blender. Add the cacao or cocoa powder and maple syrup and blend for about 20 seconds on high to combine.

4 Transfer the filling into the pastry case, cover and leave to set in the fridge for at least 20 minutes, but preferably for a few hours or overnight. Keep covered until ready to eat. Decorate the top with fresh berries just before serving.

Energy 306kcal/1274kJ; Protein 8.5g; Carbohydrate 19.9g, of which sugars 10.9g; Fat 21.9g, of which saturates 5.6g; Cholesterol 0mg; Calcium 38mg; Fibre 6g; Sodium 151mg.

Cashew lime tart

This is the perfect tart for when it's too hot to bake, as the gluten-free crust and filling are uncooked. Start preparing this the day before serving, as the cashew nuts and dates must be soaked overnight.

SERVES 8

8 dried stoned/pitted dates, soaked in water overnight
finely grated rind and juice of 1 lime
225g/8oz/2 cups cashew nuts, soaked in water for at least 4 hours or overnight
15ml/1 tbsp vanilla bean paste

For the pastry

100g/3¾oz/1½ cups desiccated/dry unsweetened shredded coconut
50g/2oz/½ cup ground almonds
thin strips of lime rind, to decorate

1 Drain the dates, reserving the soaking water. Set aside.

2 To make the pastry, put the coconut and ground almonds in a mixing bowl and stir with a spoon to combine. Gradually add enough of the soaking water from the dates just so that the dough sticks together.

3 Press the dough into a 23cm/9in-diameter round pie tin/pan lined with baking parchment. Flatten it into the bottom and up the sides of the tin in an even layer using the back of a spoon.

4 Chill the pastry case or pie shell in the fridge for at least 1 hour while you prepare the filling.

5 To make the filling, put the drained dates, grated lime rind and juice in a blender. Drain the cashew nuts, discarding the soaking water, and add them to the blender with the vanilla.

6 Blend on low, building up to medium speed. Stop the blender now and then to scrape down the sides using a silicone spatula and to gradually add the remaining date soaking water, if needed, to keep the consistency creamy.

7 Repeat until the mixture is a smooth nut cream, adding more date soaking water if necessary.

8 Remove the pastry case or pie shell from the fridge. Pour in the filling and smooth it with a palette knife until it is evenly distributed, then chill for at least 1 hour to set.

9 Remove the pie from the tin, peel off the parchment and decorate the top of the pie with thin strips of lime rind before serving.

Energy 279kcal/1159kJ; Protein 7.1g; Carbohydrate 12.8g, of which sugars 8.9g; Fat 22.5g, of which saturates 7.6g; Cholesterol 0mg; Calcium 32mg; Fibre 3.2g; Sodium 9mg.

Pumpkin & tofu tart

A classic autumnal Thanksgiving bake, updated. The crisp pastry for this tart is made with a mixture of flours: chestnut for flavour, and rice and tapioca flours for shortness.

SERVES 6–8

450g/1lb cooked mashed pumpkin
350g/12oz silken tofu
260g/9½oz/generous 1 cup soft light brown sugar
75ml/5 tbsp rapeseed/canola oil, plus extra for greasing
15ml/1 tbsp carob molasses or agave syrup
7.5ml/1½ tsp ground cinnamon
5ml/1 tsp vanilla extract
5ml/1 tsp salt
2.5ml/½ tsp ground ginger
2.5ml/½ tsp ground nutmeg
gluten-free icing/confectioners' sugar, for dusting

For the pastry

75g/3oz/⅔ cup chestnut flour
65g/2½oz/9 tbsp tapioca flour
40g/1½oz/⅓ cup rice flour
75g/3oz/6 tbsp soft light brown sugar
5ml/1 tsp ground cinnamon
2.5ml/½ tsp xanthan gum
2.5ml/½ tsp gluten-free baking powder
1.5ml/¼ tsp salt
135g/4½oz/9 tbsp hard baking margarine, diced
60–75ml/4–5 tbsp soya or other yogurt

1 Make the pastry. Combine the dry ingredients in a mixing bowl. Rub in the margarine until the mixture resembles breadcrumbs. Mix in enough yogurt to form a soft dough (you can use a dairy yogurt if you don't need the tart to be dairy-free).

2 Press the dough over the base and sides of an oiled 20cm/8in fluted tart tin/pan and chill for at least 1 hour. Preheat the oven to 180°C/ 350°F/Gas 4.

3 Mix all the filling ingredients in a food processor or blender until smooth and creamy. Pour into the pastry case and bake for 50–60 minutes, until golden.

4 Leave to cool in the tin, then chill. Remove from the tin and dust with icing sugar before serving.

Energy 434kcal/1809kJ; Protein 6.2g; Carbohydrate 35.3g, of which sugars 19.4g; Fat 30.8g, of which saturates 13.8g; Cholesterol 94mg; Calcium 108mg; Fibre 1.2g; Sodium 60mg.

Summer Bakewell tart

This traditional British tart has been reworked with a crisp gluten-free pastry case made from a combination of flours, fresh fruit instead of jam, and with a lighter almond frangipane filling. It remains an indulgent treat, but one more aligned to healthy eating.

SERVES 8

250g/9oz/2 cups raspberries
30ml/2 tbsp agave syrup
25g/1oz flaked/sliced almonds

For the pastry

60g/2¼oz/⅓ cup brown rice flour, plus extra for dusting
30g/1¼oz/¼ cup gluten-free oat flour
50g/2oz/⅓ cup potato starch
80g/3¼oz/6½ tbsp butter, frozen, plus extra for greasing

For the frangipane

50g/2oz/½ cup ground almonds
50g/2oz/½ cup fine polenta/cornmeal
50g/2oz/½ cup light muscovado/brown sugar
2.5ml/½ tsp gluten-free baking powder
2 eggs
120ml/4fl oz/½ cup whole natural/plain yogurt
1–2 drops almond extract

1 To make the filling, retain a few raspberries for decoration, then combine the raspberries and agave syrup in a mixing bowl. Set aside in the fridge to macerate for at least 30 minutes.

2 To make the pastry, sift the flours and potato starch into a mixing bowl. Grate in the butter, then mix in with your hands without rubbing it in, adding just a little iced water until the dough is wet enough to bring together in a ball, but not sticky. Cover with clear film or plastic wrap and chill for at least 1 hour, or overnight.

3 Preheat the oven to 190°C/375°F/Gas 5. Grease a 23cm/9in fluted flan tin/pan and line the bottom with baking parchment.

4 Dust a surface with rice flour, then roll out the pastry to a circle about 30cm/12in in diameter. Transfer the pastry to the tin with the rolling pin, cut away any excess, then line the top of the pastry with another circle of baking parchment. Weight it down with dry grains or baking beans and bake blind for 10 minutes.

5 Remove the beans and paper, then return the pastry case to the oven and bake for 5 minutes more. Remove from the oven and set aside for about 5 minutes.

6 Meanwhile, prepare the frangipane. Put the dry ingredients in a mixing bowl and stir to mix. Lightly beat the eggs, then beat in the yogurt and almond extract. Add to the dry ingredients and mix well.

7 Pour the macerated berries into the tart and top with the frangipane. Spread evenly, then return to the oven.

8 Bake for 20 minutes, then sprinkle the flaked almonds on the top. Return the tart to the oven and bake for 5–10 minutes more, until golden brown. Decorate with fresh raspberries before serving warm.

Variation

You can use other fruits in this tart, though it works best with ones that are slightly acidic, such as plums, rhubarb, gooseberries or blackcurrants. You may need to adjust the amount of agave syrup you use accordingly.

Energy 261kcal/1090kJ; Protein 6.1g; Carbohydrate 28.5g, of which sugars 9.9g; Fat 14g, of which saturates 6.1g; Cholesterol 79mg; Calcium 63mg; Fibre 1.9g; Sodium 96mg.

Lemon & passion fruit tart

This is a twist on the traditional lemon tart. It still has a tangy lemon flavour but is laced with passion fruit, which, along with the ground almonds, gives added texture. Using almonds also means you don't need to use any flour as a thickener, effectively creating a citrus frangipane.

SERVES 6–8

225g/8oz gluten-free pâte sucrée (see page 196) or almond pastry (see page 197), or store-bought gluten-free pastry, thawed if frozen
a litttle gluten-free plain/all-purpose flour blend, for dusting
a little oil, for greasing
2 eggs, plus 1 egg yolk
125g/4¼oz/generous 1 cup gluten-free icing/confectioners' sugar, plus extra for dusting
2 passion fruits
finely grated rind of 1 lemon and the juice of 3 lemons
50g/2oz/¼ cup butter, melted
75g/3oz/¾ cup ground almonds

1 Roll out the pastry on a lightly floured surface and use it to line a lightly greased 20cm/8in round fluted tart tin/pan. Prick the base all over with a fork, then chill in the fridge for 10 minutes.

2 Preheat the oven to 200°C/400°F/Gas 6. Line the pastry with baking parchment and baking beans and bake blind for 10 minutes.

3 Remove the paper and beans and return the pastry pie crust to the oven for 5 minutes more, until golden and dry. Remove from the oven and lower the temperature to 190°C/375°F/Gas 5.

4 Meanwhile, whisk the eggs, egg yolk and icing sugar together in a large mixing bowl.

5 Cut the passion fruits in half and spoon out the pulp, then stir this into the egg with the lemon rind and juice.

6 Stir in the melted butter and ground almonds, then pour evenly into the pastry case. Bake the tart for 20 minutes or until the filling has set and the pastry is golden.

7 Remove the tart from the oven and leave to cool on a wire rack. Remove the tart from the tin on to a serving plate and dust with icing sugar before serving.

Cook's tips

- This tart is equally delicious made with limes; you'll need the finely grated rind of 1½ limes and the juice of 5 limes.
- Most supermarkets sell slightly under-ripe passion fruit, so make sure you give them time to ripen at home (you can speed up this process by putting them in a paper bag with a ripe banana). When ripe, the skins should be very dimpled and wrinkly with slightly soft patches. They should also smell slightly fragrant.

Energy 304kcal/1267kJ; Protein 5.3g; Carbohydrate 32.3g, of which sugars 21g; Fat 17.6g, of which saturates 7.4g; Cholesterol 102mg; Calcium 38mg; Fibre 0.3g; Sodium 105mg.

Pear tarte tatin

This delectable tart is a spin on the apple classic, using juicy pears. As the fruits simmer in a buttery syrup at the bottom of the pan, the steam helps the gluten-free puff pastry to rise. Cardamom adds a warm spiciness to the fruit, but use a little ground cinnamon, if you prefer.

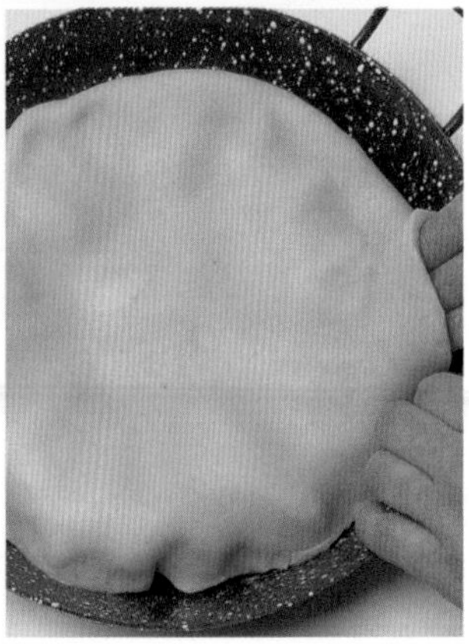

SERVES 4–6

225g/8oz gluten-free puff pastry (see page 102) or use store-bought gluten-free puff pastry, thawed if frozen
gluten-free plain/all-purpose flour blend, for dusting
50g/2oz/¼ cup butter, softened
50g/2oz/¼ cup caster/superfine sugar
seeds from 5 cardamom pods
3 ripe, large round pears
crème fraîche, whipped cream or Greek/strained plain yogurt, to serve

1 On a lightly floured surface, use a floured rolling pin to roll out the pastry to a circle slightly larger than the pan. Prick the pastry all over with a fork, place it on a baking sheet and chill for 30 minutes.

2 Preheat the oven to 220°C/425°F/Gas 7. Spread the butter over the base of an 18cm/7in heavy ovenproof frying pan. Sprinkle the sugar over the butter, then sprinkle the cardamom seeds evenly over the top.

3 Peel the pears, cut them in half lengthways and remove the cores. Arrange the pears, angled or rounded side down, in the pan. Place over medium heat and cook until the sugar melts and begins to bubble with the juice from the pears.

4 Once the sugar has caramelized, remove the pan from the heat. Carefully place the pastry on top, tucking in the edges. Bake for 25 minutes, until the pastry is puffed up and golden.

5 Leave the tart in the pan for about 5 minutes, until the juices have stopped bubbling.

6 Invert a serving plate over the pan then, wearing oven gloves to protect your hands, firmly hold the pan and plate together and quickly turn both over, gently shaking them to release the tart. If this doesn't work, flip both back again and slide a spatula underneath the pears to loosen them, then try inverting the tart on to the plate again. Be careful as hot juices may drip.

7 Allow the pear tart to cool slightly more, then serve while still warm with a dollop of crème fraîche, cream or yogurt.

Energy 265kcal/1106kJ; Protein 2.5g; Carbohydrate 30.1g, of which sugars 16.8g; Fat 15.7g, of which saturates 8.5g; Cholesterol 39mg; Calcium 34mg; Fibre 2.2g; Sodium 169mg.

Double-crust apple pie

The secret of making a successful double-crust pie is to ensure that the filling is not too wet, which would make the bottom layer of pastry soggy. Here, the apples are tossed in a mixture of gluten-free flour and sugar, to soak up and thicken the juices as the fruit cooks.

SERVES 6–8

5 apples
30ml/2 tbsp caster/superfine sugar
30ml/2 tbsp gluten-free plain/all-purpose flour blend

For the pastry

225g/8oz/2 cups gluten-free plain/all-purpose flour blend, plus extra for dusting
5ml/1 tsp gluten-free baking powder
5ml/1 tsp xanthan gum
115g/4oz/½ cup cold butter, diced, plus extra for greasing
finely grated rind of ½ lemon
75g/3oz/6 tbsp caster/superfine sugar, plus extra for sprinkling
2 eggs
15–30ml/1–2 tbsp cold water

1 For the pastry, put the flour, baking powder and xanthan gum in a food processor, then add the butter and lemon rind and process to combine. Add the sugar, then process just to mix. Lightly beat together 1 whole egg, 1 egg yolk and 15ml/1 tbsp of the water. Add to the food processor and process to a very soft dough (it firms during chilling), adding the rest of the water if needed.

2 Divide the dough into two pieces, one portion nearly double the size of the other. Pat into two flat cakes. Wrap in clear film or plastic wrap and chill for 2 hours.

3 Grease a 20cm/8in loose-based tin/pan. Place a baking sheet in the oven and preheat to 180°C/350°F/Gas 4.

4 Place the larger piece of dough on a floured piece of clear film and cover with another piece of film. Roll out to a 25cm/10in round. Remove the film and press into the tin so that it stands just clear of the top. Roll out the second piece of dough to the same size as the tin.

5 Peel, core and cube the apples. Combine the sugar and flour in a mixing bowl. Add the apple, then toss gently until evenly coated. Tip into the pastry-lined tin. Lay the pastry circle on top of the apples and tuck in the overlapping edges. Press the edges together to seal.

6 Prick the top with a fork, brush with the reserved egg white and sprinkle with sugar. Place on the baking sheet and bake for 20 minutes. Reduce the oven to 160°C/325°F/Gas 3 and bake for 25 minutes, until golden. Cool in the tin for 30 minutes, then remove and cool on a wire rack. Serve with cream or yogurt.

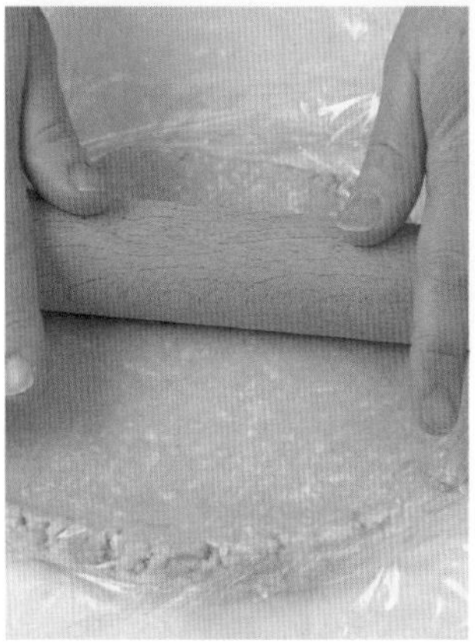

Energy 417kcal/1742kJ; Protein 4.6g; Carbohydrate 60.2g, of which sugars 28.3g; Fat 18.2g, of which saturates 10.6g; Cholesterol 105mg; Calcium 21mg; Fibre 2.4g; Sodium 143mg.

Cherry pie

Sorghum flour has a higher protein and fibre content than other flours and makes an excellent alternative to brown flour. Combined with gluten-free plain flour, it makes a wholesome golden pastry that works well with this dark-red, juicy cherry filling.

SERVES 8

450g/1lb/6 cups ripe cherries, stoned or pitted
30ml/2 tbsp gluten-free plain/all-purpose flour blend
50g/2oz/½ cup caster/superfine sugar, plus extra for sprinkling
50g/2oz/½ cup ground almonds
15ml/1 tbsp milk, for glazing

For the pastry

175g/6oz/1¼ cups gluten-free plain/all-purpose flour blend, plus extra for dusting
175g/6oz/1¼ cups sorghum flour
5ml/1 tsp xanthan gum
1.5ml/¼ tsp salt
15ml/1 tbsp caster/superfine sugar
175g/6oz/¾ cup chilled butter or hard baking margarine, diced, plus extra for greasing
90ml/6 tbsp gluten-free sour cream
15ml/1 tbsp lemon juice or white wine vinegar
2 egg yolks
75ml/5 tbsp cold water

Cook's tip

The raw pastry dough can be stored in the freezer for up to 2 weeks. Thaw in the fridge before use.

1 To make the pastry, sift the flours, xanthan gum and salt into a large mixing bowl, then stir in the sugar. Rub in the butter or hard baking margarine until the mixture resembles breadcrumbs.

2 Mix the sour cream, lemon juice or vinegar, egg yolks and water together. Add to the dry ingredients and mix to a soft dough.

3 Divide the dough into two equal discs and wrap in clear film or plastic wrap. Chill for at least 30 minutes, but preferably overnight.

4 Heat the oven to 220°C/425°F/Gas 7. Grease a 23cm/9in pie dish with butter or margarine.

5 To make the filling, put the cherries in a large glass or stainless-steel bowl and sprinkle over the flour and sugar. Mix with your hands until the fruit is evenly coated with the dry mixture.

6 Dust a surface and a rolling pin with flour, then roll out one disc of pastry into a circle about 30cm/12in in diameter and 3mm/⅛in thick. Gently transfer it to the pie dish with the rolling pin. Press in the sides to fill the corners and cut away any excess pastry with a knife.

7 Sprinkle the ground almonds inside the bottom of the pie, then pour in the cherry mixture and spread evenly.

8 Remove the second pastry disc from the fridge and roll it out in the same way. Transfer the pastry to the top of the pie and press down the edges to seal the pastry. Cut away any excess pastry, re-roll the trimmings and cut into leaf shapes or other decorations.

9 Top the pie with pastry decorations and brush with the milk. Sprinkle with sugar and bake for 15 minutes, then reduce the heat to 190°C/375°F/Gas 5. Bake for another 25 minutes, then check that the pastry crust is deep golden brown. Give it a few more minutes if not.

10 Remove from the oven and set aside for 5 minutes before serving warm, or leave to cool completely.

Energy 467kcal/1942kJ; Protein 5.5g; Carbohydrate 54g, of which sugars 16g; Fat 25.8g, of which saturates 13.6g; Cholesterol 104mg; Calcium 47mg; Fibre 1.2g; Sodium 142mg.

Plum dumplings

These sweet dumplings are made with stuffed plums that are encased in a potato-based pastry dough before being boiled and finally coated in a spiced gluten-free breadcrumb mixture. They are a wonderful way to use up a glut of plums during the autumn.

MAKES 8

For the potato pastry

675g/1½lb potatoes
250ml/8fl oz/1 cup gluten-free sour cream
25g/1oz/2 tbsp butter
2 eggs, beaten
250g/9oz/2¼ cups gluten-free plain/all-purpose flour blend, plus extra for dusting
5ml/1 tsp xanthan gum

For the filling

8 plums
90g/3½oz/¾ cup gluten-free icing/confectioners' sugar, plus extra for dusting
30ml/2 tbsp ground cinnamon, plus extra for dusting
50g/2oz/4 tbsp butter
45ml/3 tbsp gluten-free breadcrumbs (see page 18)

1 Peel and dice the potatoes, then cook in boiling water for 10–15 minutes, until soft. Drain well, leave to cool, then mash until smooth in a large mixing bowl.

2 Stir the sour cream, butter and eggs into the mash. Sift over the flour and xanthan gum and combine.

3 Turn the dough out on to a lightly floured surface and knead lightly, just to bring it together.

4 Carefully cut a slit down one side of each plum and remove the stone, keeping the plum intact. Combine the icing sugar and cinnamon in a bowl, then push a teaspoonful of the mixture inside each plum.

5 On a well-floured surface, roll out the dough until it is about 5mm/¼in thick. Cut into eight 10cm/4in squares.

6 Place a plum in the middle of each square, then bring up the dough and pinch the edges together to completely seal the plum in the dough.

7 Bring a large pan of water to the boil, then add a few of the dumplings – cook them in batches to avoid overcrowding the pan. Cook the dumplings for about 8 minutes, until they rise to the surface. Remove with a slotted spoon, transfer to a bowl and keep warm while you cook the remaining dumplings.

8 Heat the butter in a large frying pan, add the breadcrumbs and fry until golden brown.

9 Add the dumplings, turn to coat in the crumbs, then transfer to a serving plate and dust with extra icing sugar and cinnamon. Serve immediately.

Energy 331kcal/1391kJ; Protein 6.6g; Carbohydrate 58.5g, of which sugars 16.8g; Fat 8.7g, of which saturates 4.6g; Cholesterol 104mg; Calcium 54mg; Fibre 2.3g; Sodium 88mg.

Apple soufflé

This fluffy pudding consists primarily of milk, eggs and apples, with just a little gluten-free flour to thicken the roux, which is then enriched with egg yolks and lightened with whisked egg whites. This version uses apples, but other fruit in season, such as plums or pears, would be good too.

SERVES 4

4 crisp eating apples
a little lemon juice
300ml/½ pint/1¼ cups milk
40g/1½oz/3 tbsp butter, plus extra for greasing
40g/1½oz/⅓ cup gluten-free plain/all-purpose flour blend
25g/1oz/2 tbsp caster/superfine sugar
2.5ml/½ tsp vanilla extract
2 eggs, separated

1 Preheat the oven to 200°C/400°F/Gas 6. Butter an ovenproof dish 20–23cm/8–9in in diameter and 5cm/2in deep.

2 Peel, core and slice the apples. Put them in the dish and sprinkle with enough lemon juice to cover all the surfaces of the apple.

3 Put the milk, butter and flour in a medium pan. Stirring continuously with a whisk, cook over medium heat until the sauce thickens and comes to the boil.

4 Let the sauce bubble gently for 1–2 minutes, stirring well to make sure it does not stick and burn on the bottom of the pan.

5 Pour the sauce into a large mixing bowl, add the sugar and vanilla extract, then stir in the egg yolks until combined, to make a custard.

6 In a separate clean, grease-free mixing bowl, whisk the egg whites until stiff peaks form.

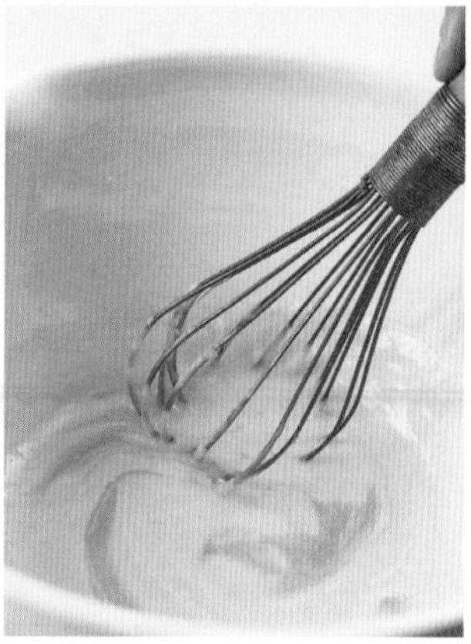

7 With a large metal spoon, gently mix one-third of the egg whites into the custard, to slacken it. Carefully fold in the rest of the egg whites, until combined, being careful not to whisk out the air. Gently pour the mixture over the apples in the dish and smooth level.

8 Put the soufflé into the preheated oven and bake for about 40 minutes, until puffed up, deep golden brown and firm to the touch.

9 Serve straight out of the oven, before the soufflé-like topping begins to fall.

Energy 210kcal/879kJ; Protein 6.7g; Carbohydrate 18g, of which sugars 18g; Fat 12.9g, of which saturates 7g; Cholesterol 141mg; Calcium 114mg; Fibre 1.6g; Sodium 137mg.

Bread & apple pudding

This modern version of bread pudding is a great way to use up slightly stale gluten-free bread. Enriched with eggs and butter, it contains dried apples and raisins and is liberally strewn with almonds, but you could use any dried fruit and nuts of your choice.

SERVES 4–6

200g/7oz gluten-free white bread slices, crusts removed
150ml/¼ pint/⅔ cup single/light cream
50g/2oz/¼ cup butter, melted
4 eggs, separated
45ml/3 tbsp caster/superfine sugar
200g/7oz sliced dried apples, roughly chopped
50g/2oz/scant ½ cup raisins
50g/2oz/¼ cup flaked/sliced almonds

1 Preheat the oven to 180°C/350°F/Gas 4 and grease a 15 x 20cm/6 x 8in ovenproof dish.

2 Process the bread in a food processor or blender until you have breadcrumbs. Transfer to a large mixing bowl and add the cream and butter, mixing well.

3 In another mixing bowl, whisk the egg yolks and sugar until light and creamy.

4 Fold the apples and raisins into the whisked egg and sugar mixture. Add this to the breadcrumb mixture, and combine thoroughly.

5 Put the egg whites into a clean, grease-free mixing bowl and whisk until they form stiff peaks. Stir a spoonful of the whites into the breadcrumb mixture to slacken it, then carefully fold in the rest of the egg whites, until combined, being careful not to whisk out the air.

6 Gently pour into the prepared dish and smooth the surface level. Sprinkle the top with the flaked almonds and bake for 25–30 minutes, or until golden and firm. Check half-way through the cooking and cover the top of the pudding with foil if the almonds start to brown too much.

Variations

• Adding a grated fresh apple to the dried apple and raisin mixture makes the pudding even more moist.
• To make a dairy-free version, use melted margarine in place of the butter, and coconut milk in place of the cream. Shake the can of coconut milk well before you open it, so that the cream and liquid coalesce.

Energy 452kcal/1893kJ; Protein 12g; Carbohydrate 50.5g, of which sugars 35.9g; Fat 23.8g, of which saturates 9.3g; Cholesterol 186mg; Calcium 147mg; Fibre 5.4g; Sodium 280mg.

Apple crumble

This warming crumble is cooked to perfection by baking in two stages. The apple layer is baked first so that it cooks thoroughly without the top burning or drying, then the gluten-free topping is sprinkled over and the dish is baked again to make the crumble crunchy and crisp.

SERVES 6

25g/1oz/¼ cup ground almonds
50g/2oz/½ cup sorghum flour
50g/2oz/½ cup gluten-free oats
2.5ml/½ tsp ground cinnamon
75g/3oz chilled butter or hard baking margarine, diced, plus extra for greasing
15ml/1 tbsp honey, plus 15ml/1 tbsp extra to sweeten (optional)
15ml/1 tbsp maple syrup, plus 15ml/1 tbsp extra to sweeten (optional)
60ml/4 tbsp apple juice
1.5ml/¼ tsp ground ginger
a pinch of ground nutmeg
4–5 medium apples

1 Preheat the oven to 180°C/350°F/Gas 4. Lightly grease a 23cm/9in square shallow baking dish.

2 Put the ground almonds, flour, oats and 1.5ml/¼ tsp of the cinnamon in a mixing bowl and mix to combine.

3 Add the butter or baking margarine and quickly rub it into the almond and oat mixture, allowing visible pea-sized pieces to remain.

4 Warm the honey and when liquid, mix 15ml/1 tbsp with the maple syrup and apple juice in a small jug or mixing bowl.

5 Sprinkle 10ml/2 tsp of the honey mixture over the almond and oat mixture and stir with a fork, until just combined. Place in the fridge to chill. Stir the ginger and nutmeg into the remaining apple juice mixture.

6 Core and quarter the apples (no need to peel unless the skins are very tough) and put them in the prepared baking dish. Pour the apple juice mixture over the top and drizzle over additional honey and maple syrup, for extra sweetness, if you like.

7 Cover with foil and bake for 30–45 minutes, then remove the foil and test the apples. The time different varieties of apples take to bake varies greatly, so use a fork to check how soft they are. When they seem almost cooked, sprinkle the chilled crumble mixture evenly over the top.

8 Raise the oven temperature to 220°C/425°F/Gas 7. Return the baking dish to the oven, uncovered, and bake for 20–30 minutes more, or until the topping is golden brown. Remove the crumble from the oven and allow to stand for about 10 minutes before serving.

Energy 239kcal/996kJ; Protein 2.8g; Carbohydrate 27.7g, of which sugars 14.9g; Fat 13.5g, of which saturates 6.7g; Cholesterol 27mg; Calcium 21mg; Fibre 2.9g; Sodium 82mg.

Sticky toffee pudding

Dates add sweetness, moisture and richness to cakes and pudding mixtures and can be used in place of flour to provide some of the substance. Sorghum flour works well here as it has a slightly sweet flavour and creamy colour, so is a good choice for darker bakes.

SERVES 15

150g/5oz/scant 1 cup chopped stoned/pitted dates
5ml/1 tsp bicarbonate of soda/ baking soda
250ml/8fl oz/1 cup boiling water
75g/3oz/⅔ cup gluten-free plain/ all-purpose flour blend
75g/3oz/⅔ cup sorghum flour
5ml/1 tsp gluten-free baking powder
50g/2oz/¼ cup butter, diced, plus extra for greasing
200g/7oz/1 cup caster/ superfine sugar
50g/2oz/½ cup walnuts, chopped
1 large egg, beaten
2.5ml/½ tsp vanilla extract

For the toffee sauce

25g/1oz/2 tbsp butter
60ml/4 tbsp soft light brown sugar
60ml/4 tbsp double/heavy cream

1 Preheat the oven to 180°C/350°F/Gas 4. Grease and line a 30 × 20cm/12 × 8in shallow baking tin/pan with baking parchment.

2 Put the dates in a bowl with the bicarbonate of soda and pour over the boiling water. Stir, then leave to cool slightly while making the cake batter.

3 Sift the flours and baking powder into a mixing bowl and add the butter. Rub between your fingertips until the mixture resembles fine crumbs.

4 Stir in the sugar and walnuts, and mix well. Add the egg, vanilla and the date mixture, and beat until smooth.

5 Spoon into the tin and smooth the top level. Bake for 25–30 minutes, or until well risen and firm to the touch. Leave to cool in the tin for 5 minutes, then turn out on to a board and peel away the lining paper.

6 Put the sauce ingredients in a pan and stir over a low heat until the sugar dissolves. Bring to the boil and boil for 1–2 minutes, until thickened.

7 Cut the pudding into pieces and serve warm, drizzled with a spoonful or two of the toffee sauce.

Variation

Serve any leftover squares as a cake, simply dusted with a little gluten-free icing/confectioners' sugar.

Energy 217kcal/908kJ; Protein 2g; Carbohydrate 33.1g, of which sugars 25.1g; Fat 9.1g, of which saturates 4.4g; Cholesterol 32mg; Calcium 18mg; Fibre 0.8g; Sodium 39mg.

Chocolate mud pudding

Guaranteed to be a big hit, this divine dessert can be made in minutes. Comprising a lot of cocoa powder and just a little gluten-free flour, it has a brownie crust topping over a thick and fudgy mousse-like base. Serve in small portions, as it is very rich.

SERVES 4–6

90g/3½oz/¾ cup gluten-free self-raising/self-rising flour blend
5ml/1 tsp ground cinnamon
75ml/5 tbsp unsweetened cocoa powder
50g/2oz/¼ cup butter, plus extra for greasing
200g/7oz/1 cup light muscovado/ brown sugar or demerara/ raw sugar
475ml/16fl oz/2 cups milk
crème fraîche, Greek/strained plain yogurt or vanilla ice cream, to serve

1 Preheat the oven to 180°C/350°F/Gas 4. Lightly grease a 1.5-litre/2½-pint ovenproof dish with butter. Place the dish on a baking sheet and set aside.

2 Sift the flour, ground cinnamon and 15ml/1 tbsp of the cocoa powder together into a large mixing bowl.

3 Place the butter in a large pan. Add 115g/4oz/½ cup of the sugar and 150ml/¼ pint/⅔ cup of the milk. Heat gently without boiling, stirring from time to time, until the butter has melted and all the sugar has completely dissolved. Remove the pan from the heat.

4 Stir in the flour mixture, mixing evenly. Pour the mixture into the prepared ovenproof dish and level the surface.

5 Mix the remaining sugar and cocoa powder in the mixing bowl you used for the rest of the dry ingredients, then sprinkle over the pudding mixture in the dish. Pour the remaining milk evenly over the top.

6 Bake the pudding for 45–50 minutes or until the sponge has risen to the top and is firm to the touch.

7 Leave the pudding to stand for 2–3 minutes, then serve hot, with crème fraîche, yogurt or ice cream.

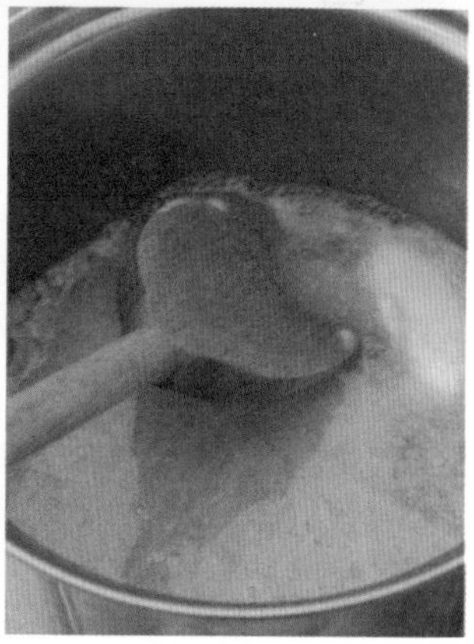

Variations

- For a mocha mud pudding, leave out the cinnamon and add 10ml/2 tsp instant coffee to the pan after heating the butter, sugar and milk. Stir until the coffee granules or powder have dissolved.
- Alternatively, keep the recipe as it is but add 2.5ml/ ½ tsp chilli powder, to spice things up.

Energy 386kcal/1625kJ; Protein 7.2g; Carbohydrate 62.4g, of which sugars 46.4g; Fat 13.3g, of which saturates 8.2g; Cholesterol 27mg; Calcium 147mg; Fibre 2.6g; Sodium 246mg.

Lemon surprise pudding

The surprise in this pudding is the pool of tangy lemon sauce that forms during cooking beneath a light sponge topping, made with just a tiny amount of gluten-free flour. Serve hot, straight from the oven, while it is still impressively puffed up and light-as-air to eat.

SERVES 4

75g/3oz/6 tbsp butter, plus extra for greasing
175g/6oz/¾ cup soft light brown sugar
4 eggs, separated
grated rind and juice of 4 lemons
50g/2oz/½ cup gluten-free self-raising/self-rising flour blend
120ml/4fl oz/½ cup milk
gluten-free icing/confectioners' sugar, for dusting

1 Preheat the oven to 180°C/350°F/Gas 4.

2 Beat the butter and sugar together in a large bowl until pale and fluffy. Beat in one egg yolk at a time and gradually mix in the lemon rind and juice.

3 Sift the flour into the lemon mixture and stir until well mixed, then gradually stir in the milk.

4 Whisk the egg whites in a clean, grease-free mixing bowl until stiff, but not dry, then lightly, but thoroughly, fold into the lemon mixture in three batches.

5 Butter a deep 20cm/8in ovenproof dish and stand it in a roasting pan. Carefully pour the mixture into the prepared dish, then pour boiling water into the pan.

6 Bake the pudding for 45 minutes, or until golden on top. Dust with icing sugar and serve immediately.

Energy 461kcal/1929kJ; Protein 9.5g; Carbohydrate 57.2g, of which sugars 47.3g; Fat 22.8g, of which saturates 12g; Cholesterol 273mg; Calcium 86mg; Fibre 0.1g; Sodium 213mg.

Raspberry & almond gratin

This delicious dessert is a great way to use up a glut of summer raspberries, or you could substitute other soft fresh fruit. The simple topping – a cross between a custard and a sponge – is made by blending gluten-free brioche crumbs with almonds, cream and eggs.

SERVES 6

butter, for greasing
115g/4oz/1 cup ground almonds
50g/2oz/1 cup gluten-free brioche breadcrumbs (see the variation for plain brioche on page 75, and blitz to fine breadcrumbs in a food processor)
50g/2oz/¼ cup soft light brown sugar
5ml/1 tsp vanilla extract
150ml/¼ pint/⅔ cup double/heavy cream
2 large eggs
500g/18oz/3⅓ cups raspberries

1 Preheat the oven to 200°C/400°F/Gas 6 and lightly butter a 20cm/8in medium square cake tin/pan.

2 Put the almonds, brioche crumbs, sugar, vanilla, cream and eggs in a food processor and blend them until combined. (Alternatively, beat the eggs, then add to the other ingredients in a mixing bowl and stir well.)

3 Spread out the raspberries over the base of the cake tin. Pour in the gratin mixture. Bake for 30 minutes.

4 Leave for 5 minutes to cool in the tin, then turn out and serve warm, accompanied by thick natural yogurt or whipped cream if you like.

Energy 347kcal/1446kJ; Protein 9g; Carbohydrate 18.3g, of which sugars 14.2g; Fat 27.1g, of which saturates 10.1g; Cholesterol 121mg; Calcium 102mg; Fibre 3g; Sodium 64mg.

Steamed pineapple puddings

An updated version of pineapple upside-down cake, these fruity individual mini puddings are made with fresh and dried pineapple instead of canned, and contain coconut flour, which adds unique flavour and texture to this dessert.

MAKES 6

15g/½oz sugar-free dried pineapple, shredded
30ml/2 tbsp coconut oil
1 fresh pineapple
115g/4oz/½ cup unsalted butter, plus extra for greasing
60ml/4 tbsp maple syrup
115g/4oz/½ cup light muscovado/brown sugar
4 eggs
115g/4oz/1 cup gluten-free plain/all-purpose flour blend, plus extra for dusting
25g/1oz/¼ cup coconut flour
10ml/2 tsp gluten-free baking powder
2.5ml/½ tsp nutmeg
grated rind of 1 lemon

1 Grease six ceramic ramekins with butter and lightly dust them with flour. Bring a double boiler or large pan of water to the boil to steam the desserts.

2 Put the dried shredded pineapple and coconut oil (see Cook's tip) in a mixing bowl. Stir to combine, then set aside to soak.

3 Peel and core the fresh pineapple, then cut into 2.5cm/1in square chunks.

4 Melt 15ml/1 tbsp of the butter in a frying pan over a high heat. Add the maple syrup and fresh pineapple and fry, stirring constantly, until the syrup has reduced and the fruit has caramelized to a golden brown.

5 Put an equal amount of pineapple and syrup into each of the prepared ramekins and set aside.

6 Cream the remaining butter and the sugar in a mixing bowl using an electric whisk on medium for about 2 minutes. Beat in the eggs one by one.

7 Sift in the flours, baking powder and nutmeg, and fold into the batter. Fold in the soaked, dried shredded pineapple and oil mixture, and the lemon rind.

8 Spoon the batter equally into the ramekins and cover with baking parchment tightly enough to seal in the moisture, but loosely enough that the desserts are able to rise above the rim of the ramekins. Tie with string.

9 Put the desserts in the top of the double boiler, or in a steamer set inside a large pan of boiling water. Steam the desserts for about 40 minutes, topping up with extra boiling water, if needed.

10 Remove the desserts from the pan and allow to cool in the ramekins for about 10 minutes.

11 Turn them out on to individual serving plates and serve warm.

Cook's tip

On a cold day, the coconut oil may solidify while soaking the fruit. If this happens, put the bowl into the top of the double boiler or in the microwave for a few seconds to melt it

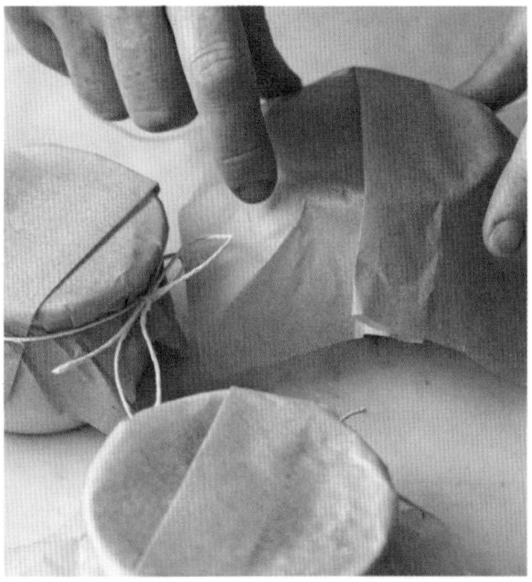

Energy 436kcal/1824kJ; Protein 6.5g; Carbohydrate 47.3g, of which sugars 28.1g; Fat 25g, of which saturates 15.3g; Cholesterol 195mg; Calcium 44mg; Fibre 0.5g; Sodium 60mg.

Small cakes & traybakes

If you are new to baking or if you are cooking with children or making cakes for a sale, small cakes are an ideal choice. Quick and easy to prepare, they cool quickly and are ready to decorate or eat in a short time. The classic way of making cakes is by creaming the fat and sugar together, then beating in eggs and folding in flour. This gives little cakes a nicely rounded top. If, however, you want flat-topped cakes, suitable for flooding with glacé icing or topping with sugarpaste, try the melted method, whereby the cool melted fat is beaten into the mixture last. You'll find both of these methods at the beginning of this chapter.

Gluten-free cakes are every bit as good as those made with wheat flour and you don't need to worry about over-beating as there is no gluten to toughen the mixture. There's a huge range of gluten-free flours to give you slightly different results for each bake. Rice flour on its own is often used in simple sponge cakes as it has a completely neutral flavour and gives a slightly crumbly and light texture. It is also sometimes blended with starchy flours, such as potato starch, which expands as it absorbs water during baking – something that can help the cake to rise. More richly flavoured ground nuts can be used to add moistness and texture.

Probably the simplest little cakes to make are Apricot Rock Cakes, which use buckwheat flour for a delicious mildly nutty and malty taste. Coconut & Blueberry Squares are substantial and filling, made with coconut flour. For a bake with a protein boost, try Flaxseed & Raisin Muffins, made with quinoa flour and ground flaxseeds.

Traybakes are easy to prepare and they can be cut into different portion sizes; smaller pieces for children and afternoon teas and larger ones for adults. They make a useful addition to lunch boxes and picnics and usually freeze well, so can be made in advance and then packed frozen, which helps keep the rest of the food cool until you're ready to eat. Try Lime & Coconut Drizzle Traybake, or Sweet Potato Brownies; the latter is still rich and chocolatey, but with healthier ingredients rather than lots of butter and sugar, so you can have your cake and eat it too!

Basic sponge: creamed method

In this cake-making method the butter is beaten with the sugar until very creamy, then combined with the gluten-free rice flour and any flavourings. The resulting cake has a moist, dense crumb. The beating can be done with a wooden spoon or an electric mixer, the latter being quicker.

MAKES 12 CUPCAKES

115g/4oz/⅔ cup rice flour
5ml/1 tsp gluten-free baking powder
115g/4oz/½ cup softened butter or soft baking margarine
115g/4oz/⅔ cup caster/superfine sugar
5ml/1 tsp vanilla extract
2 eggs, lightly beaten
15–45ml/1–3 tbsp milk

1 Preheat the oven to 190°C/375°F/Gas 5. Line a 12-cup tin/pan with paper cases.

2 Sift the rice flour with the baking powder into a mixing bowl.

3 Cream the butter or margarine in a separate mixing bowl for a few minutes, until soft and pale. Add the sugar and continue to beat until the mixture is pale and fluffy.

4 Add the vanilla extract to the eggs and then gradually add to the butter and sugar mixture, beating well between each addition. Add a teaspoon of the rice flour mixture with the last two additions to avoid curdling.

5 Fold in the dry ingredients and enough milk so that the mixture drops slowly off the spoon. Divide between the paper cases.

6 Bake for 15 minutes until risen, lightly browned and a knife tip inserted into the middle comes out clean. Allow to cool in the tin for a few minutes, then remove and cool on a rack before serving or decorating.

VARIATIONS

• For a large sponge cake, double the quantities and divide the mixture equally between two lined and greased 20cm/8in shallow cake tins/pans. Bake for 20–25 minutes or until well risen and the cakes spring back when lightly pressed. Loosen the cake edges and leave in the tins for 5 minutes. Turn out, remove the lining paper and cool on a wire rack. Fill the two layers with jam and whipped cream for a classic Victoria sponge cake.

• If you prefer, you could use the quicker all-in-one method to make the sponge, although the results are sometimes not quite as light. Instead of creaming the butter and sugar and then adding the remaining ingredients, you simply put all the ingredients in a large mixing bowl and beat them until just combined. Ensure the butter or baking margarine is really soft so that it is easy to blend with the other ingredients.

• For chocolate sponge, replace 30ml/2 tbsp of the flour with unsweetened cocoa powder, and add a splash more milk. Sift the cocoa, flour and baking powder to ensure there are no lumps before you stir them into the butter and sugar mixture, which avoids knocking out air.

Energy 161kcal/673kJ; Protein 2g; Carbohydrate 18.2g, of which sugars 10.6g; Fat 9.1g, of which saturates 5.3g; Cholesterol 59mg; Calcium 14mg; Fibre 0.3g; Sodium 74mg.

Basic sponge: melted method

Here, the butter is melted and left to cool slightly. The remaining ingredients are combined, and the butter is folded in last. The resulting cakes will have a soft sponge-like texture and will rise evenly to give a flatter top suitable for glacé icing and sugarpaste toppings.

MAKES 12 CUPCAKES

2 eggs
115g/4oz/½ cup caster/superfine sugar
50ml/2fl oz/¼ cup double/heavy cream
5ml/1 tsp vanilla extract
115g/4oz/1 cup gluten-free self-raising/self-rising flour blend
2.5ml/½ tsp gluten-free baking powder
50g/2oz/¼ cup butter, melted

1 Preheat the oven to 180°C/350°F/Gas 4. Line a 12-cup tin/pan with paper cases.

2 Whisk the eggs and sugar until pale and foamy. Whisk in the cream for 1 minute, then add the vanilla.

3 Sift the flour with the baking powder, then fold it lightly into the mixture, followed by the melted butter.

4 Three-quarters fill the paper cases with the cake mixture, ensuring they are evenly filled.

5 Bake in the middle of the oven for 12–15 minutes until risen and golden brown. Test by lightly pressing the middles of the cakes with your fingers: the sponge should lightly spring back. Alternatively, insert the tip of a sharp knife or a skewer into one of the cakes; it should come out clean.

6 Remove from the oven and leave to cool in the bun tin for 5 minutes, then turn the cakes out on to a wire rack to cool completely before icing and decorating them.

CARROT CAKE

Gluten free • Dairy free

Grated, puréed or mashed fruit and vegetables, such as carrots and bananas, add texture and flavour, and help bind ingredients together in gluten-free cakes.

MAKES 18CM/7IN CAKE

225g/8oz/2 cups gluten-free self-raising/self-rising flour blend
10ml/2 tsp gluten-free baking powder
150g/5oz/scant 1 cup soft light brown sugar
225g/8oz carrots, grated
2 small ripe bananas, mashed
2 eggs
150ml/¼ pint/⅔ cup sunflower oil, plus extra for greasing

1 Grease and line a 18cm/7in cake tin/pan. Preheat the oven to 180°C/350°F/Gas 4.

2 Sift the flour, baking powder and sugar into a large mixing bowl.

3 Squeeze as much liquid out of the grated carrots as you can and add to the flour mixture. Add the bananas and stir to combine. Beat the eggs and oil together, then stir into the flour. Pour into the tin.

4 Bake for 1–1¼ hours, until a skewer comes out clean. Remove from the tin. Cool on a wire rack.

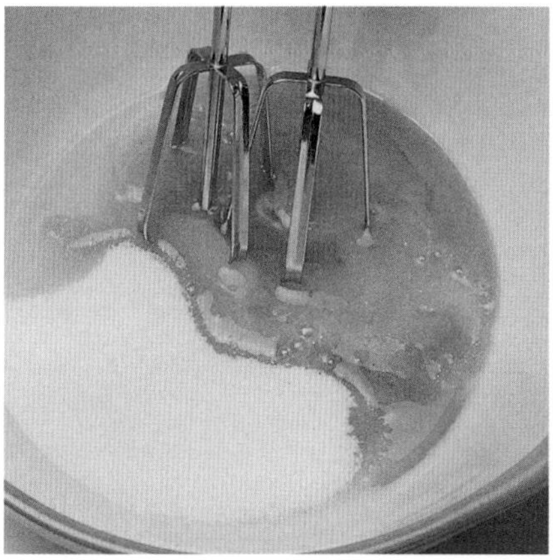

Basic: Energy 166kcal/694kJ; Protein 2.2g; Carbohydrate 21.3g, of which sugars 12.2g; Fat 8.3g, of which saturates 4.7g; Cholesterol 64mg; Calcium 14mg; Fibre 0.1g; Sodium 49mg.
Carrot: Energy 2729kcal/11394kJ; Protein 29.6g; Carbs 384.3g, of which sugars 200.4g; Fat 127.4g, of which saturates 18g; Cholesterol 462mg; Calcium 218mg; Fibre 11.8g; Sodium 272mg.

Chocolate banana cupcakes

As well as being gluten and dairy free, these cupcakes are made without eggs, using ground flaxseeds instead. They are sweetened primarily with bananas, so make sure you choose very ripe ones, with skins starting to turn black and very soft inside.

MAKES 12

4 large, ripe bananas
150ml/¼ pint/⅔ cup sunflower oil
90ml/6 tbsp brown rice malt syrup
90ml/6 tbsp coconut milk
10ml/2 tsp vanilla extract
115g/4oz/1 cup brown rice flour
75g/3oz/½ cup buckwheat flour
45ml/3 tbsp ground flaxseeds/linseeds
35g/1½oz/¼ cup carob flour
35g/1½oz/¼ cup raw cacao powder or unsweetened cocoa powder
25g/1oz/¼ cup ground almonds
5ml/1 tsp bicarbonate of soda/baking soda
2.5ml/½ tsp xanthan gum
2.5ml/½ tsp ground cinnamon
2.5ml/½ tsp salt

1 Preheat the oven to 180°C/350°F/Gas 4. Line a 12-cup tin/pan with paper cases.

2 Mash the bananas in a medium mixing bowl. Add the oil, brown rice malt syrup, coconut milk and vanilla extract, then combine using a fork.

3 Mix all of the other ingredients together in a separate large mixing bowl.

4 Add the wet ingredients to the dry ingredients and mix to combine, using a spoon, working quickly.

5 Spoon the batter into the paper cases so that they are about three-quarters full.

6 Bake for about 25 minutes in the middle of the oven, until they spring back when lightly pressed, and a skewer inserted into the middle comes out clean.

7 Remove from the oven and place on a wire rack to cool before serving.

Cook's tips

• Carob flour, also known as carob powder, is similar to unsweetened cocoa powder, but paler and sweeer. It's a great ingredient to use alongside cocoa powder as together they produce a smooth, more chocolatey flavour.

• The coconut milk and brown rice malt syrup help sweeten the cupcakes and make them moist. If you can't find brown rice malt syrup, you can substitute agave syrup/nectar or date syrup instead.

Energy 257kcal/1068kJ; Protein 3.7g; Carbohydrate 28.2g, of which sugars 13.4g; Fat 14.5g, of which saturates 2.4g; Cholesterol 0mg; Calcium 51mg; Fibre 2.3g; Sodium 67mg.

Orange polenta cupcakes

Made with polenta (cornmeal) instead of flour, these little cakes are extremely moist yet have a light-as-air texture and a tangy citrus flavour. They are topped with an orange glaze made with fresh orange juice, marmalade and a little icing sugar to thicken and sweeten.

MAKES 12

175g/6oz/¾ cup softened butter or soft baking margarine
175g/6oz/scant 1 cup caster/superfine sugar
finely grated zest of ½ orange
3 eggs, lightly beaten
165g/5½oz/scant 1½ cups fine polenta/cornmeal
7.5ml/1½ tsp gluten-free baking powder
15ml/1 tbsp orange juice

For the glaze

juice and finely grated rind of ½ orange
75ml/5 tbsp gluten-free icing/confectioners' sugar
10ml/2 tsp orange marmalade

1 Preheat the oven to 190°C/375°F/Gas 4. Line a 12-cup tin/pan with paper cases.

2 Put the fat and sugar in a large mixing bowl and beat together until creamy, pale and fluffy.

3 Whisk the orange zest and eggs together and mix, a little at a time, into the creamed mixture. Combine the polenta and baking powder, add to the creamed mixture and start to fold in.

4 When the ingredients are almost mixed, add the orange juice, then gently stir everything together.

5 Spoon the mixture into the paper cases and bake for 20 minutes, until golden and firm. Leave the cakes in the tins for 5 minutes, then transfer to a wire rack and leave to cool.

6 To make the glaze, put the juice and rind in a bowl and beat in the icing sugar and marmalade. The mixture should cover the back of a spoon, but be thin and fluid. Drizzle the glaze in a loose zig-zag over the tops of the cakes just before removing from the tin and serving.

Variation

For chocolate orange cupcakes, substitute 40g/1½oz/⅓ cup of unsweetened cocoa powder for the same amount of polenta/cornmeal. Instead of the orange glaze, dust the tops with gluten-free icing sugar or drizzle with melted chocolate.

Energy 268kcal/1119kJ; Protein 3.3g; Carbohydrate 33g, of which sugars 22.9g; Fat 14.1g, of which saturates 8.1g; Cholesterol 89mg; Calcium 16mg; Fibre 0.4g; Sodium 112mg.

Flaxseed & raisin muffins

Quinoa flour and ground flaxseeds (or linseeds) are used in place of flour in these wholesome muffins, which are packed with protein, essential Omega 3 fats and soluble fibre, so they keep you feeling fuller for longer, as well as tasting delicious.

MAKES 12

250ml/8fl oz/1 cup buttermilk (see Cook's tips)
150ml/1/4 pint/2/3 cup vegetable oil
2 eggs
175g/6oz/1 1/2 cups quinoa flour
115g/4oz/1 cup ground flaxseeds/linseeds
5ml/1 tsp gluten-free baking powder
5ml/1 tsp ground cinnamon
5ml/1 tsp ground nutmeg
115g/4oz/2/3 cup caster/superfine sugar
50g/2oz/1/3 cup raisins
30ml/2 tbsp whole flaxseeds/linseeds, for sprinkling

1 Preheat the oven to 200°C/400°F/Gas 6. Combine the buttermilk, oil and eggs in a jug or pitcher.

2 Sift the quinoa flour into a large mixing bowl, then stir in the ground flaxseeds, baking powder, cinnamon, nutmeg, sugar and raisins.

3 Make a well in the middle of the dry ingredients, then pour in the buttermilk and egg mixture, stirring briefly to just combine the ingredients. The mixture needs to be of a dropping consistency to ensure a soft crumb, so add a little extra buttermilk if required.

4 Divide the muffin mixture between 12 muffin tins/pans, lined with paper cases if you wish.

5 Sprinkle the top of each muffin with a few whole flaxseeds, and use the end of a teaspoon to push any exposed raisins into the batter to avoid them scorching as the muffins bake.

6 Bake for 18–20 minutes, until the muffins are well risen and firm to the touch. Remove from the tins and cool slightly on a wire rack. Serve warm.

Cook's tips

- If you can't find buttermilk, make sour milk by adding 15ml/1 tbsp lemon juice to 250ml/8fl oz/1 cup full-fat/whole milk. Leave to stand for 5 minutes, after which it will be ready to use in the same way as buttermilk.
- It is easy to grind flaxseeds/linseeds in a coffee bean grinder or food processor, but make sure that you use one specifically for gluten-free foods to avoid cross-contamination. Store in an airtight container in the fridge.

Energy 287kcal/1197kJ; Protein 6g; Carbohydrate 25g, of which sugars 14g; Fat 19g, of which saturates 3g; Cholesterol 23mg; Calcium 51mg; Fibre 2g; Sodium 24mg.

Blueberry & pumpkin seed muffins

These muffins are made with ground quinoa and pumpkin seeds in place of flour, and naturally sweetened with honey and both fresh and freeze-dried blueberries. Nutritionally dense, the latter are light and dry, but when cooked in these muffins, they become juicy.

MAKES 16

175g/6oz/1 cup quinoa
185g/6½oz/1½ cups pumpkin seeds
2.5ml/½ tsp salt
5ml/1 tsp ground cinnamon
7.5ml/1½ tsp bicarbonate of soda/baking soda
120ml/4fl oz/½ cup cold water
45ml/3 tbsp pumpkin seed or other nut or seed oil
2 eggs
175g/6oz/½ cup honey
150g/5oz/1½ cups fresh blueberries (or frozen blueberries if out of season)
50g/2oz/½ cup freeze-dried blueberries

1 Preheat the oven to 190°C/375°F/Gas 5. Line a muffin tin/pan with paper cases.

2 Grind the quinoa in a food processor for 5 minutes. It will become a mixture of fine flour and larger visible pieces of the grain. When it is as fine as possible, tip it into a large mixing bowl.

3 Grind 130g/4½oz/1 cup of the pumpkin seeds in the food processor for 1 minute, then add them to the quinoa. Mix in the salt, cinnamon and bicarbonate of soda.

4 Put 25g/1oz/¼ cup of the remaining pumpkin seeds with the water and oil in a blender, process to combine, then pour into a separate bowl.

5 Add the eggs and honey and mix in with a fork. Gently fold in the fresh and dried blueberries, and the remaining whole pumpkin seeds.

6 Stir the wet ingredients into the dry ingredients very quickly to make a loose batter. Don't worry about any lumps, it's more important to work fast.

7 Pour the batter into the muffin cases and bake for 18–25 minutes, until the tops of the muffins are golden brown and a toothpick inserted into the middle comes out clean. Remove from the tins and cool slightly on a wire rack. Serve warm.

Cook's tip

You can use this combination of ground quinoa and seeds in other types of muffin, but not in fine-textured cakes – ready-mixed gluten-free flour is best for those.

Energy 173kcal/722kJ; Protein 5.5g; Carbohydrate 16.9g, of which sugars 9.8g; Fat 9.6g, of which saturates 1.5g; Cholesterol 29mg; Calcium 26mg; Fibre 1.4g; Sodium 82mg.

Apricot rock cakes

A cross between a cake and a cookie, this is one of the simplest types of bake to make. This version is made with buckwheat flour, which adds fluffiness, and is sweetened with dried apricots.

MAKES 10–12

100g/3¾oz/1 cup dried apricots
30ml/2 tbsp apple juice or water
100g/3¾oz/scant 1 cup gluten-free self-raising/self-rising flour blend
100g/3¾oz/scant 1 cup buckwheat flour
50g/2oz/¼ cup erythritol
10ml/2 tsp gluten-free baking powder
10ml/2 tsp vanilla bean paste (optional)
2.5ml/½ tsp ground cinnamon
1.5ml/¼ tsp salt
115g/4oz/½ cup unsalted butter, at room temperature, plus extra for greasing
1 egg, lightly beaten
15ml/1 tbsp almond milk

1 Preheat the oven to 190°C/375°F/Gas 5. Grease a baking sheet with butter or line it with baking parchment.

2 Chop the apricots then put in a mixing bowl with the apple juice or water. Turn the apricots with your fingers so that they are covered in liquid, then set aside to soak.

3 Put the flours, erythritol, baking powder, vanilla if using, cinnamon and salt in a large mixing bowl and mix to combine. Add the butter and rub it in with your fingers until it resembles breadcrumbs.

4 Mix in the soaked apricots, which should have plumped up. Mix the egg and 10ml/2 tsp of the milk together. Stir into the mixture, adding a little more milk, if needed, to make the dough moist enough to mould.

5 Make little uneven mounds of dough on the baking sheet, about the size of fresh apricots.

6 Bake in the preheated oven for 18–20 minutes, until firm to the touch. Leave to cool on a wire rack before serving. These are best eaten on the day they are made, or can be stored for 2 days.

Energy 163kcal/677kJ; Protein 2.2g; Carbohydrate 19.6g, of which sugars 5.9g; Fat 8.7g, of which saturates 5.2g; Cholesterol 40mg; Calcium 14mg; Fibre 1.2g; Sodium 71mg.

Coconut & blueberry squares

Coconut flour has a delicious flavour and makes a substantial bake. It will soak up the blueberry juices as they cook, so that the squares remain crisp and crunchy.

MAKES 9

250g/9oz/2¼ cups coconut flour
20ml/4 tsp gluten-free baking powder
250g/9oz/scant 1⅓ cups coconut crystals/sugar or soft light brown sugar
75g/3oz/1 cup desiccated/dry unsweetened shredded coconut
200g/7oz/1 cup cold coconut oil, diced, plus extra for greasing
2 eggs, beaten
200g/7oz/1½ cups fresh blueberries

1 Preheat the oven to 180°C/350°F/Gas 4. Grease the sides of a 20cm/8in square baking tin/pan with coconut oil and line the base with baking parchment.

2 Put the flour, baking powder, coconut crystals or sugar and dried coconut in a large bowl and mix to combine.

3 Add the coconut oil, and rub it in with your fingers until only small pea-size pieces remain.

4 Set aside about 250ml/8fl oz/1 cup of the mixture, then stir in the eggs.

5 Pour the batter into the tin and smooth down with your fingers. Drop the blueberries evenly over the surface. Scatter the remaining dry coconut mixture over the top, allowing some of the berries to be left revealed. Pat down quickly, just enough to make contact.

6 Bake for 50 minutes–1 hour, until golden brown and a skewer inserted into the middle comes out clean but moistened with crumbs. Leave to cool in the tin, then cut into squares before serving.

Energy 347kcal/1446kJ; Protein 5.3g; Carbohydrate 29.8g, of which sugars 19.8g; Fat 23.8g, of which saturates 11.4g; Cholesterol 78mg; Calcium 59mg; Fibre 1.5g; Sodium 105mg.

Mini Victoria sponges

These dainty little cakes are simplicity itself to make, yet pretty enough for a special afternoon tea table. The sponge is egg-free, with air and lightness added by the bicarbonate of soda and baking powder, and moisture by the yogurt.

MAKES 24

225g/8oz/1 cup softened butter or soft baking margarine
225g/8oz/generous 1 cup caster/superfine sugar
300g/10oz/2⅔ cups gluten-free self-raising/self-rising flour blend
2.5ml/½ tsp bicarbonate of soda/baking soda
5ml/1 tsp gluten-free baking powder
120ml/4fl oz/½ cup milk
250ml/8fl oz/1 cup whole natural/plain yogurt
5ml/1 tsp vanilla extract
60–90ml/4–6 tbsp raspberry, strawberry or cherry jam
gluten-free icing/confectioners' sugar, for dusting

1 Preheat the oven to 180°C/350°F/Gas 4. Line a 35 x 25cm/14 x 10in deep baking tin/pan with a piece of baking parchment.

2 Cream the butter or margarine and sugar in a large mixing bowl for about 5 minutes, until very light and creamy. It is important to whisk in as much air as possible as this will give lightness to the cake.

3 Sift together the flour, bicarbonate of soda and baking powder and then gently whisk or fold the mixture into the creamed butter mixture. Add the milk, yogurt and vanilla and gently whisk or fold in.

4 Spoon the mixture into the prepared tin and bake for 30–40 minutes, until the cake is firm and springs back to your touch and a skewer comes out clean when inserted into the middle of the cake.

5 Remove the tin from the oven, leave it to stand for 5 minutes, then lift out the cake using the baking parchment and place it on a wire rack to cool. Carefully peel off the baking parchment.

6 Once it is completely cold, carefully split the cake in half using a serrated knife so that you have two large rectangles of even depth. Spread the jam evenly over the cut side of one of the halves. Place the second rectangle on top to sandwich, then dust with a little icing sugar.

7 Cut into 24 even-sized squares. This cake will keep for up to 2 days in an airtight container.

Variations

This recipe can be adapted in many ways – from adding finely grated lemon or orange rind to the batter to swapping the jam for lemon curd or chocolate spread.

Energy 165kcal/692kJ; Protein 1.4g; Carbohydrate 22.6g, of which sugars 12.6g; Fat 8.1g, of which saturates 5g; Cholesterol 20mg; Calcium 28mg; Fibre 0.1g; Sodium 67mg.

Lime & coconut drizzle traybake

Sweet and moist, these tangy squares are made by whisking eggs and sugar until voluminous, then gently folding in naturally gluten-free ground almonds and shredded coconut in place of flour. The texture and flavour is similar to coconut macaroons, soft and slightly chewy.

MAKES 24

5 eggs
115g/4oz/⅔ cup caster/superfine sugar
115g/4oz/1 cup ground almonds
grated rind and juice of 2 limes
100g/3½oz/1⅓ cups soft shredded coconut
50g/1¾oz/⅓ cup gluten-free icing/confectioners' sugar, sifted

1 Preheat the oven to 180°C/350°F/Gas 4. Line a 35 x 25cm/14 x 10in deep baking tin/pan with a piece of baking parchment.

2 Place the eggs and sugar in a stand mixer bowl or use a large mixing bowl and a hand-held electric whisk. Whisk for about 5 minutes, until the mixture is very thick and creamy.

3 Gently fold the ground almonds and grated lime rind into the egg mixture, until incorporated.

4 Pour the mixture into the tin and spread level with a spatula. Sprinkle the coconut over the top of the cake.

5 Bake for 30–35 minutes, until lightly golden brown on top and the cake springs back to your touch. If the coconut starts to brown too much before the cake is cooked, cover loosely with a sheet of foil.

6 In a pan, heat the lime juice and icing sugar and bring to the boil. Drizzle over the cake and leave to cool.

7 Cut the cake into 24 squares. Slide a sharp knife under each square of cake to release it from the paper. It will store for up to 2 days in an airtight container but is best eaten on the day it is made.

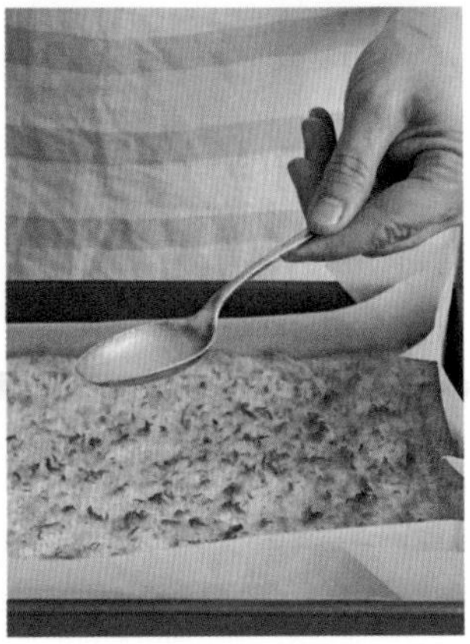

Variation

This cake also works beautifully with pink grapefruit, lemon or orange.

Cook's tip

Soft shredded coconut is different from desiccated/dry unsweetened shredded coconut, but if you are unable to find it, you can use desiccated coconut in its place as it will soften slightly once the drizzle is poured over.

Energy 103kcal/428kJ; Protein 2.9g; Carbohydrate 8g, of which sugars 7.9g; Fat 6.8g, of which saturates 2.8g; Cholesterol 48mg; Calcium 22mg; Fibre 0.8g; Sodium 20mg.

Grapefruit & poppy seed polenta traybake

This gluten-free traybake is sure to be a crowd-pleaser, with its bright, zesty flavour and nubbly texture thanks to the use of ground almonds and fine polenta. It works equally well with other citrus fruits, but grapefruit is just a bit different and well worth a try.

MAKES 24

225g//1 cup softened butter or soft baking margarine
170g/6oz/scant 1 cup caster/superfine sugar, plus 90g/3½oz/½ cup for candying
50g/2oz/¼ cup soft dark brown sugar
grated rind of 1 red grapefruit, plus extra for candying
3 eggs
200g/7oz/scant 2 cups ground almonds
150g/5oz/generous 1 cup fine polenta/cornmeal
1 tsp/5ml gluten-free baking powder
120ml/4fl oz/½ cup natural/plain yogurt
30ml/2 tbsp poppy seeds
juice of 2 red grapefruits
30ml/2 tbsp gluten-free icing/confectioners' sugar
24 red grapefruit segments, to decorate

1 Preheat the oven to 180°C/350°F/Gas 4. Line a 35 x 25cm/14 x 10in deep baking tin/pan with baking parchment.

2 Cream the butter or margarine and sugars until light and fluffy. Add the grapefruit rind and eggs and beat until incorporated. Add the almonds, polenta and baking powder along with the yogurt and whisk in. Fold through the poppy seeds and pour the mixture into the baking tin.

3 Bake for 30–40 minutes until the top is golden brown and the cake springs back to your touch. Remove from the oven.

4 Prepare a drizzle by mixing the grapefruit juice and icing sugar in a pan and bringing just to the boil. Spoon the hot drizzle over the warm cake, making sure that the whole top is covered. Do not oversoak the cake; you may not need all of the drizzle depending on how much juice your grapefruits contain. Leave to cool.

5 To make the candied rind for decoration, simmer 250ml/8fl oz/1 cup water with the 90g/3½oz/½ cup sugar until the sugar has dissolved. Peel thin strands of rind with a julienne peeler, making sure that you have the rind only and not the pith. Simmer for 2–3 minutes in the hot syrup, until the rind is soft.

6 When cool, cut the traybake into 24 squares and decorate with grapefruit segments and candied rind.

Energy 225kcal/938kJ; Protein 4.3g; Carbohydrate 22.5g, of which sugars 16.2g; Fat 14.2g, of which saturates 5.6g; Cholesterol 49mg; Calcium 64mg; Fibre 0.7g; Sodium 73mg.

Coconut blondie brownies

These gluten-free brownies are succulent and gooey, and are enjoyed by everyone. They have a pretty striped effect with both a blondie and brownie layer, although if you prefer you can just make them with plain chocolate.

MAKES 24

200g/7oz plain/semisweet chocolate
250g/9oz/1 cup plus 30ml/2 tbsp softened butter or soft baking margarine
200g/7oz white chocolate
5 eggs
400g/14oz/2 cups caster/superfine sugar
200g/7oz/2⅔ cups soft shredded coconut
200g/7oz/generous 1⅔ cups gluten-free plain/all-purpose flour blend

1 Preheat the oven to 180°C/350°F/Gas 4. Line a 35 x 25cm/14 x 10in deep baking tin/pan with a piece of baking parchment.

2 Break the plain chocolate into small pieces and place in a heatproof bowl with half of the butter over a pan of simmering water. Heat until the chocolate and butter have melted and you have a smooth, glossy sauce.

3 Do the same with the white chocolate and remaining butter so that you have both a melted white chocolate mixture and a plain chocolate mixture. Remove both from the heat and leave to cool.

4 Place the eggs and sugar in a stand mixer bowl or use a large mixing bowl and a hand-held electric whisk. Whisk for about 5 minutes, until the mixture is very thick and creamy.

5 Divide into two bowls and fold the white chocolate mixture into one and the plain chocolate mixture into the other with a spatula. Fold half of the coconut and flour into each bowl so that everything is incorporated.

6 Pour the plain chocolate batter into the tin and spread out in an even layer. Pour the white chocolate mixture on top, taking care that the two layers do not mix.

7 Bake for 25–30 minutes, until a crust has formed on top but the blondie brownies still feel a little soft underneath. Leave to cool in the tin, then remove the paper and cut into 24 squares to serve.

Variation

If you do not have soft shredded coconut use desiccated/dry unsweetened shredded coconut instead.

Energy 317kcal/1321kJ; Protein 3.5g; Carbohydrate 34.6g, of which sugars 27.9g; Fat 19g, of which saturates 12g; Cholesterol 74mg; Calcium 40mg; Fibre 1.2g; Sodium 100mg.

Sweet potato brownies

Brownies are traditionally made with lots of melted butter and sugar – this healthier version is made with steamed sweet potato and mashed banana, with just a few tablespoons of maple syrup, and contains no flour.

MAKES 12

350g/12oz/about 2 small sweet potatoes, peeled and cut into small chunks
50g/2oz dark/bittersweet chocolate, broken into pieces, plus 25g/1oz, diced, to decorate (optional)
45ml/3 tbsp smooth unsweetened peanut butter
45ml/3 tbsp coconut oil
45ml/3 tbsp maple syrup
1 large banana, peeled and broken into pieces
5ml/1 tsp vanilla extract
2.5ml/½ tsp ground cinnamon
3 eggs
50g/2oz/½ cup unsweetened cocoa powder
7.5ml/1½ tsp gluten-free baking powder
50g/2oz/scant ⅓ cup brazil nuts, roughly chopped

1 Preheat the oven to 180°C/350°F/Gas 4. Line a shallow 20cm/8in square cake tin/pan with a piece of baking parchment.

2 Cook the sweet potato in a steamer for 10–15 minutes, until just soft when pressed with a knife.

3 Meanwhile, put the dark chocolate, peanut butter, coconut oil and maple syrup in a small pan and heat gently, stirring, until the chocolate has melted and the mixture is smooth. Take off the heat.

4 Transfer the sweet potato to a food processor, add the banana and blend until smooth. Add the vanilla and cinnamon, then gradually mix in the eggs. Add the melted chocolate mixture and beat until smooth.

5 Mix the cocoa and baking powder together. Add to the food processor and blend again until smooth.

6 Spoon into the lined tin. Sprinkle over three-quarters of the nuts and spread level, then sprinkle on the rest of the nuts. Bake for 20–25 minutes, until well risen and cracked around the edges with a slightly soft middle.

7 Put the tin on to a wire rack and sprinkle with a little extra diced chocolate, if using. Leave to cool in the tin.

8 Lift the paper and brownies out of the tin, peel off the paper and cut into 12 bars. Store in a paper-lined plastic box in the fridge for up to 3 days.

Energy 176kcal/734kJ; Protein 4.8g; Carbohydrate 14.4g, of which sugars 8.6g; Fat 11.4g, of which saturates 5.3g; Cholesterol 58mg; Calcium 34mg; Fibre 2.1g; Sodium 86mg.

Large cakes & gâteaux

Gluten-free cakes are often made in a slightly different way to conventional ones. In order to overcome a dry texture, vegetable oil or yogurt are included in the cake batters to help keep the crumb softer and moister, as seen in Vanilla & Chocolate Yogurt Cake. Ground almonds or seeds, grated fruit and vegetables are all helpful for adding moisture, too, as well as replacing all or much of the flour and providing the bulk of the cake. Bulk is also provided by alternative ingredients such as gluten-free puffed rice or blitzed-up gluten-free flapjacks, for easy-to-make no-bake showstoppers. Mixtures that are made with gluten-free flour or an alternative, such as quinoa flour, tend to thicken and stiffen soon after mixing, as these products absorb more liquid, so make sure you transfer these cake batters to the pan and get it in the preheated oven straight away.

If you follow these simple rules, you can make all manner of wonderful cakes and gâteaux. From classic everyday sponges to elaborate tortes, there are cakes in this chapter to rival any store-bought confection. Some, such as Lemon Drizzle Loaf Cake, are perfect with mid-morning coffee or for a tea break, while others are ideal for an energy boost. These include nutrient-rich Oat & Fruit Loaf Cake, which is packed with fresh bananas and plumped-up dried fruit and nuts that have been soaked overnight. Others, such as Blueberry Streusel Ice Cream Cake and feather-light Coffee & Almond Quinoa Roulade, make unforgettable dessert-type cakes for serving at the end of a meal. There are also celebration cakes for birthdays, Christmas and other special occasions, like Chocolate Almond Truffle Cake, White Christmas Cake, and Layered Sponge Supreme.

There's truly something here for everyone, and every occasion, and all the cakes are every bit as delicious as you could hope for. So what are you waiting for – get baking!

Lemon drizzle loaf cake

Gluten free because of the ground almonds and oat flour, this is pleasantly sticky yet light as a feather, and one of the moistest cakes you can imagine. It is delicious as it is for afternoon tea, or served with some fruit and cream or yogurt for dessert.

SERVES 8

finely grated rind and juice of 2 lemons, plus extra strips of rind to decorate
175g/6oz/¾ cup unsalted butter, softened, or soft baking margarine, plus extra for greasing
225g/8oz/generous 1 cup coconut crystals/sugar or soft light brown sugar
3 eggs
100g/3¾oz/scant 1 cup gluten-free oat flour
15ml/1 tbsp gluten-free baking powder
75g/3oz/¾ cup ground almonds
150ml/¼ pint/⅔ cup milk or Greek/strained plain yogurt

1 Preheat the oven to 180°C/350°F/Gas 4. Grease a 900g/2lb loaf tin/pan, and line it with baking parchment.

2 Put half the lemon rind in a large mixing bowl. Add the butter or margarine and mix them together along with 175g/6oz/scant 1 cup of the sugar.

3 Add 1 egg to the butter mixture, and 5ml/1 tsp of the flour, and beat to combine, using an electric whisk if you have one. Continue adding each of the eggs, adding a teaspoon of flour with each. Sift in the remaining flour, baking powder and ground almonds.

4 Fold the ingredients together, working quickly, using a spatula. Mix in the milk or yogurt little by little until the mixture is just thin enough to fall off the spoon, but no more. It's unlikely you'll need all of the liquid.

5 Spoon the batter into the loaf tin, and bake in the preheated oven for 40–55 minutes.

6 Meanwhile, mix the lemon juice and remaining rind with the remaining sugar. Set aside to dissolve.

7 Remove the cake from the oven. It's done when a skewer inserted into the middle comes out clean. Immediately prick the surface of the hot cake with a fork.

8 Evenly pour the lemon juice mixture over the cake, allowing it to sink in before pouring more on. The cake will be able to absorb all of it. Leave to cool inside the tin, then lift out of the tin by the edges of the paper and decorate with thin strips of lemon rind.

Energy 424kcal/1769kJ; Protein 7.3g; Carbohydrate 40.2g, of which sugars 30.8g; Fat 27.1g, of which saturates 12.7g; Cholesterol 134mg; Calcium 77mg; Fibre 1.1g; Sodium 179mg.

Oat & fruit loaf cake

Vegan, heart-healthy and full of fibre thanks to the gluten-free oat flour, this teabread is particularly good served in toasted slices, spread with nut butter. It is sweetened with date syrup and caramelized ripe bananas, which also give it a lovely moist texture.

SERVES 8

115g/4oz/scant 1 cup sultanas/golden raisins
120ml/4fl oz/½ cup hot tea
12 cashew nuts
15ml/1 tbsp coconut oil, plus extra for greasing
3 ripe bananas, halved lengthways
juice of ½ lemon
45ml/3 tbsp apple juice
120ml/4fl oz/½ cup date syrup
225g/8oz/2 cups gluten-free oat flour
10ml/2 tsp bicarbonate of soda/baking soda
2.5ml/½ tsp salt
5ml/1 tsp ground cinnamon
5ml/1 tsp ground ginger
2.5ml/½ tsp ground nutmeg

1 Put the sultanas in a mixing bowl and cover with the tea. Put the cashew nuts in another bowl and cover with warm water. Set both aside to soak for 4 hours or overnight.

2 Preheat the oven to 180°C/350°F/Gas 4. Grease a 900g/2lb loaf tin/pan and line with baking parchment.

3 Melt the coconut oil in a frying pan over a medium heat and fry the bananas for 1–2 minutes, until golden. Turn them over and repeat on the other side. Remove the pan from the heat and set aside.

4 Put the lemon juice and apple juice in a blender. Discard the soaking water from the cashews. Add the cashews, caramelized bananas with any liquid that's collected in the frying pan, and the date syrup. Blend on high for 20–30 seconds, until combined, then pour the banana mixture into a large mixing bowl.

5 Sift the oat flour, bicarbonate of soda, salt, cinnamon, ginger and nutmeg over the banana mixture, and then add the sultanas and their soaking juices.

6 Combine together quickly with a spatula or a spoon. Pour the batter into the loaf tin and smooth the top.

7 Bake for about 35–40 minutes, until a skewer inserted into the middle comes out clean.

8 Lift the loaf out of the tin using the baking parchment, and set aside to cool completely on a wire rack. Cut into slices to serve, with a spread of your choice.

Energy 229kcal/973kJ; Protein 4.8g; Carbohydrate 49.6g, of which sugars 28.3g; Fat 2.7g, of which saturates 0.1g; Cholesterol 0mg; Calcium 54mg; Fibre 4.3g; Sodium 20mg.

Madeira cake

This fine-textured gluten-free cake is a good choice for a birthday or celebration cake, as it is firm but light, which makes it the perfect base for decorating. Serve plain as is, or split and sandwiched with buttercream.

SERVES 8–10

200g/7oz/scant 1 cup butter, softened, plus extra for greasing
200g/7oz/1 cup caster/superfine sugar
4 eggs
25g/1oz/¼ cup ground almonds
finely grated rind and juice of ½ lemon
150g/5oz/1¼ cups gluten-free self-raising/self-rising flour blend
1.5ml/¼ tsp xanthan gum

1 Preheat the oven to 160°C/325°F/Gas 3. Grease and line the base of an 18cm/7in round deep cake tin/pan.

2 In a large mixing bowl, beat the butter and sugar until light and fluffy, then beat in the eggs one at a time, adding 15ml/1 tbsp almonds after each egg. Beat well.

3 Add the lemon rind and beat for a few more seconds, then sift in the flour and xanthan gum and fold in until half-mixed. Sprinkle over the lemon juice and continue to gently fold in the flour until everything is combined.

4 Spoon the mixture into the prepared tin and smooth the top level with the back of the spoon.

5 Bake for 1¼–1½ hours, until golden, or until a skewer inserted into the middle comes out clean. Leave to cool in the tin for 45 minutes, then turn out on to a wire rack to go cold. Remove the paper and serve.

Cook's tip and variations

- The top of the cake should be a dark golden colour. If it starts to get too brown before the cake is cooked through, cover the top with a piece of foil.
- For a vanilla cake, leave the lemon zest out of the cake and add 30ml/2 tbsp milk and 15ml/1 tbsp vanilla extract instead of the lemon juice.
- If you want to ice the cake, make a simple buttercream frosting by beating 450g/1lb/4 cups sifted icing/confectioners' sugar with 150g/5oz unsalted butter, at room temperature, in a freestanding electric mixer with a paddle attachment (or a hand-held electric whisk) on a low speed until the mixture comes together. Add 30ml/2 tbsp milk a little at a time. Once all the milk has been incorporated, turn the mixer up to high speed and continue beating until the frosting is light and fluffy.

Energy 332kcal/1384kJ; Protein 4.5g; Carbohydrate 33.2g, of which sugars 21.2g; Fat 20.7g, of which saturates 11.3g; Cholesterol 135mg; Calcium 29mg; Fibre 0.2g; Sodium 156mg.

Buttermilk sponge cake

This sponge has a soft and light texture because it is made with rice flour, and it is moist thanks to the use of buttermilk, which lends the cake a slightly tangy flavour that partners especially well with jam or buttercream, or for a special occasion, cream and fresh fruit.

SERVES 8–10

115g/4oz/½ cup butter, softened, plus extra for greasing
300g/11oz/1½ cups caster/superfine sugar
2 eggs
300g/11oz/2½ cups white rice flour
5ml/1 tsp xanthan gum
5ml/1 tsp bicarbonate of soda
300ml/½ pint/1¼ cups buttermilk
15ml/1 tbsp white wine vinegar
icing/confectioners' sugar, for dusting

For the filling

225g/8oz fruity jam of your choice,
115g/4oz/½ cup butter, softened
115g/4oz/½ cup icing/confectioners' sugar
OR
150ml/¼ pint/⅔ cup double/heavy cream
225g/8oz/2 cups fresh soft fruit, such as raspberries, strawberries (quartered or halved, depending on their size) and blueberries

1 Preheat the oven to 180°C/350°F/Gas 4. Lightly grease the sides and line the bases of two 20cm/8in cake tins/pans with baking parchment.

2 Beat the butter and sugar in a large mixing bowl until light and fluffy. Add the eggs, one at a time, beating well between each addition.

3 Sift together the flour, xanthan gum and bicarbonate of soda. Mix the buttermilk and vinegar in a jug or bowl.

4 Add half of the flour mixture to the butter mixture along with half the buttermilk and gently fold in until almost combined. Add the rest of the flour and buttermilk mixtures and fold in.

5 Divide the mixture evenly between the two tins and level the surface. Bake in the middle of the oven for 30–35 minutes, or until a skewer inserted into the middle of the cakes comes out clean.

6 Leave the cakes in the tins for 5 minutes, then turn out on to a wire rack to go cold. Peel off the paper.

7 If filling with buttercream, beat the butter and icing sugar together until light and fluffy. Put one cake on a serving plate and spread with the buttercream and jam. Place the other cake on top to make a sandwich, and dust with more icing sugar.

8 If filling with cream and soft fruit, put the cream in a large mixing bowl and beat with an electric whisk, until the mixture holds its shape but isn't too stiff; it will thicken further as it stands. Spread the cream over the bottom layer of the cake and top with the fruit. Put the second layer of cake on top of the first, then dust the top with icing sugar before serving.

Variations

For a really spectacular gâteau, top with more whipped cream, add a layer of soft fruit and glaze with sieved apricot jam.

Energy 568kcal/2377kJ; Protein 5.4g; Carbohydrate 77.5g, of which sugars 53.5g; Fat 27.3g, of which saturates 16.5g; Cholesterol 112mg; Calcium 82mg; Fibre 1.1g; Sodium 125mg.

Vanilla & chocolate layer cake

Here, a combination of three types of gluten-free flour, together with olive oil and yogurt, create a light and moist sponge. The chocolate frosting has a base of cream cheese, so is not as sweet or rich as a classic buttercream, and is used for filling and covering the top of the cake.

SERVES 16

550ml/18fl oz/2¼ cups Greek/strained plain yogurt
150ml/¼ pint/⅔ cup olive oil, plus extra for greasing
200g/7oz/1 cup coconut crystals/sugar or soft light brown sugar
15–20ml/3–4 tsp vanilla extract
5 eggs
225g/8oz/2 cups brown rice flour
90g/3½oz/¾ cup sorghum flour
125g/4¼oz/generous 1 cup potato starch
15ml/1 tbsp gluten-free baking powder
5ml/1 tsp salt

For the chocolate cream

450g/1lb/2 cups cream cheese, at room temperature
225g/8oz/1 cup butter, softened
200g/7oz/1½ cups agave powder
20g/¾oz/¼ cup raw cacao powder or unsweetened cocoa powder
30ml/2 tbsp agave syrup

1 Preheat the oven to 180°C/350°F/Gas 4. Grease two 25cm/10in round springform baking tins/pans.

2 To make the cakes, put the yogurt, oil, sugar and vanilla in a large mixing bowl. Using an electric whisk on low, add the eggs one by one, incorporating each one before adding the next.

3 Add the rest of the ingredients to the bowl and stir gently to combine.

4 Pour half the batter into each of the cake tins, and smooth with a silicone spatula. Bake for 45 minutes, until golden brown and the edges have shrunk away from the tins.

5 Remove the cakes from the oven and allow to cool in the tins for about 15 minutes, then remove the springform sides, peel off the lining paper and leave the cakes to cool on a wire rack.

6 Make the chocolate cream. Put all of the ingredients into a large mixing bowl and cream together for about 2 minutes, using an electric whisk on medium.

7 Put one of the cold cakes on a large plate or a cake stand. Spread half the chocolate cream evenly over the top. Carefully put the second cake on top, to create a sandwich. Spread the top with the remaining chocolate cream, using a silicone spatula or spoon to create a swirl to decorate, then serve.

Energy 541kcal/2247kJ; Protein 7.5g; Carbohydrate 43g, of which sugars 15g; Fat 38.2g, of which saturates 19.8g; Cholesterol 135mg; Calcium 96mg; Fibre 7.3g; Sodium 235mg.

Maize cake

It is best to use a very finely milled maize flour for this simple-to-make, everyday cake. It is essentially a light sponge mixture, in which regular flour has been replaced with golden, naturally sweet and gluten-free maize flour. Serve it plain, or with cream, yogurt or even chocolate sauce.

SERVES 12

225g/8oz/1 cup butter, softened, plus extra for greasing
225g/8oz/1 cup caster/superfine sugar
4 eggs, separated
125g/4¼ oz/generous 1 cup fine maize flour
finely grated rind of 1 lemon or 1 orange
125g/4½oz/generous 1 cup gluten-free self-raising/self-rising flour blend

1 Preheat the oven to 190°C/375°F/Gas 5. Grease and flour the sides of a 20cm/8in springform cake tin/pan, and line the base with baking parchment.

2 In a large bowl, cream the butter and sugar together until light and fluffy. Add the egg yolks one at a time to the mixture, ensuring each is fully incorporated before you mix in the next one.

3 Add the fine maize flour and the grated lemon or orange rind to the bowl, and beat for another minute.

4 In a separate bowl, whisk the egg whites until stiff peaks form, then gently fold them into the yolk and sugar mixture. Sift the flour over the mixture and fold it in carefully with a metal spoon.

5 Spoon the cake mixture into the prepared tin and smooth the surface level. Bake for 30–40 minutes, until the cake is firm to the touch.

6 Remove the cake from the oven and allow to stand in the tin for 10 minutes before turning out on to a wire rack. Serve while still warm.

Cook's tip

This cake is best enjoyed while it is still slightly warm, and is especially good served with small cups of strong espresso coffee.

Energy 332kcal/1358kJ; Protein 6g; Carbohydrate 35.3g, of which sugars 20; Fat 19.2g, of which saturates 1.1g; Cholesterol 121mg; Calcium 92mg; Fibre 0.9g; Sodium 209mg

Orange & almond cake

Made with whole oranges, which are simmered until very tender and then puréed and combined with sugar and ground almonds – instead of flour – this cake has a moist texture and fresh citrus flavour. Serve it drizzled with luxurious chocolate sauce for a special occasion.

SERVES 12

3 medium or 2 large oranges
coconut oil, for greasing
6 eggs
450g/1lb/2¼ cups coconut crystals/sugar or soft light brown sugar
500g/18oz/5 cups ground almonds
7.5ml/1½ tsp gluten-free baking powder
chocolate sauce, to serve (see Cook's tip)

1 Bring a large pan of water to the boil over a high heat. Add the whole oranges, put the lid on the pan, reduce the heat and simmer for 30 minutes.

2 Remove the oranges from the water with a slotted spoon and discard the cooking water. Leave the fruit to cool.

3 Preheat the oven to 180°C/350°F/Gas 4. Oil a 23cm/9in round springform cake tin/pan with the coconut oil.

4 When the oranges are cool enough to handle easily, cut them in half along their circumferences. Remove the pips. Transfer them to a blender, and process for about 20 seconds on high until puréed.

5 Put the eggs in a large mixing bowl and add the coconut sugar. Gently beat with a fork to combine, then add the orange purée and mix it in with a large spoon or a silicone spatula.

6 Add the ground almonds and baking powder and fold in, working quickly.

7 Pour and scrape the batter into the prepared cake tin, smoothing the top.

8 Bake for about 50 minutes, until a skewer inserted into the middle comes out clean. If it's cooked a little longer, the outside may be darker in colour, but it will have a richer flavour.

9 Leave the cake in the tin to cool completely, then remove and put it on a serving plate. Serve the cake on its own, or with a rich chocolate sauce, if liked (see Cook's tip).

Cook's tip

For a simple chocolate sauce, put 100g/3½oz chopped plain/semisweet chocolate, 50g/2oz/4 tbsp butter (or margarine for dairy free), cut into small pieces, and 90ml/6 tbsp water into a heatproof mixing bowl set over a pan of steaming but not boiling water. Stir frequently until melted and smooth. Remove from the heat, leave to stand and thicken for a few minutes, then serve warm.

Variation

You could also use large, juicy lemons to make this cake, if you like – Amalfi lemons are especially good.

Energy 481kcal/1999kJ; Protein 14.4g; Carbohydrate 43.5g, of which sugars 39.4g; Fat 29g, of which saturates 3.1g; Cholesterol 103mg; Calcium 149mg; Fibre 0.8g; Sodium 164mg.

Coffee & almond quinoa roulade

This dessert is transformed by using toasted quinoa in place of flour, the nutty flavour of which complements the almonds and coffee. Although the result looks impressive, it isn't too difficult to make and can be done in advance. Delight guests with this gluten-free version of a classic.

SERVES 6–8

75g/3oz/½ cup quinoa
500ml/17fl oz/2 cups water
4 eggs
150g/5oz/¾ cup caster/superfine sugar, plus extra for sprinkling
75g/3oz/¾ cup ground almonds
25g/1oz/¼ cup cornflour/starch
5ml/1 tsp gluten-free baking powder
30ml/2 tbsp flaked/sliced almonds, toasted
fresh berries, to serve

For the filling

300ml/½ pint/1¼ cups whipping cream
15ml/1 tbsp instant coffee dissolved in 30ml/2 tbsp boiling water

1 Preheat the oven to 180°C/350°F/Gas 4. Grease and line a 30 x 22cm/12 x 9in Swiss roll tin or jelly roll pan.

2 Spread the quinoa on a baking sheet and toast for 6–8 minutes under a medium grill or broiler, until golden. Place in a pan, add the water, bring to the boil and cook for 12–14 minutes, until soft. Drain the quinoa if necessary and set aside to cool completely.

3 Whisk the eggs and sugar until light and frothy. Fold in the ground almonds, cornflour, baking powder and quinoa. Spread evenly in the tin and bake for 12–15 minutes, until golden, and springy when touched. Cover with a dish towel and cool for 5–10 minutes.

4 For the filling, whip the cream until firm but soft. Blend with the coffee and set aside in the fridge.

5 While the roulade is slightly warm, cut a piece of parchment larger than the sponge. Sprinkle with the flaked almonds and a tablespoon of sugar. Turn the roulade on to the paper, then peel off the paper from the back. Make a shallow slit, without cutting all the way through the sponge, 2cm/¾in in from a long edge.

6 With the paper in place, start to roll the roulade from the same side as the slit, making it as tight and straight as you can. Leave to cool completely.

7 Unroll, remove the paper and spread the middle with coffee cream. Re-roll, arranging any dislodged flaked almonds on the top. Sprinkle with more sugar. Serve.

Energy 309kcal/1279kJ; Protein 8.6g; Carbohydrate 10g, of which sugars 2.1g; Fat 26.3g, of which saturates 11g; Cholesterol 155mg; Calcium 78mg; Fibre 0g; Sodium 61mg.

Chocolate roulade

Moist and intensely chocolatey as a result of the use of both cacao and carob flour in place of wheat flour, this version of a Swiss roll is perfect at any time of year. Served in summer, it can be garnished with fresh fruit, and at Christmas it becomes a Yule log.

SERVES 8–10

40g/1½oz/⅓ cup raw cacao powder or unsweetened cocoa powder
40g/1½oz/⅓ cup carob flour
25g/1oz/2 tbsp coconut oil, melted if solid, plus extra for greasing
6 eggs
1.5ml/¼ tsp cream of tartar
150g/5oz/¾ cup coconut crystals/sugar or soft light brown sugar
ground cinnamon, to taste
300ml/½ pint/1¼ cups whipping cream
30ml/2 tbsp gluten-free icing/confectioners' sugar, for dusting

1 Preheat the oven to 190°C/375°F/Gas 5. Grease a 30cm x 22cm/12in x 9in Swiss roll tin or jelly roll pan with oil, then line the base and sides with baking parchment.

2 Sift the cacao and carob flour into a large mixing bowl, then pour in the coconut oil. Mix thoroughly with a metal spoon and set aside.

3 Separate the eggs, putting the whites in a spotlessly clean large bowl. Add the cream of tartar to the whites.

4 Add the egg yolks to the cacao mixture, then stir in the sugar and set aside.

5 Whisk the egg whites and cream of tartar to form stiff peaks, but no more, using an electric whisk on high. Set aside.

6 Beat the egg yolk and cacao mixture for 2–3 minutes, until creamy. The mixture will leave thick trails when the whisk is lifted.

7 Gently stir about 30ml/2 tbsp of the egg whites into the mixture, then carefully fold the remaining egg whites into the chocolate with a metal spoon, retaining as much of the air as possible.

8 Pour the batter into the tin, then gently tilt the tin from side to side until the batter is level.

9 Bake in the preheated oven for 18–20 minutes until risen and firm to the touch. Remove from the oven, and leave in the tin to cool.

10 When the cake is cool, wash and dry the beaters, then pour the cream into a clean bowl, and whisk on high until thick enough to hold fairly stiff peaks, without overwhisking it. Spread the cream over the cake using a metal spoon, leaving a 2.5cm/1in border.

11 Starting with one of the shorter edges, roll the cake, using the baking parchment. Peel the paper away as the cake rolls from one side of the tin to the other.

12 Put the finished roll on a serving platter, and dust with icing sugar before serving.

Energy 296kcal/1230kJ; Protein 7.4g; Carbohydrate 20g, of which sugars 18.6g; Fat 21.2g, of which saturates 12.4g; Cholesterol 170mg; Calcium 58mg; Fibre 1.9g; Sodium 173mg.

Walnut & chestnut cake

Two autumnal nuts are used in this recipe, in the chestnut flour, and the walnuts, used both toasted and chopped in the filling and as halves to decorate. This fabulous light sponge cake is filled and covered with a fluffy white meringue-style frosting.

SERVES 12
oil, for greasing
6 eggs, separated
200g/7oz/1 cup caster/superfine sugar
200g/7oz/scant 1 cup gluten-free crème fraîche
100ml/4fl oz/scant ½ cup whole natural/plain yogurt
10ml/2 tsp vanilla extract
190g/6½oz/1⅔ cups chestnut flour
15ml/1 tbsp gluten-free baking powder
75g/3oz/¼ cup toasted chopped walnuts

For the buttercream
75g/3oz/6 tbsp unsalted butter
5ml/1 tsp vanilla extract
175g/6oz/1½ cups gluten-free icing/confectioners' sugar

For the frosting
2 large egg whites
350g/12oz/1¾ cups golden caster/superfine sugar
pinch of salt
pinch of cream of tartar
15ml/1 tbsp warm water
walnut halves, to decorate

1 Preheat the oven to 160°C/325°F/Gas 3. Grease and line two 20cm/8in round shallow cake tins/pans with baking parchment.

2 Put the egg yolks and sugar in a large mixing bowl and whisk until light and fluffy and the mixture leaves a trail when the whisk is lifted. Stir the crème fraîche, yogurt and vanilla together, then fold into the mixture.

3 Sift over the flour and baking powder and gently fold in. Whisk the egg whites until stiff, then fold into the mixture with the toasted walnuts. Divide between the two tins and level the tops with the back of a spoon.

4 Bake for 25 minutes, or until golden and springy to the touch in the middle.

5 Allow the cake to stand for 5 minutes, then turn out on to a wire rack to go cold. Remove the lining papers. Carefully cut each cake in half horizontally using a long-bladed sharp knife.

6 To make the buttercream, in a large mixing bowl, beat the butter, vanilla extract and icing sugar together until light and fluffy.

7 Spread a third thinly over one sponge half and place a sponge layer on top, then continue layering the sponges with the buttercream. Put the cake on to a serving plate.

8 To make the frosting, put the egg whites in a large heatproof bowl and add the sugar, salt, cream of tartar and water. Put the bowl over a pan of hot water and whisk with an electric mixer for 7 minutes, or until the mixture is thick and stands in peaks.

9 Immediately, use a metal spatula to swirl the frosting over the top and sides of the cake. Arrange the walnut halves on top and leave the frosting to set for 10 minutes before serving.

Variation
Pecan nuts work well in this cake, too, being similar in texture and with a sweet, slightly caramel flavour.

Energy 491kcal/2070kJ; Protein 6.7g; Carbohydrate 75.4g, of which sugars 66.3g; Fat 20.1g, of which saturates 9.3g; Cholesterol 148mg; Calcium 74mg; Fibre 1.9g; Sodium 69mg.

White Christmas cake

This light gluten-free sponge has a moist texture and zesty flavour thanks to the coconut and lime, is filled with a tangy lemon curd, and coated with a sumptuous frosting. Make the sponge bases a day ahead, or bake and freeze ready for decorating. Eat on the day of assembly.

SERVES 12

finely grated rind and juice of 2 limes
75g/3oz block creamed coconut, grated, or 150ml/¼ pint/⅔ cup coconut cream
225g/8oz/1 cup unsalted butter, softened, plus extra for greasing
225g/8oz/generous 1 cup caster/superfine sugar
4 large eggs
225g/8oz/2 cups gluten-free self-raising/self-rising flour blend
2.5ml/½ tsp xanthan gum

For the filling & decoration

200g/7oz/scant ¾ cup lemon curd
225g/8oz/1 cup cream cheese
75g/3oz/6 tbsp unsalted butter
275g/10oz/2½ cups gluten-free icing/confectioners' sugar
finely grated rind of 1 lime
175g/6oz/2 cups shredded coconut
frosted bay leaves, rosemary and cranberries, to decorate

1 Preheat the oven to 180°C/350°F/Gas 4. Grease and line two 20cm/8in round cake tins/pans.

2 Put the lime juice and 45ml/3 tbsp water in a pan with the creamed coconut. Heat gently to dissolve, then cool.

3 Put the lime rind, butter, sugar, eggs, flour, xanthan gum and cooled coconut mixture into a bowl and whisk for 2–3 minutes or until smooth and soft.

4 Divide the batter equally between the cake tins and smooth the tops level.

5 Bake for 20–25 minutes or until golden and risen and firm to the touch in the middle. Leave to cool in the tin for 5 minutes, then turn out to cool on a wire rack and peel away the lining papers.

6 Cut each cold cake in half horizontally with a sharp knife, then sandwich each together with lemon curd. Put one cake on a plate, spread the top with the remaining curd and sandwich both cakes together.

7 To make the coating, put the cream cheese, butter, icing sugar and lime rind in a bowl and beat until smooth. Spread over the top and sides of the cake.

8 Sprinkle the coconut over the top and pat on to the sides, then tidy the base. Decorate with sprigs of bay, rosemary and cranberries.

Energy 661kcal/2771kJ; Protein 5.1g; Carbohydrate 70g, of which sugars 51.1g; Fat 41.4g, of which saturates 27.3g; Cholesterol 152mg; Calcium 41mg; Fibre 1.6g; Sodium 103mg.

Layered sponge supreme

Four cakes, layered one on top of the other, are presented here as a towering centrepiece fit for any party. The trick to keeping this gluten-free recipe fluffy is to make the batter a little runnier than if you were making it with wheat flour.

SERVES 12

450g/1lb/2 cups butter, softened, plus extra for greasing
275g/10oz/1⅓ cups coconut crystals/sugar or soft light brown sugar
20ml/4 tsp vanilla extract
6 eggs
450g/1lb/4 cups gluten-free plain/all-purpose flour blend
15ml/1 tbsp gluten-free baking powder
500ml/17fl oz/generous 2 cups almond milk or full-fat/whole milk
gluten-free icing/confectioners' sugar, for dusting
fresh edible flowers, to decorate (optional)

For the filling

900g/2lb fresh strawberries, hulled and quartered
juice of ½ lemon
50ml/2fl oz/¼ cup raw agave syrup
475ml/16fl oz/2 cups coconut cream (put the can in the fridge to chill) or whipping cream

1 For the filling, combine the strawberries, lemon juice and agave syrup in a non-reactive bowl. Cover and macerate in the fridge for at least 4 hours, or overnight.

2 To make the cakes, preheat the oven to 180°C/350°F/Gas 4. Lightly grease two non-stick 23cm/9in round 5cm/2in-deep cake tins/pans (unless you have four pans and sufficient room in the oven).

3 Cream half of the butter, half of the sugar, and half of the vanilla extract in a mixing bowl with a wooden spoon. One by one, mix in 3 of the eggs.

4 Sift in half of the flour and half of the baking powder, and stir. Little by little, add half of the milk.

5 Pour the batter equally into the cake tins and bake for about 45 minutes, until a skewer inserted into the middle comes out clean.

6 Turn the cakes out on to a wire rack and set aside to cool. Repeat these steps to use up the rest of the cake ingredients and bake two more cakes, so there are a total of four. (If you have enough cake tins and oven space you can of course mix and bake all four at once.)

7 When all four cakes have been baked, cooled, and are ready to be assembled, remove the coconut or dairy cream from the fridge. Whisk until it is thick and stiff peaks form, using an electric whisk or hand whisk.

8 Put one of the cakes on to a serving plate or a tiered cake stand. Spread one-third of the cream on top of the cake using a spatula or a palette knife. Spread one-quarter of the macerated strawberries on top. Put the second cake on top to make a sandwich.

9 Spread an equal amount of the whipped cream on top of the second cake evenly. Top with an equal amount of strawberries. Put the third cake on top, and spread over the remaining cream. Add an equal amount of the strawberries. Top the fourth cake and finish with the remaining strawberries.

10 Leave for about 1 hour, so that the cake has a little time to absorb some of the cream and strawberry juices. Dust with sugar and decorate with fresh flowers, if liked.

Energy 755kcal/3137kJ; Protein 8.7g; Carbohydrate 65.1g, of which sugars 32.2g; Fat 51.9g, of which saturates 31.4g; Cholesterol 243mg; Calcium 117mg; Fibre 1.5g; Sodium 306mg.

Angel food cake

This snowy white American tea-time classic is great for those on a gluten-free diet since it contains very little flour. The cream of tartar helps to aerate the egg whites, and the addition of sugar creates a light meringue texture that is springy but slightly sticky. It is also very low in fat.

SERVES 10–12

65g/2¼oz/generous ½ cup gluten-free plain/all-purpose flour blend
15ml/1 tbsp cornflour/starch
225g/8oz/1 cup caster/superfine sugar
10 egg whites
5ml/1 tsp cream of tartar
7.5ml/1½ tsp vanilla extract

For the frosting

2 egg whites
115g/4oz/generous ½ cup caster/superfine sugar
10ml/2 tsp golden/light corn syrup
2.5ml/½ tsp vanilla extract
grated rind of 1 orange, to decorate

1 Preheat the oven to 180°C/350°F/Gas 4.

2 In a large bowl, sift together the flour, cornflour and 50g/2oz/¼ cup of the sugar two or three times, so that the texture is very, very light.

3 Put the egg whites and cream of tartar into a large, clean, grease-free bowl and whisk together with an electric whisk until they form stiff peaks.

4 Gradually whisk in the remaining sugar, 15ml/1 tbsp at a time, until the mixture becomes thick and glossy and you can't see any grains of sugar.

5 Using a metal spoon, gently fold the sifted flour and sugar mixture and the vanilla extract into the egg whites until combined. Use a figure-of-eight movement with the spoon, and try not to knock out too much air.

6 Gently pour and scrape the mixture into a 25cm/10in non-stick ring mould and smooth it out so it is level. Bake for 35–40 minutes, or until risen and golden.

7 Remove from the oven, invert the cake in its mould on to a wire rack, and leave to go cold.

8 To make the frosting, put the egg whites into a large, clean, grease-free bowl and whisk with an electric whisk until stiff and dry. Set aside.

9 Heat the sugar and 60ml/4 tbsp water in a small pan, stirring constantly until the sugar dissolves. As soon as this happens, stop stirring. Increase the heat and boil until the syrup reaches 115°C/240°F on a sugar thermometer. As soon as this temperature is reached, remove the pan from the heat.

10 Carefully pour the sugar syrup into the egg whites, whisking constantly as you do so, until the mixture is thick and glossy. Add the golden syrup and vanilla, and continue beating for 5 minutes, until the frosting is really light and fluffy.

11 Lift the mould off the cake and put the cake on a serving plate. Quickly spread the frosting all over the cake and sprinkle with orange rind to decorate. Serve immediately, or store the cake in the fridge for up to 5 days.

Energy 177kcal/5007kJ; Protein 3.1g; Carbohydrate 27.7g, of which sugars 21.4g; Fat 0.1g, of which saturates 0g; Cholesterol 0mg; Calcium 24mg; Fibre 0.3g; Sodium 49mg.

Chocolate almond truffle cake

This dark chocolate cake contains almonds and only a little gluten-free flour, meaning it is dense and moist. It's also cooked until only just set, to retain its fudgy texture. Covered with chocolate ganache and finished with caramelized almonds, it is very rich, so serve it in thin slices.

SERVES 12

150g/5oz/¾ cup unsalted butter, plus extra for greasing
200g/7oz dark/bittersweet chocolate, chopped
6 large eggs, separated
150g/5oz/⅔ cup soft light brown sugar
30ml/2 tbsp gluten-free plain/all-purpose flour blend
115g/4oz/1 cup ground almonds

For the ganache

150ml/¼ pint/⅔ cup double/heavy cream
200g/7oz dark/bittersweet chocolate, chopped

For the topping

200g/7oz/1¾ cups blanched almonds
150g/5oz/¾ cup caster/superfine sugar

1 Preheat the oven to 180°C/350°F/Gas 4. Grease a 20cm/8in round cake tin/pan and line it with some baking parchment.

2 Melt the butter in a pan over low heat. Remove from the heat and add the chocolate, stirring constantly so that it melts in the hot butter. Leave to cool.

3 In a large mixing bowl, whisk the egg yolks and sugar together with an electric whisk, until thick and pale. Add the chocolate mixture and mix well. Sift in the flour and ground almonds and carefully mix together.

4 Put the egg whites into a clean, grease-free mixing bowl and whisk until they form soft peaks. Fold the egg whites carefully into the mixture to retain as much air as possible in the batter.

5 Pour the batter into the prepared tin and bake for 25 minutes. The cake will be set but slightly wobbly in the middle. Leave to cool in the tin.

6 To make the chocolate ganache (see Cook's tip), heat the cream to almost boiling point. Immediately remove from the heat and add the chopped chocolate. Stir until all of it is amalgamated.

7 Set aside to cool and thicken, then pour the ganache over the cake to glaze. Leave to set.

8 To make the almond topping, first toast the almonds in a low oven for a few minutes on a baking sheet. Put the sugar and 100ml/3½fl oz/scant ½ cup water in a pan and cook until lightly caramelized. Remove from the heat and add the toasted almonds. Stir briefly to coat. Using tongs, and working quickly, take out small clusters of the sticky nuts and put on a prepared greased sheet of baking parchment to cool.

9 Top the cake with the almond clusters and serve.

Cook's tip

Chopping chocolate helps it melt more quickly – dark/bittersweet chocolate is best divided into nut-size pieces. To avoid scorching the chocolate, put it in a heatproof bowl and set it over a pan of hot water. Do not let the water touch the bowl. Stir so that it melts evenly.

Energy 635kcal/2652kJ; Protein 11.4g; Carbohydrate 51.3g, of which sugars 48.3g; Fat 43.9g, of which saturates 18.1g; Cholesterol 161mg; Calcium 105mg; Fibre 1.1g; Sodium 52mg.

Crispy cake with berries

A crispy cake doesn't just have to be just for children, and using gluten-free rice crispies held together with melted marshmallows is an easy, no-bake way to replace wheat flour and quickly produce a tempting treat. For the best flavour, use seasonal fresh fruit.

SERVES 8

225g/8oz/6 cups gluten-free marshmallows
50g/2oz/¼ cup butter, plus extra for greasing
100g/3½oz/3½ cups gluten-free rice crispies
100g/3½oz white chocolate
225g/8oz/1 cup clotted or thick whipped cream
400g/14oz fresh berries, such as raspberries, strawberries (quartered or halved) and blueberries
gluten-free icing/confectioners' sugar, for dusting

1 Grease and line a 23cm/9in round springform tin/pan.

2 Place the marshmallows and butter in a pan over a gentle heat until they have melted and are combined, stirring all the time. Add the rice crispies to the pan and stir well so that all the crispies are coated in the marshmallow mixture.

3 Spoon the crispy mixture into the prepared tin and press down to an even layer with the back of a spoon.

4 Break the white chocolate into pieces and place in a heatproof bowl over a pan of simmering water. Leave to melt, making sure that the base of the bowl does not touch the water. Spread the melted chocolate over the top of the crispy cake layer and leave to set.

5 When you are ready to serve and the chocolate has set, take the cake out of the tin and remove the paper. Place on a plate and cover the chocolate with the cream. Top with the berries and a light dusting of icing sugar.

6 Serve it straight away or store in the fridge. This cake should be eaten on the day it is made.

Energy 440kcal/1837kJ; Protein 3.8g; Carbohydrate 46g, of which sugars 30.4g; Fat 28.1g, of which saturates 17.4g; Cholesterol 64mg; Calcium 111mg; Fibre 0.9g; Sodium 157mg.

Blueberry streusel ice cream cake

This is a great no-bake dessert that you can prepare ahead and keep in the freezer, just making the streusel topping and blueberry compote a little while before you want to serve. The dessert uses ready-made gluten-free flapjacks, although you can make your own (see page 192).

SERVES 8

350g/12oz gluten-free soft flapjacks
500ml/17fl oz/2 cups vanilla ice cream
250g/9oz/2 cups blueberries
50g/2oz/¼ cup caster/superfine sugar
juice of 2 limes

For the streusel topping

50g/2oz gluten-free amaretti
50g/2oz gluten-free flapjacks
50g/2oz golden or white gluten-free marzipan
50g/2oz/¼ cup butter

1 Using your fingers, press the flapjacks for the case into a round pie dish measuring about 23cm/9in, so that there are no gaps and the flapjack is in an even layer. You need to ensure that the flapjacks you use are soft so that they can be easily pressed into shape, and choose a pie dish that will fit your freezer.

2 Place the flapjack case in the freezer for 10 minutes to chill it – this will help to prevent the ice cream from melting when you spread it over the top, and the case from crumbling as you spread the ice cream over it.

3 Bring the vanilla ice cream to room temperature so that it is just soft enough to spoon out. Fill the flapjack case with the ice cream and smooth level. Return to the freezer until you are ready to serve.

4 Meanwhile, for the compote, place the blueberries, sugar and lime juice in a pan and simmer for about 5 minutes, until the fruit has burst and the sauce is thick. Set aside to cool completely.

5 For the topping, crush the amaretti into small pieces with your hands in a mixing bowl. Add the flapjack and mix together with your hands. Break the marzipan into small pieces and add to the bowl.

6 Melt the butter in a pan and while it is still hot, pour it over the topping mixture. Mix everything together with your hands so that the streusel forms small clumps.

7 To serve, carefully remove the cake from the freezer and top with the compote and then the streusel topping. Serve immediately and eat on the day of assembling.

Energy 498kcal/2084kJ; Protein 5.4g; Carbohydrate 64g, of which sugars 45.3g; Fat 26.5g, of which saturates 9.9g; Cholesterol 29mg; Calcium 96mg; Fibre 2.7g; Sodium 230mg.

Rum & raisin brownie torte

Using ready-made gluten-free brownies means this dessert requires minimal effort and yet the result is a rich and indulgent rum and raisin truffle fridge cake. You could also of course make your own gluten-free chocolate brownies (see page 245).

SERVES 16

oil, for greasing
120ml/4fl oz/½ cup dark rum
150g/5oz/1 cup raisins and sultanas (golden raisins)
2 eggs
375ml/13fl oz/1½ cups double/heavy cream, plus extra whipped, to serve
120ml/4fl oz/½ cup milk
350g/12oz plain/semisweet chocolate, plus extra for grating
15ml/1 tbsp golden/light corn syrup
150g/5oz gluten-free chocolate brownies
whipped cream, to serve

1 Grease and line a 23cm/9in loose-bottomed cake tin/pan. Place the rum in a pan and heat until just warm then tip in the raisins and sultanas; do not boil. Remove from the heat and leave to cool. The raisins should become plump.

2 Place the eggs, cream and milk in a large jug or bowl and whisk together, then pour into a pan. Break up 300g/11oz of the chocolate into small pieces and add to the cream mixture.

3 Heat over a gentle heat, whisking all the time, for about 4–5 minutes, until the chocolate is melted and the ganache is thick and glossy.

4 Stir in the rum-soaked raisins and golden syrup and set aside while you prepare the base.

5 Break the brownies into small pieces and spread out over the base of the tin. It does not matter if there are small gaps. If the seal of your tin is not tight, wrap the base and sides of the tin in foil to ensure that the ganache does not leak out.

6 Pour the rum and raisin ganache over the brownie base and chill in the fridge overnight to set.

7 When you are ready to serve, remove the cake from the tin by sliding a sharp knife around the edge, then remove the sides. Place the cake on a serving plate.

8 Decorate with dollops of whipped cream and a good sprinkling of grated chocolate. This torte will store for up to 3 days in the fridge.

Energy 312kcal/1299kJ; Protein 3.4g; Carbohydrate 25.4g, of which sugars 24.2g; Fat 21.8g, of which saturates 13.3g; Cholesterol 71mg; Calcium 40mg; Fibre 1.3g; Sodium 55mg.

Blueberry cheesecake torte

Instead of crushed cookie crumbs or pastry, this cheesecake base is made from pulverized walnuts and dates. It is also light in fat as the creamy filling is made with ricotta. Together, they give this classic dessert a healthier and more modern twist.

SERVES 12

For the base

150g/5oz/scant 1 cup fresh or dried stoned/pitted dates
115g/4oz/1 cup chopped walnuts, soaked in water overnight in the fridge

For the filling

250g/9oz/2 cups blueberries
45ml/3 tbsp honey
1kg/2¼lb/4 cups ricotta cheese
150g/5oz/¾ cup raw cane crystals
5ml/1 tsp grated lemon rind
10ml/2 tsp vanilla extract
1.5ml/¼ tsp salt
4 eggs

1 Preheat the oven to 180°C/350°F/Gas 4. To make the base, soak the dates in a bowl of warm water for 10 minutes, until plumped up.

2 Drain the dates and discard the soaking liquid. Put them in a food processor with the drained walnuts and process for about 30 seconds, until combined.

3 Press the walnut and date mixture into the bottom of a 23cm/9in springform cake tin/pan with the back of a spoon and chill while you prepare the filling.

4 Mix the blueberries with the honey in a small mixing bowl and set aside to macerate.

5 Put the ricotta, cane crystals, lemon rind, vanilla and salt in a mixing bowl and beat with an electric whisk for 2 minutes on medium, until combined.

6 Whisk in the eggs one by one, incorporating each one before adding the next.

7 Pour the batter over the base, smooth the top, then bake for about 1 hour, until the cake has risen around the sides, the top is brown and it's still moist and not entirely firm in the middle. Allow to cool in the tin on a wire rack.

8 Remove the outer ring from the tin and pour the macerating juices from the blueberries over the cake. Decorate the top with the blueberries and allow to stand at room temperature for 20 minutes before serving.

Energy 322kcal/1346kJ; Protein 12.2g; Carbohydrate 29.6g, of which sugars 28.5g; Fat 18.1g, of which saturates 7.1g; Cholesterol 119mg; Calcium 230mg; Fibre 1.8g; Sodium 115mg.

Index

almonds 30
Almond Florentines 177
Almond milk 38
Almond pastry 197
Chocolate almond truffle cake 264
Coffee & almond quinoa roulade 256
Orange & almond cake 255
Raspberry & almond gratin 227
amaranth flour 26–27
Angel food cake 263
apples
Apple batter pudding 145
Apple crumble 222
Apple shortcake slice 190
Apple soufflé 220
Bread & apple pudding 221
Buckwheat & apple pancakes 150
Cranberry, chia & apple muesli bars 193
Double-crust apple pie 215
apricots
Apricot & pecan flapjack 192
Apricot rock cakes 238
Oaty apricot slice 191
arrowroot powder 24

Bagels 70
Bakewell tart, summer 211
baking 18–19
baking blind 100
bananas
Chocolate banana cupcakes 234
Sesame & banana fritters 154
batters 18, 126–159
Beef & mushroom suet pudding 124
Beef & pine nut filo pie 116
Belgian waffles with fruit 152
bell peppers 83, 122
berries
Berry & yogurt scones 166
Blueberry cheesecake torte 269
Blueberry & pumpkin seed muffins 237
Blueberry streusel ice cream cake 267
Coconut & blueberry squares 239
Cranberry, chia & apple muesli bars 193
Crispy cake with berries 266
Layered sponge supreme 260
Raspberry & almond gratin 227
Summer Bakewell tart 211
Bhajis, onion 141
Blinis, buckwheat 132
Bread & apple pudding 221
breadcrumbs, gluten-free 18
breads & doughs 40–75
Brioche, chocolate & chestnut 75
Brown loaf, simple 45
Brownie torte, rum & raisin 268
Brownies, coconut blondie 244
Brownies, sweet potato 245
buckwheat flour 26–27
Buckwheat & apple pancakes 150
Buckwheat blinis with mushroom caviar 132
Buckwheat noodles 80
Spicy buckwheat noodles 94
Sprouted buckwheat loaf 54
buttermilk 55
Buttermilk sponge cake 251

cakes
large cakes & gateaux 246–269
small cakes & traybakes 230–245
calcium 13
Calzoni 63
Cappuccino swirls 181
Caraway scones 163
Carob chip shortcake cookies 175
carob flour 26–27
Carrot cake 233
Cashew lime tart 208
Chard pie, double-crust 118
Cheese & dill puff pastries 107
Cheese choux gougères 106
Cheese & mushroom cannelloni 86
Cheesecake, blueberry 269
Cheesy cornbread 57
Cheesy fish goujons 142
cherries
Cherry pie 217
Chocolate cherry cookies 184
chestnut flour 26–27
chestnuts 30, 75, 258
chia seeds 32
Chicken & mushroom noodle soup 92
Chicken & mushroom pie 121
chickpeas
Chickpea flour flatbreads 65
Pasta & chickpeas 84
children 17
chocolate
Chocolate almond truffle cake 264
Chocolate avocado tart 207
Chocolate banana cupcakes 234
Chocolate cherry cookies 184
Chocolate & chestnut brioche 75
Chocolate éclairs 202
Chocolate macaroons 182
Chocolate mud pudding 225
Chocolate popcorn slice 186
Chocolate roulade 257
Churros with hot chocolate 155
Coconut blondie brownies 244
Dark chocolate hazelnut tart 206
Mississippi mud pie 204
Nut butter cookies 183
Rum & raisin brownie torte 268
Sweet potato brownies 245
Vanilla & chocolate layer cake 252
Choux pastry 101, 106, 202
Christmas cake, white 259
Christmas stars 199
Churros with hot chocolate 155
coconut
Chocolate macaroons 182
Coconut blondie brownies 244
Coconut & blueberry squares 239
coconut flour 29
Coconut milk and coconut cream 38
Coconut mint slice 188
Coconut pastry 104, 122
Lime & coconut drizzle traybake 242
Mango & coconut filo baskets 200
White Christmas cake 259
coeliac disease 8, 10–11, 14, 16, 17
coffee
Cappuccino swirls 181
Coffee & almond quinoa roulade 256
cookies & slices 172–193
Cornbread, cheesy 57
cornflour 24
cornmeal 22
Courgette & feta pasties with quinoa pastry 110
Courgette linguine, minty 82
Crackers, multiseed 170
Crackers, sun-dried tomato 171
Crêpe batter 128 *see also* batters
Crêpes, quinoa 149
Crêpes, ricotta-filled 151
cross-contamination of foods 16
Crumble, apple 222
Crumpets 159

dairy alternatives 36–9
dates
date syrup 35

Date & walnut cookies 176
Sticky toffee pudding 224
Deep-frying, batter for 131
dermatitis herpetiformis 11
desserts 194–229
Doughnuts, baked ring 156
Drop scone batter 129
Drop scones, dairy-free 129
Dumplings, plum 218

eating out 16
Éclairs, chocolate 202
erythritol 35

Feta & courgette pasties with quinoa pastry 110
Filo pastry 105
Beef & pine nut filo pie 116
Lemon & ricotta rolls 201
Mango coconut baskets 200
Potato & pea samosas 108
fish & seafood
Cheesy fish goujons in beer batter 142
Salmon puff pastry pie 120
Smoked salmon quiche with potato pastry 113
Tempura butterflied prawns 143
Flatbreads, chickpea 65
Flapjack cookies 185
flapjacks 191–193
Flaxseed & raisin muffins 236
flaxseeds 32
Florentines, almond 177
flours 20–33
Focaccia 58
food labelling 14
fritters 140, 147, 154
Fruit & millet cookies 174
Fruit teabread, rich 73
Fruit turnovers 198

Ginger cookies 180
gluten
adverse reactions to 10–11
gluten-containing foods 15
gluten-free foods 14
types of 8–9
gluten-free baking 18–19
gluten-free flours 20–33
glutinous rice flour 25
gram flour 26–27
Grapefruit & poppy seed polenta traybake 243
Gougères, cheese choux 106

hazelnut pastry 112, 206
hazelnuts 31, *see also* nuts
healthy diet 12–13
hemp flour 26–27
hot-water crust pastry 109

Lasagne with pesto & potatoes 90
Leek & tofu tart 112
lemons
Lemon & passion fruit tart 212
Lemon & raisin sorghum pancakes 148
Lemon & ricotta rolls 201
Lemon drizzle loaf cake 248
Lemon surprise pudding 226
Madeira cake 250
Lime & cashew tart 208
Lime & coconut drizzle traybake 242
linseeds 32

Macaroons, chocolate 182
Madeira cake 250
Maize cake 254
maize flour 22
Mango & coconut filo baskets 200
millet flour 22
Millet & sorghum loaf 51
Mississippi mud pie 205
Muffins 236, 237
Multiseed crackers 170
mushrooms
Beef & mushroom suet pudding 124
Buckwheat blinis with mushroom caviar 132
Chicken & mushroom noodle soup 92
Chicken & mushroom pie 121
Chinese veggie vermicelli 95
Two-cheese & mushroom cannelloni 86
Naans 61
non-coeliac gluten sensitivity 11
noodles & pasta 76–97
nut and seed flours 30–3
nuts
Apricot & pecan flapjack 192
Cashew lime tart 208
Dark chocolate hazelnut tart 206
Hazelnut praline slice 187
Nut butter cookies 183
Peanut butter cookies 178
see also almonds; walnuts

oat flour 25
oats, oatmeal
Flapjack cookies with ginger & turmeric 185
Herby seeded oatcakes 169
Oat & cinnamon rolls 66
Oat & fruit loaf cake 249
Oaty apricot slice 191
onions
Caramelized onion & walnut scones 164
Onion bhajis 141
Red onion tart with polenta pastry 115
oranges
Angel food cake 263
Maize cake 254
Orange & almond cake 255
Orange pastry 197
Orange polenta cupcakes 235
Orange quinoa cookies 179

Pancake batter 128 *see also* batters
pasta & noodles 76–97
Fresh egg pasta 78–79
pastry
savoury 98–125
sweet 194–229
Pâte sucrée 196
Peanut butter cookies 178
peanuts 31
Pear tarte tatin 214
pecans 31, 192
pies *see* pastry
Pineapple puddings, steamed 229
pistachios 31
Pittas 60
Pizza 62
plums & prunes
Christmas stars 199
Fruit turnovers 198
Plum dumplings 218
polenta 22
Polenta bread 56
Polenta cupcakes, orange 235
Polenta pastry, red onion tart with 115
Polenta traybake 243
Popcorn, chocolate slice 186
pork
Cellophane noodles with pork 97
Mini pork pies 109
Vietnamese spring rolls 137
potato flour 25
potato starch 24
potatoes
Filled rice flour pancakes 138
Lasagne with pesto & potatoes 90
Potato buns 68
Potato & dill pancakes 133
potato pastry 113
Potato & pea samosas 108
Thin potato breads 64
psyllium husk 19
puddings *see* desserts
Puff pastry 102
Puffed fritters in syrup 147
pumpkin seeds 33, 237
Pumpkin & tofu tart 209

Quiche Lorraine with rice flour pastry 114
quinoa
Courgette & feta pasties with quinoa pastry 110
Orange quinoa cookies 179
Quinoa crêpes 149
Quinoa & poppy seed twists 168
Seeded quinoa bread 53
quinoa flakes 28
quinoa flour 28
Ravioli, spinach & ricotta 89
rice crispies 266

rice flour 22
Rice flour pancakes 138
Rice flour pastry, quiche Lorraine 114
Rice noodles 81, 92, 93, 95, 96
Rice-wrapper summer rolls 136
Rice wrappers 128
ricotta cheese
Blueberry cheesecake torte 269
Lemon & ricotta rolls 201
Ricotta-filled crêpes 151
Spinach & ricotta ravioli 89
Rock cakes, apricot 238
Roulade 256, 257

Samosas, potato & pea 108
scones & savoury crackers 160–171
Scones, classic 162
Seeded quinoa bread 8
sesame seeds 32
Shortcake, apple slice 190
Shortcrust pastry 100
Soda bread 55
sorghum flour 28
Sorghum pancakes, lemon & raisin 148
Sorghum & millet loaf 51
Soufflé, apple 220
sourdough
Brown sourdough loaf 50
Classic sourdough 47
Sourdough baguette 48
Sourdough starter 46
spinach
Pancake roll with spinach 135
Spinach & ricotta ravioli 89
Sponge, basic
creamed method 232
melted method 233
spring rolls 136, 137
Sprouted buckwheat loaf 54
Steamed buns 69
Steamed pineapple puddings 229
Sticky toffee pudding 224
Suet pudding, beef & mushroom 124
sugar and sweeteners 34–35
sunflower seeds 33
Sweet potato brownies 245
Sweet potato scones 165
Swiss chard pie, double-crust 118

tapioca flour 25
Tapioca pancakes 134
Tarte tatin, pear 214
tarts *see* pastry
Teabread, rich fruit 73
Teacakes 72
teff flour 28
Teff pancakes 134
Tempura batter 131
Tempura, butterflied prawns 143
Toad-in-the-hole 130, 144
Toffee sauce 224
tofu
Leek & tofu tart 112
Pumpkin tart 209
Tofu soup with rice noodles 93
Veggie toad-in-the-hole 144
traybakes 230–245
Triticum aestivum 11

ultratex 19

vanilla 232, 233, 240, 252, 258, 260, 263
Vanilla & chocolate layer cake 254
Vegan 'sausage' rolls 122
Veggie toad-in-the-hole 144
Vegetable fritters 140
Vermicelli, Chinese veggie 95
Victoria sponge 232–3, 240, 260
Vietnamese spring rolls 137
vitamins 12–13

Waffles, Belgian with fruit 152
walnuts 31
Caramelized onion & walnut scones 164
Date & walnut cookies 176
Walnut & chestnut cake 258
wheat allergy 10–11
wheat and bread making 8–9
white bread flour blend 42
White loaf, simple 42
wholegrain bread flour blend 45

xanthan gum 19

Yorkshire pudding batter 130

Published by Lorenz Books
an imprint of Anness Publishing Ltd
www.lorenzbooks.com; info@anness.com

Publisher: Joanna Lorenz
Editorial and layout: Lucy Doncaster
Design: Adelle Mahoney
With thanks to the additional recipe contributors and photographers
Special photography: William Shaw
Nutritional consultant: Clare Emery
Index: Marie Lorimer

COOK'S NOTES

For all recipes, quantities are given in both metric and imperial measures and, where appropriate, in standard US cups and spoons. Follow one set of measures, but not a mixture, because they are not interchangeable. Standard spoon and cup measures are level. 1 tsp = 5ml, 1 tbsp = 15ml, 1 cup = 250ml/8fl oz. Australian standard tablespoons are 20ml. Australian readers should use 3 tsp in place of 1 tbsp for measuring small quantities. American pints are 16fl oz/2 cups. American readers should use 20fl oz/2½ cups in place of 1 pint when measuring liquids. Bracketed terms are intended for American readers. Since ovens vary, you should check with your manufacturer's instruction book for guidance.

The nutritional analysis given for each recipe is calculated per portion (i.e. serving or item), unless otherwise stated. If the recipe gives a range, such as Serves 4–6, then the nutritional analysis will be for the smaller portion size, i.e. 6 servings. The analysis does not include optional ingredients, such as salt added to taste.

A CIP catalogue record is available from the British Library.